Entertaining Politics

Communication, Media, and Politics

Series Editor
Robert E. Denton, Jr., Virginia Tech

Recent Titles in the Series

Forthcoming

Entertaining Politics

New Political Television and Civic Culture

Jeffrey P. Jones

ROWMAN & LITTLEFIELD PUBLISHERS, INC.
Lanham • Boulder • New York • Toronto • Oxford

ROWMAN & LITTLEFIELD PUBLISHERS, INC.

Published in the United States of America
by Rowman & Littlefield Publishers, Inc.
A wholly owned subsidiary of The Rowman & Littlefield Publishing Group, Inc.
4501 Forbes Boulevard, Suite 200, Lanham, Maryland 20706
www.rowmanlittlefield.com

P.O. Box 317, Oxford OX2 9RU, UK

Photograph permissions: Bill Maher on cover courtesy of HBO; Jon Stewart
on cover and photographs on pp. 6, 55, 59, 110, 111, and 116 courtesy of Comedy
Central; pp. 68 and 78 courtesy of *Politically Incorrect with Bill Maher*; p. 80
courtesy of Chris Polk/FilmMagic.com; p. 84 courtesy of Nick Ut/AP Photo; and
p. 95 courtesy of AP/Wide World Photos.

British Library Cataloguing in Publication Information Available

Library of Congress Cataloging-in-Publication Data
Jones, Jeffrey P., 1963–
  Entertaining politics : new political television and civic culture / Jeffrey P. Jones.
    p. cm. — (Communication, media, and politics)
  Includes bibliographical references and index.
  ISBN 0-7425-3087-6 (cloth : alk. paper) — ISBN 0-7425-3088-4 (pbk. : alk. paper)
  1. Television in politics—United States. 2. Television and politics—United States.
  3. Talk shows—United States. 4. Political culture—United States. I. Title. II. Series.
  HE8700.76.U6J66 2005
  306.2'0973—dc22

                                                                              2004006968

Printed in the United States of America

♾™ The paper used in this publication meets the minimum requirements of
American National Standard for Information Sciences—Permanence of Paper for
Printed Library Materials, ANSI/NISO Z39.48-1992.

For Shana

Humour is the only test of gravity, and gravity of humour, for a subject which will not bear raillery is suspicious, and a jest which will not bear serious examination is false wit.

—Aristotle

Contents

Part IV: Audiences for New Political Television

Preface

When I first saw the program *Politically Incorrect,* I wasn't particularly en-amored of it. I didn't disdain it like some of my colleagues; I was simply in-trigued. Now *here* is something different, I thought, something that is overtly violating the implied rules of televised political talk. Although I never partic-ularly enjoyed watching the Sunday morning talk shows or the shouting matches of the overly conservative hosts on cable television, they did define the standard. Here, though, was a comedian with a mullet discussing politics with the guy who played Batman on television when I was a kid. Say what? I, like other viewers, initially enjoyed seeing this odd mixture of celebrities from various public venues presented in a different light, hearing what they had to say and marveling at their intelligence, articulateness, or outright stu-pidity.

But, as I watched, what increasingly became clear to me was that this pro-gram was not operating under the same linguistic or epistemological guide-lines that I had come to accept as the normative ideal in discussing politics. Instead, it sounded like political discussions found in most every venue out-side of the institutions of television or the university—shortsighted, ahistori-cal, laced with the latest media buzz, prone to diverting comments, and gen-erally dependent on the "truths" offered by personal experiences. It also was refreshingly honest, impassioned, diverse, stimulating, witty, and smartly commonsensical when push came to shove. Indeed, the prevalence of com-mon sense as the primary means for thinking through and arguing political issues is what hooked me intellectually. I had previously studied Rush Lim-baugh and his claim to commonsense thinking in the populist early 1990s, but his talk never seemed very commonsensical to me—it was just mean-spirited bigotry driven by fear.

As I began to watch, listen to, and study *Politically Incorrect*, however, I realized that this program, which had recently moved from cable to network television, was truly something different. Whenever I overheard conversations about the show or mentioned it to people outside the academy, I realized that many of them enjoyed it for the humor, guests, and issues it debated. They seemingly didn't entertain the logic used in the dismissals of the show by political elites and cultural critics that this was some unholy marriage of entertainment with politics, primarily because they didn't take it *too* seriously (which critics always did). At some level, they seemed rhetorically engaged in the conversation it offered as well as generally amused by this televised cocktail party.

This book, then, began as a project to study this program in greater detail, including my perceptions of a disjunction between audience appreciation for the show and academic/elite disdain for it. The project, however, changed considerably from its first appearance as a dissertation to include other programming from the same mold—*Dennis Miller Live* and *The Daily Show*. What's more, the world also changed during that process, beginning with a presidential impeachment and continuing through to election debacles, horrific terrorist attacks, and stunning foreign policy initiatives. What became clear during this time is that what I call New Political Television— with its biting humor and satire and its honest and commonsensical talk by people not directly linked to the political establishment—has been a central location on television for the interrogation of political issues from a critical perspective. Here I have found voices on television that consistently question and ridicule the patronizing lies, twisted logic, and taken-for-granted assumptions of both government and news media in a time of crisis.

What follows, then, is an in-depth look at new political talk shows and their audiences, the humorous entertainment talk programming that appeared in the 1990s in the programs *Politically Incorrect with Bill Maher*, *Dennis Miller Live*, and *The Daily Show with Jon Stewart*. These shows, I argue, have challenged normative assumptions about who gets to speak about politics on television, what issues will be covered and in what manner, and how audiences can engage politics on television beyond simply deferring to expert knowledge. Furthermore, they challenge the boundaries between "serious" and "entertaining" programming erected in the network era, which increasingly have come to be seen as artificial. Finally, the shows have become a primary location for new public rhetors that consistently challenge the policies advanced by political elites and the sense-making on which those policies are founded.

In this process, the reader will note that I have attempted to bridge the fields of political communication and cultural studies—theoretically, methodologically, and rhetorically. Political communication and political science's interest in civic participation and political norms, values, and culture are linked here with cultural studies' recognition of culture as a complex process of meaning-making. By my reading, cultural studies has retreated from its early beginnings as a means of interrogating the relationship of cultural production directly to the state. Similarly, political science continues to expend energy focusing on the formal political arena with minimal attention to the cultural factors that often precede political action. The traditional bounded nature of politics (culturally *and* academically) has transformed into a more porous position in media and culture, and our methods, approaches, and targets of analysis should reflect those changes.

I have attempted to be both expansive and narrow in my analysis, perhaps to the dissatisfaction of readers who are overly committed to one particular approach within these fields of study. Although I discuss *Dennis Miller Live* and *The Daily Show* as part of this move toward a hybrid genre of political talk, I have intensified the investigation of *Politically Incorrect* to examine the specificity of its production decisions, content, and audiences who watched it. And although I examine issues related to civic engagement, the focus is clearly on how this particular slice of television programming is a contributor to our overall political culture. Again, detail and specificity necessarily sacrifice an analysis of a wider range of texts and a wider range of subjects in a book this size.

Acknowledgments

Many people have contributed to the writing of this book, for which I am very grateful. Professors Roderick Hart, Sharon Strover, John Downing, and Bob Jensen at the University of Texas at Austin deserve special thanks for their assistance with this project in its first manifestation as a dissertation. Central to this book is Horace Newcomb, who helped me understand many a thing I thought I already knew. A person could not ask for a better teacher, mentor, and friend, and I feel extraordinarily fortunate to have had the opportunity to work with him. He shepherded this project from its nascent beginnings and deserves credit for helping make it a reality. He may not have cared too much for the television program I first found interesting, but he clearly cares that we understand and appreciate the central role that television plays in our common culture and in the lives of viewers—including our lives as citizens.

I also owe much gratitude to the creators and staff of *Politically Incorrect*, including Bill Maher, Scott Carter, Chris Kelly, Doug Wilson, Carol Chouinard, Lizzy Scherer, and Avrielle Gallagher, for granting me time for interviews and access to their production facilities. In particular, I want to acknowledge the generous support of Sheila Griffiths, coexecutive producer of *Real Time with Bill Maher* and longtime member of *Politically Incorrect with Bill Maher*'s creative team. Sheila was instrumental in providing access to all facets of the show, and in the process, exhibiting great kindness, openness, honesty, and a willingness to assist in this project in every way. She embodies the meaning of a true democrat, believing in the importance of accessible and meaningful political discourse and the need for television to facilitate it. This book would not have been possible without her.

Special thanks also goes to all of my colleagues in the Department of Communication and Theatre Arts at Old Dominion University for their support and assistance. In particular, much appreciation goes to Gary Edgerton for helping me find the time to complete this project and for his extraordinarily sane and smart leadership, and to Kyle Nicholas, a good friend for many years. Heartfelt thanks also goes to my dear friend and colleague Mary Marchand, whose numerous gestures of support and love over the duration of this project as a book can never be repaid. Thanks also to colleagues Jane Bennett and William Connelly for their support and helpful advice, and my students Nick Riddle, Richard Thor, Mindy Howard Dunn, Cody Brownson Katz, and Dexter Marcelino for their interest, conversations, and assistance with various aspects of this project. Finally, gratitude goes to my parents Grace and Allen for their abiding faith in me, and my loving and beautiful spouse, friend, editor, counselor, and lifeline, Shana, to whom this book is dedicated.

I

TELEVISION AND POLITICS TODAY

1

Introduction: The Changing Face of Politics on Television

One week after the 9/11 terrorist attacks on the World Trade Center and the Pentagon, the late-night talk shows of network television went back on the air after a brief pause from the national shock. *Politically Incorrect with Bill Maher*, the political discussion-entertainment show on the ABC network, began in somber tones with all comedy segments removed and a vacant chair for a guest killed in the attacks while traveling to Los Angeles for a taping of the program. Host Bill Maher and panelist Dinesh D'Souza began a discussion of whether President Bush's labeling of the terrorists as "cowards" was an accurate characterization. D'Souza argued that the word was misplaced, and Maher agreed saying, "We have been the cowards, lobbing cruise missiles from 2,000 miles away. That's cowardly. Staying in the airplane when it hits the building, say what you want about it, it's not cowardly." Although Maher was referring to American military conduct during the Clinton administration, radio talk show hosts used the statement the following day to excoriate Maher as an unpatriotic traitor.[1] Amid the public outcry, a reporter asked White House Press Secretary Ari Fleischer if President Bush had a comment on Maher's remarks. Fleischer noted that the president had not seen the show, but nevertheless chided, "It's a terrible thing to say, and it's unfortunate. There are reminders to all Americans that they need to watch what they say, watch what they do, and this is not a time for remarks like that; there never is." Although supposedly an "entertainment" program that some critics had attacked for years as providing little more than uninformed drivel,[2] *Politically Incorrect's* political talk, it seems, warranted special attention from the White House during a national security crisis. Indeed, the talk it produced was now deemed a "threat."

If Maher felt his performance on the show had a special connection to the White House in some way, that feeling certainly wasn't new. Several years earlier, Maher had waged an almost nightly campaign in defense of President Bill Clinton during the presidential scandal over sexual relations with an intern. Seeing the scandal as part of a right-wing campaign against the Clintons, Maher considered himself one of the president's leading defenders. The program routinely debated the scandal and subsequent impeachment, focusing on what Maher considered to be the persecution of America's leading official over nothing more than his lying about oral sex. In an interview, Maher commented on what he hoped might be a forthcoming exchange between himself and the soon-to-be ex-president: "I would like to think that when he's out of office, we could have a conversation with him. And I'd like to think he might say, 'Hey, I appreciated the support during that rough period, that little tough time I had. I appreciated you saying some of the things I couldn't say myself.'"[3] Again, although it was considered an "entertainment" show for many, Maher was convinced that his program provided a needed contribution to American political debate simply because it said what others would not. He firmly believed that he helped the president receive a more balanced airing of public opinion on the matter than that given in other television forums.

Whether Presidents Bush and Clinton personally paid much attention to a program watched by two to three million people every weeknight, or whether they felt comforted or threatened by discussions occurring there, is not known.[4] What most certainly has occurred, however, is that new forms and forums of politics on television (such as *Politically Incorrect*) have altered the television landscape over the preceding decade. Politics is now appearing on numerous and disparate channels and is packaged in a variety of formats and genres, including sitcoms, satires, parodies, town halls, roundtable discussions, talking-head debates, and viewer-participation programs. The conventional lines between the "serious" and the "entertaining" in television programming have become remarkably blurred, and the location for where institutional politics now resides within those lines is questionable. Discussions on television about a presidential scandal or terrorist attacks no longer occur solely among Washington insiders and the news media. Instead, the nightly sense-making of events is processed in new ways by new voices, and rarely operates by the previous assumptions that guided televised political discourse.

For decades, politics on television was largely controlled by the network oligopoly, in particular, network journalists and news bureaus. Through intense competition in the cable marketplace in the 1990s, however, politics gained currency as a programming strategy for television producers who offered new alternatives for viewers seeking political discussion, information, and entertainment.[5] Although talk radio was perhaps the first (rude) awakening to a new type of mediated political discourse that could be popular with audiences, televisual changes seemed most noticeable when new forums for politics played an increasingly important role in the 1992 presidential campaign. Candidates began appearing with great frequency on "entertainment" talk shows, while critics were aghast at what they considered a degradation of the electoral process, widely proclaiming this the "entertainmentization" of politics.[6]

A decade later, however, changes in the relationship between politics and television were much starker. In 2002, for example, prime-time network television programming with government institutions as the central theme or setting included three shows on the CIA, one on the FBI, one on the White House, two on the Supreme Court, one on City Hall, two on the U.S. armed forces, and one on an American embassy.[7] As one journalist noted in expressing his surprise at this new spate of government-related programming, "As far as TV was concerned, there were once three branches of government: lawyers, judges and hard-nosed cops who played by their own set of rules. Otherwise, government was ratings death."[8] Over the course of the preceding decade, cable channels such as Comedy Central, MTV, Court TV, Bravo, HBO, MSNBC, Fox News, CNN, and CNBC attempted a variety of different programs that addressed differing viewer interests and pleasures in politics. For instance, Comedy Central ran a sitcom/parody, *That's My Bush*, which brutally ridiculed a moronically portrayed President George W. Bush and his wife shortly after he assumed office. Bravo ran Michael Moore's left-wing populist program of documentary vignettes called *The Awful Truth*, and in August 2004, Showtime planned to air a reality program in the mold of *American Idol* called *American Candidate*, in which citizens would compete as candidates in a faux political campaign for president.[9]

In 2000, both Democratic and Republican presidential candidates appeared on a special prime-time edition of *Saturday Night Live* the night before the election—formerly the place where they were satirized; now they participated in satirizing themselves *during* a campaign. In 2003, movie star Arnold Schwarzenegger announced his candidacy for governor of California on *The Tonight Show with Jay Leno* and Senator John Edwards announced his candidacy for president of the United States on *The Daily Show with Jon Stewart*. By early 2004, most of the Democratic presidential candidates were guests on either *Real Time with Bill Maher* or *The Daily Show* (or both), being interviewed by comedian-hosts who rarely operate within traditional journalistic boundaries or mindsets.[10]

Other political players have increasingly come to recognize the influence that these new forms of political programming can have. Appearances by politicians are not simply limited to candidates looking for free airtime or a format that can help them look more "real" and less constructed to the voters. HBO aired a program in 2003 called *K Street* (shot in a video *verité* style to enhance its documentary feel) that centered on a make-believe lobbying firm and featured a mixture of actors and real life politicos (such as political consultants James Carville and Mary Matalin, but also cameos by lawmakers

Senator Joseph Lieberman appearing on The Daily Show with Jon Stewart.

such as Senators John McCain, Hillary Clinton, and Orrin Hatch).[11] Both of the political comedy-entertainment shows *Real Time* and *The Daily Show* have interviewed a variety of political guests, such as former UN Ambassador Madeleine Albright, former U.S. Ambassador to Iraq Joseph Wilson, former CIA Director R. James Woolsey, Senate Minority Leader Tom Daschle, House Minority Leader Richard Gephardt, and Senators Joseph Biden and Hillary Clinton, among others. Even *ABC World News Tonight* anchor Peter Jennings is a fan of *The Daily Show* and has acknowledged that the program's host, Jon Stewart, can enunciate important things about politics and politicians that the norms of objectivity won't allow Jennings to say.[12] And during the 2000 presidential election, Al Gore's advisers made him watch a *Saturday Night Live* skit (as he prepared for a debate) that parodied his debating style.[13] In many of these instances, there seemingly is an underlying recognition that new political television expresses a measure of truth, honesty, or realness that is missing from more formulaic political coverage. These political figures aren't bemoaning some loss of credibility because of a changed political culture—they are embracing it, contributing to it, and as might be expected, attempting to exploit it.

Perhaps the most revealing change at the intersection of popular culture and political culture, however, occurred when the Bush administration took several unconventional opportunities for addressing the American people in the aftermath of the 9/11 terrorist attacks. The FBI sought leads or tips on twenty-two terrorist suspects via a special edition of *America's Most Wanted*, the program dedicated to catching criminals by enlisting the viewing audience's assistance.[14] The Pentagon then attempted to explain the concept and workings of military tribunals via the CBS dramatic program *JAG*, providing more details and explanations of the workings of such tribunals to the program's scriptwriters than that offered to reporters.[15] The State Department even sought diplomacy with young citizens of the world by sending Colin Powell to appear in a live "town hall" meeting on MTV's *Be Heard*, fielding questions from young adults in seven countries.[16] Finally, the producers of a program called *D.H.S.—The Series* (about the Department of Homeland Security) attempted to sell the pilot to prospective networks by noting that the counterterrorism agencies that are depicted in the show (the White House, DHS, FBI, EPA, etc.) "have rallied their resources and support behind the vision of *D.H.S.—The Series*, including President G. W. Bush and Homeland Security Secretary Tom Ridge, who both endorse and contribute sound bites to the introductions of the series."[17] In short, the administration obviously recognized the power and potential benefits in circumventing traditional channels of communication (namely, journalists and news networks) to speak directly to American and global citizens through a variety of entertainment programming. As the travails of Bill Maher that opened this chapter also suggest, entertaining political programming now *interacted* with formal politics—and vice versa—at an unprecedented level.

What we are experiencing, then, is a fundamental change in political communication in America. We have passed a point in which entertainment television would only occasionally dip into politics (such as *Rowan & Martin's Laugh-In*, *The Smothers Brothers Comedy Hour*, *Saturday Night Live*, etc.). Politics is now clearly an integral part of entertainment programming these days, and as such, its cultural location has broken the traditional bounded nature of programming assumptions about politics. Yet these changes are often derided and dismissed with simple statements that politics and entertainment have become one and the same. Since it is quite easy (and often popular) to view both politicians and the entertainment industry with cynical disdain, it is also tempting to let normative desires (i.e., that politicians should not act like politicians, or that the entertainment industry should offer "better" programming) overcome serious analysis of the changes that are occurring and the effect of such changes on our political culture. To label the changes outlined above *Entertaining Politics*, as I have done in the title of this book, is to risk the scorn of numerous academic and cultural critics who have decried the encroachment of television, celebrity, and entertainment into politics. Admittedly, these critics may have a point when we witness a wealthy pop superstar like Arnold Schwarzenegger waltzing through a populist campaign for governor by simply smiling broadly, touching his fans, and avoiding tough questions by repeating lines from movies. Or perhaps such criticism is merited when we see a former political apparatchik like

George Stephanopoulos elevated to the role of "journalist"/host on a pundit talk show simply because of his good looks and youthful appeal.

Yet critics go too far when they lay the blame for increased interactions between politics and entertainment (and the supposed "effects" that result) at the feet of television, a medium that is often seen as *inherently* detrimental to democracy. For instance, Robert Putnam's problem with television is ontological—citizens have forgotten the importance of social connections and the benefits those connections have in producing a rich, democratic polity because we have divorced ourselves from each other through our isolated acts of watching entertainment television. For Neil Postman, the problem is epistemological—television is an inferior (even dangerous) means of knowing the arena of politics. Due to the technological biases of electronic communication (as opposed to his privileging the written word), television offers little more than amusement, entertainment, and distraction because the medium is incapable of helping us think in any other way. For Roderick Hart, the problem is phenomenological—television is a cynical medium that may encourage us to *feel* engaged or empowered politically, but ultimately it provides feelings that are false, temporal, and certainly not residual. These critics maintain a certain normative standard of rational-critical discourse that should be found (although rarely is) in the public sphere of television. The changes in mediated politics noted above, therefore, are likely to be viewed skeptically by those who find these critiques of television affirming.

These criticisms are faulty, however, in several important regards, the first being the long history of association between entertainment and politics. Politics is drama, and as such has always had entertainment value for individuals, communities, and the nation.[18] Politicians are showmen, and they depend upon similar rhetorical and performative tools and techniques that show business hucksters use to create and sustain their audience.[19] Second, politics (as it is practiced) is increasingly crafted through and for media spectatorship, and hence the desired separation between media and politics no longer exists. The conduct of politics is rarely conceived and executed without consideration of the actions themselves as communicative events, including how they will "play" across the myriad of media channels and forms. And third, such criticisms are rarely built upon analyses of actual audiences. Critics freely make claims about entertainment television's supposed detrimental effects on democracy, but they almost never conduct or refer to direct studies of audiences to prove their point.[20] The study offered here asks that we interrogate this conjoining of politics and popular culture by engaging in intensive scrutiny of exactly what is occurring and why. To do so, we must recognize that the medium of television is a multifaceted communication medium that allows for numerous performative, rhetorical, perceptive, and disseminative positions for presenting, understanding, celebrating, and critiquing politics. We must also be aware of the multivocality of media texts, as well as make an attempt to understand the complex readings and relationships that audiences both make and have with television, including their abilities to negotiate, appropriate, and appreciate many different types of programming forms that include politics.

Entertaining Politics suggests a double meaning: one is that television producers, audiences, and politicians have shown their desire or willingness to *entertain* politics in newly creative ways. From dramatic narratives to debates, to parodies, to investigative reports from a satirical perspective, politics has become a subject area that is more frequently contemplated in a myriad of televisual formulations. Two, entertaining politics highlights the fact that politics can be *pleasurable*, and that engaging or contemplating it need not always be the equivalent of swallowing bitter medicine. Politics is naturally interesting, dramatic, strange, unpredictable, frustrating, outrageous, and downright hilarious in ways that far exceed the reductive formulations of politics as horse races, policy maneuvers, and palace court intrigue that insider presentations of politics tend to emphasize. What the success of new forms of political programming suggests—whether it is *The West Wing*, *The Awful Truth*, or *The Daily Show*—is that television has begun to explore multiple avenues for presenting politics in imaginative ways, treatments that can offer voices, positions, and perspectives not found in traditional television presentations of politics. It also suggests that audiences are receptive to (if not hungry for) political programming that is meaningful and engaging to them, programming that connects with their interests and concerns, provides new ways of thinking about politics, and speaks to them through accessible and pleasurable means.

Finding politics meaningful and engaging is no small matter. Numerous scholars have pointed to a legitimacy crisis in Western democracies, that is, the increasing disaffection from politics among citizens, as measured by declining voting rates, low opinions of politicians, lack of trust and declining confidence in government, political apathy, low levels of political knowledge, and declining rates of civic volunteerism.[21] Yet, other scholars contend that these traditional measures of civic vitality may not paint a complete picture of contemporary political culture. They point instead to postmodern approaches to civic engagement and changing conceptions of citizenship that include redirected political activity more closely connected to people's lives and identities (such as new social movements and identity politics).[22] There is also a recognition that media's role in contemporary processes of citizenship formation and maintenance is changing, including the strong commitments and relationships people maintain with popular culture. These issues, as well as the role and place of new political television in such debates, are discussed in chapter 2.

What this book offers, then, is an investigation into new manifestations of entertaining political programming on television. It seeks to understand why such programming is produced, what it presents, why audiences are at-tracted to it, and what this means for American democracy. In order to limit the investigative focus within the broad array of genres and fictional and nonfictional programming mentioned above, I concentrate on new forms of political *talk* on television, specifically *humorous* political talk shows. Political talk (including news) has traditionally been the defining form of political sense-making on television and is also widely considered one of the most important and accessible means of involvement with politics (beyond voting). I have also chosen new political talk because of its radical departure from the types of programs typically offered in this genre. These shows are markedly different from pundit political talk programming (e.g., *The McLaughlin Group, Crossfire*) where "experts" discuss narrowly defined issues with much gravity. New political talk also offers something more complex than the simple jokes about politicians found in the monologues of late-night talk show comedians (e.g., Jay Leno and David Letterman) or in the political skits of sketch-comedy shows such as *Saturday Night Live*. These shows are also different from the personal politics found on afternoon audience participation shows (e.g., *Oprah* and *Donahue*), which generally do not stray into formal political processes.

Programs such as *Politically Incorrect with Bill Maher* (Comedy Central and ABC), *Dennis Miller Live* (HBO), *The Daily Show with Jon Stewart* (Comedy Central), and more recently, *Real Time with Bill Maher* (HBO), and *Dennis Miller* (CNBC), are entertainment programs—first and foremost—yet with political talk as their central compositional and discursive feature. They offer direct and specific talk (by entertainment television standards) about the formal, institutional political process and its players and outcomes, yet do so by eschewing the "insider" perspectives offered elsewhere. Instead, they feature comedians and nonexperts on politics (i.e., political "outsiders") discussing, arguing, satirizing, parodying, laughing, and ranting about political events and issues in a serious yet entertaining manner. They are also highly intent on speaking truth to power, whatever partisan or ideological stripes such power represents. It is in these shows that new modes of political discussion on television are located, and hence these programs are at the center of discussions in chapters 3, 4, and 5.

Several chapters intensify the investigation by focusing specifically on *Politically Incorrect with Bill Maher* (*P.I.*). These sections of the book offer the specificity typical of cultural studies through a detailed analysis of the factors that comprise the show and its audience. *P.I.* was the earliest, most successful, and perhaps defining show in this move toward entertaining politics in the last decade. Indeed, I argue that the show led the way for television producers to take risks with the programming of politics in innovative ways. The program receives extended treatment here for several reasons. First, *P.I.*'s beginnings on a comedy channel and subsequent move to network television is informative in understanding the production and programming decisions behind an *entertainment* channel's selection of a hybrid program that blended several genres of television talk while ignoring the traditional separation between entertainment programming and serious public affairs programming.[23] Why Comedy Central (where *P.I.* began) bought the show and what the channel wanted from it, as well as why it was picked up by ABC as a follow-on program to its long-running public affairs program *Nightline*, illustrates the intentions within the industry in utilizing political programming with an entertainment bent as a programming strategy (including what such programming would accomplish irrespective of the show's success or failure). The show's subsequent cancellation by ABC amid controversy over Maher's 9/11 comments also speaks to the particular demands and limits of network television as a source for innovative and politically provocative programming.

Second, both the types of guests and the types of discourse on politics produced on *P.I.* are outside the norm of conventional talk about politics on television. *P.I.* boldly included guests who are typically not experts on politics discussing politics (indeed, their nonexpertise was largely the show's premise and draw). The producers aimed to create a televised cocktail party with guests from numerous areas of public life (television, politics, sports, music, interest groups, publishing, etc.) debating current events. The show invited viewers to identify and link names and faces seen in other public forums with the guests' opinions on politics and social issues. By centering the show on celebrities and public persons discussing topical issues, the show does not stand apart from other media and cultural offerings. Culture and politics mix, and audiences are not encouraged to see the arbitrary boundaries traditionally constructed between the two. Instead, they are encouraged to relate these texts (via the show's eclectic guests, topics, and sensemaking strategies) to other things that confer meaning in their lives, such as tastes in music and literature, political issues (such as animal rights or gun control), sources of information (such as op-ed columns or talk radio), or simple life experiences. Indeed, I argue, it is this conjoining of popular culture and politics that represents the fundamental shift in political programming on television.

Because the majority of guests are also not political experts, they tend to utilize the same means for making sense of public issues as the viewing audience. Specifically, they discuss politics in a language resembling more of what would be found in a bar or basement or barbershop than what occurs at the National Press Club or on *Meet the Press*—a common vernacular that is accessible and familiar. Furthermore, the guests apply more commonsensical notions to what politics means to them than the conventional elite discourse on television that is largely derived from insider knowledge and concerned with political maneuverings. As social psychologist Michael Billig argues, common sense is a means through which publics think through and discuss deeper "ideological dilemmas" that often lie at the heart of public issues and events.[24] Also, part of that freedom to think and talk in common-sensical terms is the opportunity to make fun of or satirize both politicians and other guests who "just don't get it." Humor, often lacking on most political talk shows, becomes an important tool of political critique, especially if political events seem surreal or absurd (e.g., the Clinton-Lewinsky scandal, the 2000 presidential election, Bush flying a war plane, etc.). Examining *P.I.* provides the opportunity to analyze the mixture of humor and serious political discourse—and how that is attractive to certain audiences—while determining if that discourse is nonsense or perhaps some other form of sense.

Which leads to the third point about why *P.I.* receives extended attention here among the programs available for investigation: the audiences that enjoy this type of programming and the reasons why they watch. To study audience behavior toward any television program qualitatively, one could analyze fan mail and conduct interviews with audiences (as is done here). What makes *P.I.* also ripe for investigation is an on-line discussion forum on the program that allows viewers to debate and discuss the show, its guests, and the issues presented there after the show goes off the air (and into the following days and weeks).[25] It is a forum for political discussion that other shows don't share to such a degree, and the political discussions that occur there often derive from discussions that originate on the program. In sum, *P.I.* provides multiple avenues for examining fan thinking and behavior related to the show, ultimately leading us to answers about why audiences watch this type of programming and how they employ the show for their own political needs through their interactions with it in their private and public lives.

This book, then, sets out to study new political television by interrogating issues related to these shows' production, content, and audiences. Some of the questions of production taken up in chapters 3, 4, and 5 include: Why did television producers turn to *politics* in search of new and original programming when prima facie evidence suggested that voters were "sick and tired" of politics in the populist 1990s?[26] What role has the individual creative talent, or comedian-host, played in shaping these shows? Why did the producers feel comfortable in mixing humor and politics? Why have these shows generally originated and appeared on cable television more than on the broadcast networks? How have technology (such as fax machines, satellite link-ups, the Internet), politics (such as populism, terrorist attacks, and military invasions), economics (such as increased competition in television and the need for inexpensive programming), and culture (such as the liberal versus conservative culture wars) influenced the decisions producers have made in offering such programming?

Questions of content are examined in chapters 5, 6, and 7, including: What makes such programming "popular"? That is, what type or quality of talk about politics occurs on these programs that viewers might find appealing (such as parody and satire, impassioned narratives, discursive drama, ideological diversity, etc.)? Does the programming entertain issues and concerns not regularly discussed in pundit political programming? Is the language spoken there more accessible, or does it make "sense" of these events in ways that are different from the sense made in more traditional political formats? How is the political content affected by the entertainment and celebrity system in which it exists? Does the comedian-host as political commentator have a different license to speak from that of newscasters and other traditional voices of political commentary on television, thereby operating outside the bounds of the traditional discursive structures and frameworks constructed and maintained by the latter?

Chapter 8 examines audiences for new political television by asking: Why do viewers watch such programming? Do they locate people or issues there that they identify with or who they feel represent them and their concerns in some way? What do they take away from this programming, and how does it affect their relationship to politics? Are they engaged by the programming (behaviorally or cognitively), and if so, how is that manifested? How is it linked to their ritual attendance to television and their affective relationships with popular culture more generally? Does the blending of politics and entertainment worry them in some way? What do they think this programming contributes to the realm of public talk in America? Answers to these questions are key to developing an understanding of the changes in political programming that have occurred over the last decade, why it has appeared, why it has been successful, and what this means for us as citizens.

Which leads to the concluding chapter in which these analyses are situated within the framework of what Peter Dahlgren calls our "civic culture." He defines civic culture as the "dispositions, practices, and processes" that are "pre-conditions" for citizen participation in public life and offers a typology for the six factors he believes comprise that culture—values, knowledge, affinity, practices, identities, and discussion.[27] I find Dahlgren's theorization a helpful heuristic for measuring and evaluating the ways in which new political television contributes to public life at the level of citizenship. For ultimately, the point of primary interest here is not that what is appearing on television is "new and different" for television's sake, but how such political texts and symbolizations that are occurring in the public sphere engage or affect the body politic in meaningful ways. What these changes in television programming suggest is that the role of popular culture in shaping citizen understandings, expectations, behaviors, attitudes, and commitments to democratic governance—in short, our civic culture—is a significant role that should no longer be ignored or dismissed.

This book, then, advances five main arguments. First, entertaining politics allows for political life to be evaluated in different terms: humorously, based on common sense thinking, with values, beliefs, and experiences at the forefront of the analysis; in short, the components of meaning-making rarely featured or explored elsewhere on political television. Second, entertaining politics allows for different people to evaluate political life on television. Comedian-hosts with a different license to speak offer political critiques beyond the scope of what news and pundit political talk have previously imagined. Similarly, celebrities talking politics (including these comedian-hosts) offer a special representative appeal for viewing audiences. Third, comedy is not just frivolous entertainment. It is a narrative, a story we tell each other to make sense of our common world. The "serious" discourse of pundit television is one such narrative or story, but so are the narratives of new political television that are driven by humor—narratives that can be brutally honest and damningly forthright. Fourth, the combination of information and entertainment that occurs in entertaining politics offers the same complex mixing of interests and competencies citizens maintain in their daily lives, yet which television has tended to segregate in the past. Finally, entertaining politics provides pluralist forums of social conversation that invite engagement and interactivity with the texts, offering linkages between and across the public and private aspects of citizens' lives. In short, entertaining politics offers a *cultural* site where new issues, languages, approaches, and audience relationships to politics on television are occurring. This book shows how and why that is the case, and what such changes mean for our common political culture.

2

Rethinking Civic Engagement in
the Age of Popular Culture

> If citizens are home watching television or its future counterpart, they cannot be out participating in politics.
>
> —Norman Nie, political scientist

Of the many claims that can be made about media and politics in late modern society, two points are indisputable: one is that television continues to be an enormously popular and powerful cultural presence in American society, and the second is that traditional measures of democratic vitality—voting, political party affiliation, trust in leaders, political knowledge, voluntary activism—all register signals of "decline." The question, of course, is whether these two things are related. That is to ask, Is television, as the central arena of America's public sphere, in some way "responsible" for producing this state of "civic malaise"? The question of television as a negative social and political influence has, in one form or fashion, dogged the medium almost from its beginnings. In recent years, however, there has been no shortage of scholars and social commentators willing to spill ink (and sell some books) in suggesting a causal link between the two. With alarmist titles such as *Seducing America, Remote and Controlled, The Sound Bite Society, Amusing Ourselves to Death,* and *Life: The Movie,* these authors have trumpeted the dangers they believe television presents to American political and social life.[1]

Robert Putnam's argument concerning our supposed civic disengagement from the body politic—and television's primary role in that withdrawal—has perhaps attracted the most attention of late. He contends that participation in voluntary civic associations has greatly decreased during the past forty years, and when combined with other data, suggests a weakening of the social

15

bonds (or "social capital") that are crucial in supporting democracy. The thesis works under the catchy yet paradoxical slogan, "Bowling Alone," that neatly sums up the dilemma—how can you engage in a group activity with just one person? Well, you can't—at least not as a "group." So where is everybody instead of participating in life's communal activities? At home watching television. That was the singular conclusion offered in the original journal article that first announced the argument, although by the time of its arrival in book form, Putnam had included other explanatory factors beyond television.[2] Nevertheless, his arguments about television continue to dominate the proposition. Here are his conclusions about television's primary role in civic disengagement:

> Americans at the end of the twentieth century were watching more TV, watching it more habitually, more pervasively, and more often alone, and watching more programs that were associated specifically with civic disengagement (*entertainment*, as distinct from news). The onset of these trends coincided exactly with the national decline in social connectedness, and the trends were most marked among the younger generations that are . . . distinctively disengaged. . . . At the very least, television and its electronic cousins are willing accomplices in the civic mystery we have been unraveling, and more likely than not, they are ringleaders. (Emphasis added)[3]

Putnam admits his evidence is circumstantial and correlational in this regard, not causational. Yet, to extend the metaphor, he is still willing to assert the conclusion that television—especially *entertainment* television—is the chief culprit in the crime.[4]

Several scholars have offered rebuttals to Putnam from a variety of intellectual perspectives. From a behavioral perspective, Pippa Norris contends that the civic malaise theory, at least in regard to news media, is wrong because news programming, in conjunction with political party activities, is actually an activating force for the politically engaged.[5] From a cognitive perspective, Doris Graber mounts a defense of television news programming by arguing that audio-visual materials are quite important in individual learning about politics, and that citizens are therefore engaged with politics when processing political information that appears on television.[6] From a historical perspective, Michael Schudson suggests that theories of decline (such as Putnam's) have ignored the changing norms and practices of American civic culture that have occurred from the nation's founding to the present.[7] Americans have operated under several different models for what constitutes proper behavior by "good citizens," he argues, only one of which is the normative model from which Putnam believes we have strayed (and which Schudson believes we have moved beyond).

What we must first recognize is the state of contemporary citizenship that so frustrates Putnam and others—that daily citizen *engagement* with politics is more frequently *textual* than organizational or "participatory" in any traditional sense. For better or worse, the most common and frequent form of political *activity*—its actual practice—comes, for most people, through their choosing, attending to, processing, and engaging a myriad of media texts about the formal political process of government and political institutions as they conduct their daily routines. Media are our primary points of access to politics—the "space in which politics now chiefly happens for most people," and the place for political encounters that precede, shape, and at times determine further bodily participation (if it is to happen at all).[8] Furthermore, those encounters occur through a panoply of media forms (books, magazines, newspapers, newsletters, billboards and advertisements, direct mail, radio, film, e-mails, websites, blogs, chat rooms, and, of course, cable and network television) and across numerous fictional and nonfictional genres, and comprise what communication scholars call our "media ensemble."[9] Such encounters do much more than provide "information" about political ideas, issues, events, or players. They constitute our mental maps of the political and social world outside our direct experience. They provide a reservoir of images and voices, heroes and villains, sayings and slogans, facts and ideas that we draw upon in making sense of politics. They provide the constituent components of the narratives we construct for organizing, interpreting, explaining, understanding, and adjudicating the realities and illusions we find within the media, but also within our lives. They are ritual encounters with public life that help in our understanding of who and what we are as individuals, a community, a public, and a nation.[10]

But if we recognize that attending to media presentations of politics in all its myriad forms is central to most citizens' daily engagement with politics, it is also helpful to recognize that (perhaps as a result) media are "the center of gravity" for the conduct of politics in general.[11] As Peter Dahlgren argues, "Politics no longer exists as a reality taking place outside the media. . . . Rather, politics is increasingly organized as a media phenomenon, planned and executed for and with the co-operation of the media."[12] Indeed, politics and popular culture are essentially opposite sides of the same coin. John Street argues that for politicians,

> politics, like popular culture, is about creating an "audience," a people who will laugh at their jokes, understand their fears and share their hopes. Both the popular media and politicians are engaged in creating works of popular fiction which portray credible worlds that resonate with people's experiences. To this extent, therefore, political performance has to be understood in similar terms to those applied to popular culture.[13]

This intertwined relationship and logic of contemporary politics and popular culture includes notions of representation, popularity, "the people," and identity that they both share.[14] Street contends that politicians not only use the arts and techniques of popular culture in instrumental ways, but that in doing so, politicians "are also being changed—in their language and their priorities, and in the way they are 'read' by their citizens."[15]

The point here is that politics is increasingly a textual practice, both in how it is constructed and presented for publics and how it is consumed or "read" by audiences. But as texts, this engagement does not happen in a vacuum. It happens in the swirl of other images, narratives, and ritual practices with which we invest our time and make commitments through all forms of popular culture. And it happens in the context of our primary social relationships—among our families, friends, or colleagues and in our homes, workplaces, or gathering spots. Politics occurs for many people in what one author calls our "media surround": the forms, types, places, and contexts in which media are inserted into our lives.[16] It is this complexity to our relationship with politics *via* media—its simultaneously private and public nature—that provides a location for reexamining the notion of television's role in civic (dis)engagement.

The situation I am posing, therefore, extends beyond Putnam and the critics of television noted above. What they represent, in my mind, is the broader desire by scholars and social critics to realize a normative ideal of the citizen as a "rational-critical actor" in public life. It is what Schudson calls the "informed citizen" model, a Progressive Era construction of the voter as "independent, informed, public-spirited and above partisanship."[17] By extension, this model includes the desire to segregate various forms of media practice by citizens. That is, this model advocates a strict separation between the "serious" information needed for citizens to be informed, deliberative, interrogational, and empirically reasoning thinkers, and the "entertainment" programming that is threatening because it is supposedly none of these things.

Yet this normative ideal, I contend, is rarely found in the practices of modern citizenry and is an unrealistic standard for the types of behavior that currently hold much interest for many citizens. What's more, it does not represent the multitude of ways in which people exchange, process, and engage political material in their day-to-day lives, ways that just as easily can be crude, limited, dismissive, trivial, playful, and emotional as they can be thoughtful, wide-ranging, generous, complex, rational, serious, and high-minded. Nor does it accurately represent the ways in which people *attend* to politics—in passing, cursorily, mixed in with other activities, from various media and across numerous subjects. In short, holding onto a conception of citizenship born from a rational-critical standard is perhaps noble, but it is an inappropriate means for assessing the relationship of television to politics. Instead, I agree with Schudson when he argues, "We require a citizenship fit for our own day."[18]

Schudson advances the concept of a "monitorial citizen," one who "engages in environmental surveillance more than information-gathering." As he describes it, "Monitorial citizens scan (rather than read) the information environment in a way so that they may be alerted on a very wide variety of issues for a very wide variety of ends and may be mobilized around those issues in a large variety of ways."[19] These citizenship practices are actually quite similar to the arguments made by media researchers for understanding how media are used in everyday life.[20] For instance, H. Bausinger contends that there are four ways in which audiences engage media: that we construct and consume a daily "media ensemble"; that we do not always give our full attention and concentration to media as they are used (for instance, we skim while reading, zap while watching television, and scan while listening to radio); that media are incorporated into our daily routines (such as meals, driving, at the dentist's office); and that media usage is not an isolated process but often occurs in the presence of—and under the influence of—other people (for instance, the male's typical control of the television remote).[21]

What this chapter offers, then, is some reflection on contemporary citizenship practices that involve media and popular culture generally, and television specifically, practices that challenge the assumptions held by critics of the medium. I first explore the conditions of our contemporary political culture—our beliefs, attitudes, and behaviors toward political practice that have reconstituted the norms and practices of citizenship. I briefly examine what theorists have posited as a postmodern citizenship in which traditional forms of political engagement and previous relationships with media have changed. I then review several studies that examine the role of television in the lives of citizens (television being the most popular form of media engagement), studies that support the claims made above regarding media as a constitutional force in maintaining our relationship to political life. These studies exemplify how politics is increasingly seen as a discursive activity, as well as how monitorial citizens behave when their fundamental values have been challenged by what they see and hear on television. The chapter concludes by examining this question: If politics is increasingly a textual practice for citizens, how are television narratives involved in the construction of political "meaning making"? The case is made for television as a pluralist forum of social conversation that offers accessible interpretive procedures for making sense of the world. That argument is linked to the recognition of the importance of popular culture as a central location of our affective commitments in public life, as a familiar site where political life can be made meaningful.

THE VICISSITUDES OF MEDIA AND POLITICAL CULTURE

Peter Dahlgren has offered one of the most concise yet instructive summations of contemporary political practice by citizens, describing what some scholars have called "postmodern politics."[22] This political culture is increasingly marked by a lack of commitment to traditional institutions (such as political parties, labor unions, and civic associations), yet composed of temporary alliances around issues and values linked to everyday life (such as morality, identity, and worldview). These alliances can be associated with new social movements (e.g., environmentalism or the ethical treatment of animals) or "identity politics" (e.g., race, sexuality, gender), but are generally ones that offer more individualistic forms of expression.[23] This approach to politics, Dahlgren notes, is part and parcel of the larger reflexive project of the emergence of "self," an "ongoing process of the shaping and reshaping of identity, in response to the pluralized sets of social forces, cultural currents and personal contexts encountered by individuals."[24] This project of the self results in multiple identities we each maintain—again, one of which is as "citizen" (although, as he notes, that word itself may not resonate with many people).

Citizens increasingly act as *bricoleurs* in their beliefs and ideological commitments, constructing their own a la carte politics through adhocing, mixing, and individualizing social and political positions. Of course, this can be criticized as a "consumerist" approach to communal life, and indeed is probably shaped by both public and private sector appeals to the public as "consumers" more so than as "citizens."[25] Nevertheless, many citizens are more comfortable constructing their own "frameworks rather than inherit(ing) culturally received 'packages.'"[26] John Gibbins and Bo Reimer see this as a tendency toward direct representation in public life by individuals who value dialogue, discussion, and dissension, and who demand "the voicing of one's view and having it heard." Politics in postmodernity, they argue, is "recognized to be constructed in language; politics *is* language."[27]

Concurrent with these changes have been changes in media that accentuate and perhaps even accelerate these tendencies. We live now, according to Jay Blumler and Michael Gurevitch, in a world of media abundance. As such, the audience has moved beyond its role as simple receptor of top-down political communication as traditionally established by elite gatekeepers (journalists, politicians, experts, etc.). Because of technologies such as satellites, the Internet, cable, and video and digital recorders, audiences are now smaller and more fragmented, with more choice and control in what information they do and don't consume. With that said, such media abundance also means that it is much easier to "bump up against" the political in one's daily life. Such changes have led to a porous relationship between politics and popular culture, where "politics has undoubtedly broken out of the shells of respect, deference, and distance from people's daily lives in which it had formerly been enclosed. There is now a less identifiable core of what counts in some delimited sense as 'the political.'"[28] There has also been a blossoming of populist media formats with an increased presence of the voices and images of ordinary citizens expressing their political opinions. All of these changes have altered how audiences are addressed by media, therefore affecting what they find politically "interesting, relevant and accessible."[29] The new political communication system that has emerged from this process, Blumler and Gurevitch conclude, results from three root sources:

> A widespread belief that democracy as conventionally interpreted is in trouble and that shortcomings of mainstream media coverage of politics are largely to blame for its 'crisis'; the rising tide of populism in cultural, political, and media quarters, which upgrades the value of heeding the views and preferences of ordinary people; and an impression that certain qualities of the new media could be enlisted behind more active forms of political participation.[30]

It is important to note at this point that, in subsequent chapters, we see how these changes are visible at every level of production, content, and consumption of new political television: the lack of commitment to traditional political bodies and the rejection of elite formulations about politics, including the exclusionary language used by experts and political insiders; the mix-and-match approach to political values and ideas by new television commentators and public alike; the populist impulse to project and hear the voices of ordinary people (including oneself) and the usage of new media and communication technologies to achieve this; the small and fragmented yet committed audiences attentive to new offerings in political communication; and the porous nature of politics within and across popular cultural formats.

The question still to be considered now, however, is what do we know about audience engagement with television given these changes in political culture and the media landscape? Several studies of audiences suggest that the viewing public's political relationship to television is much more complex than critics of the medium either understand or express.

STUDIES OF TELEVISION AND CITIZENSHIP

Media researcher Kevin Barnhurst has conducted several studies of young people (generally college-level students) and their habits of news consumption.[31] His findings buttress the observation that young people are disconnected from traditional sources of political information—namely, the news. He finds that they generally disdain the displays of political opinion on television news programs, considering them little more than "reality-based variety shows" and something not to be taken seriously. Similarly, he finds that young people largely find newspapers irrelevant to their lives because newspapers' version of "news" has little meaning within the localities where these young citizens live. As he notes, "The news floats past them, unanchored."[32] Instead, he argues, citizenship for young people is lived from the personal into the public. Their knowledge, understandings, and concerns for public life emanate from personal bonds with family and friends, but also from their personal relationship with popular media. "Their understanding of political life seems primarily discursive," he notes, "existing in the ideas that emerge from local interactions in the presence of the media. Their practical knowledge is rooted in media savvy rather than in the traditional modes of political action."[33] This is why, he notes, young people use "many genres (especially entertainment media) to make sense of the political world."[34] Their understanding of political life as primarily discursive is also seen in their belief that "the essence of political life for them is the expression of opinions and preferences."[35]

Similar results are reported by Michael Delli Carpini and Bruce Williams in their examination of television's effect on how citizens process information and formulate opinions on environmental issues. They conducted a series of focus group discussions with citizens of all ages and found that television is a constituent part of people's understandings of public life, a central reference in their thinking and arguing about political issues. They found that citizens make few distinctions between fictional and nonfictional television, and tend to refer to both in making knowledge claims—even more so than their own personal experiences. Furthermore, people retain an enormous variety and array of television-related personalities in their heads (from Ted Turner, Bill Cosby, and Bob Barker to Sally Struthers, Nadia Comaneci, and Bette Midler), and use these figures as reference when talking politics, almost to the total *exclusion* of politicians and government officials.[36] That is, rather than explain environmental issues by referencing the politicians who craft or manage regulatory policies, they instead use a repertoire of other figures from popular culture as communal signifiers to make their point. Popular culture, then, clearly comprises many people's constellations of meaning, even in regard to political life.

The narratives of popular culture are significant in their provision of characters, plots, outcomes, and morality tales that can be employed in people's construction of their own narratives about politics. Television not only instigates conversation, then, but in their engagement with it, citizens construct their own opinions or views *through* these narratives. As Delli Carpini and Williams argue, "Citizens often 'discover' their political views in the give-and-take of discussions with others. Television plays a central role in this process in that it is engaged in an ongoing political conversation: when we turn our set on, we dip into this conversation."[37] And it matters not whether the conversation arises from fictional or nonfictional programming. For viewers, it is all part of the same narrative flow that is "television."

What this study reveals is that the conversation citizens have with television exists in three ways. People talk *to* television, speaking back to the set (whether alone or in groups), just as television talks to them. Sometimes that conversation is a silent one, but it is a conversation nonetheless.[38] People also talk *about* television with others (what they have watched there) with great regularity. And people talk *with* television, using its narratives as part of how the world is to be understood and explained. Delli Carpini and Williams conclude that, "in many ways, television serves as a privileged member in public discourse, one to whom citizens feel an obligation to respond."[39] In other words, television is leading the discussion, or what political communication scholars have generally referred to as the agenda-setting function of media (not what to think, but what to think *about*). Here, though, the concept should be extended to recognize not just what to *talk* about, but the impetus to speak about politics publicly at all.

An important study by sociologist Ron Lembo, although not specifically focused on political communication, investigates the ways in which we "think through television." By interviewing and observing television viewers in their homes, his work is focused on examining television's use in everyday life, developing what he refers to as the "sociality of the viewing culture."[40] He contends that the viewing culture "encompasses the formation of attitudes and opinions that emerge from television use and that people may carry around in their heads and draw upon in making sense of themselves and their world, especially the world beyond their own day-to-day experiences."[41]

Lembo investigates the factors that are involved as people engage the medium, and how they go about relating to, accepting, or dismissing what is found there. One of the most important of these factors is the narrative's plausibility: does it ring true with their experiences or understanding of people, situations, and the world, "a world that they know in common with others—family, friends, co-workers"?[42] Like Delli Carpini and Williams, Lembo finds people engaged in a conversation with the medium—either silently, directly to the set, or with other people. When watching with other people, he reports, a comment or criticism tended to set off a series of interactions and extended discussions about the program, other programs, real life, and so on. People associate what they are watching with other aspects of their lives, both textual and "real."[43] As such, people make the choice to be mindfully engaged with television "in a way that is not simply oriented around escaping thoughts of their own real-life circumstances."[44] When they believe narratives are plausible, they incorporate the discourses of television as their own understanding of the world. When not seeing social reality, they see formula, and disengage from what they consider commercial product and manipulated images. Lembo concludes that when people watch television, "they can identify with or be critical of what is presented to them, but, either way, they enter into a process in which they are continually judging, monitoring, and evaluating things."[45] In other words, people *engage* the medium and what they find there.

Another illuminating study of how audiences engage with politics on television comes from an examination of citizen reactions to the televised hearings and media reports of the Iran-Contra scandal.[46] Using citizen correspondence (both letters and telephone calls) to members of Congress over the matter, historian David Thelen investigates how citizens were mobilized by watching the hearings and news, objecting to or applauding what they saw there, and feeling an immense need to have their voices heard as a result. He summarizes the process viewers took by noting that "viewers talked about what they saw on television with the people around them, and they became so troubled by public officials or journalists that they felt compelled to interrupt them, to add their own voices, and to try to make talk on television more nearly resemble everyday talk."[47] Indeed, Thelen argues that it was a perceived "disconnect" by politicians and journalists from the fundamental principles and values of everyday life that motivated viewers to take action, which usually began in conversation with others first.

Instead of finding the primary places for participation in public life to be large-scale social institutions (such as political parties, pressure groups, churches, unions), Thelen contends that the most meaningful participation in politics now occurs in intimate relationships, the places where people make sense of and actually take part in politics through their conversations.[48] It is here that the viewers in his study found "standards for authenticity and authority, so that those [primary] relationships became powerful sites from which to challenge the construction of the mass media."[49] In turn, they contacted the members of Congress they saw on television in an effort to assert that "the values that shaped their everyday relationships ought to shape the [political] conversation."[50]

It is this intimacy between public and private life that occurs with, through, and because of the medium of television that deserves our attention here. Television is invited into our homes, and the pageantry of public life becomes intimate and accessible. As noted by Barnhurst, citizenship is lived from the personal into the public. Thelen argues that citizens wanted the conversations on television to resemble those that occur in their homes, including the usage of their language, their conversational style, and their value-driven (not issues- or policy-driven) discourse.[51] And he notes that "Viewers participated in the hearings, as in real life, not so much *in* a topic as *with* a person," wanting desperately to engage in a conversation.[52] He goes on to describe how the articulated desires between private principles, actions, and behaviors and a specific vision of public life became the motivation for engagement with the actors they found in the national drama. This particular engagement, in the end, tethers them to the nation and revives the democratic spirit. The description deserves to be quoted at length:

> The issue at the core of popular participation was whether the trust that people sought in their personal relationships could become the kind of bond they felt with citizens they did not know and, through them, with their nation and government. To help them turn personal trust into public trust and public trust into democratic hope, citizens needed someone they could trust to carry their vision

into government. During the hearings, Americans were thrilled to find representatives who spoke for their distinctive worlds instead of to common denom-
inators. They needed these people to think as they did, to have access to government, and to fight courageously for their views. By their letters they tried to
draw these people into their personal worlds. They offered their newfound
champions encouragement, advice, and information just as they did to people
around them.

By defending their values at the hearings their champion encouraged citizens
to feel connected once again to each other and to government. . . . By expressing what the writers thought, their champion reconnected them with the traditions that mattered most to them. The thrill at hearing their thoughts come
through the voice of a defender they had brought into their intimate worlds—
the voice of a fellow citizen—was the thrill of renewed confidence in the community.[53]

Thelen concludes that "the core of democracy was the confidence that
their interests, beliefs, and feelings were fully represented in public life."[54]
Citizenship, then, becomes an assertion of one's values that have become
threatened and must be reestablished in a public way. That representation
occurs through texts, through words that are publicly displayed and made
available to all. The creation of texts is perhaps what politics is all about for
the postmodern citizen. As Sonia Livingstone and Peter Lunt argue, "Political
participation as narrowly defined is a minority activity. . . . A more discursive
notion of participation may be as significant for involving the majority of the
public in the fairly undemanding activity of talk and opinion formation."[55]

One last point from this study deserves mention. Much of what Thelen reports also corroborates the claims about television audiences made in the
studies cited above. His study reveals that citizen-viewers (1) find much of
what journalists and politicians do has little relevance to their daily lives;
(2) are critically engaged with what they find on television ("cheering, mod-
ifying, dismissing, or ridiculing");[56] (3) examine content for plausibility, asking if it rings true with their experiences and understandings, and if it is
related to the world they share in common with family and friends; (4) feel
an obligation to respond to television when it doesn't correspond to their realities; and (5) believe that the central political practice available to them is
discursive, that is, expressing their political opinions and having them heard
publicly.

To summarize these studies in relation to the conception of postmodern citizenship described above (including our changed relationships with media),
we see from Barnhurst's study that young citizens have a personalized engagement with politics and conceive of political activity as primarily discursive (and populist) in nature ("politics *is* language"). Media plenitude provides opportunities to brush up against politics in ways that shape these
young citizens' understandings of political issues and events. The findings by

Delli Carpini and Williams exemplify the fluid boundaries between politics and popular culture as citizens spliced together political meanings from a myriad of media representations. Furthermore, they contend that the citizenry's political views are not "received" packages but are "discovered" through discursive interactions with television and others in their everyday lives. Lembo's research also emphasizes the ways in which audiences use media as a means of discursive engagement with others. Their activities of judging, critiquing, incorporating or dismissing media narratives exemplify the *bricoleurs* at work, constructing meanings that ring true with their experiences. Finally, Thelen's study also highlights an active brigade of citizen-viewers who fashioned the public sphere in the image of their private relationships and discursive interactions.[57] Political action was seen as discursive, driven by personal values, and based on their engagement with the "characters" that media provided and with whom they identified. As such, television narratives brought politics vividly *to life* (and into their lives), to a place where citizens felt comfortable or emboldened enough to participate.

POLITICAL MEANING AND TELEVISION NARRATIVES

From these studies, then, we see how television serves as a significant source for the public's relationship to politics. For many citizens, politics is a textual practice that exists in the interplay between media representations and the discursive interactions that then occur between television and themselves within their intimate relationships. As a textual *practice*, however, we should focus our attention on how the "meaning" of politics is produced by citizens through their systematic interpretations of media offerings. As psychologist Jerome Bruner succinctly put it, culture "*gives meaning to action* by situating its underlying intentional states in an interpretive system. It does this by imposing the patterns inherent in the culture's symbolic systems—its language and discourse modes, the forms of logical and narrative explication, and the patterns of mutually dependent communal life."[58] Obviously, television has become a (if not *the*) dominant purveyor of communal life through the various languages, discourses, and narratives that citizens ritually attend to now in late modern society. But as Bruner also notes, "What makes a cultural community is not just shared beliefs about what people are like and what the world is like or how things should be valued"—all things that television ritually provides. Instead, "What may be just as important to the coherence of a culture is the existence of interpretive procedures for adjudicating the different construals of reality that are inevitable in any diverse society."[59] Of the languages, discourses, and narratives that television provides, how do we make sense of them, how do we chose what "realities" to believe and which to reject, and on what basis?

The most common interpretive procedure we utilize, Bruner argues, is "common sense" (what he also calls "folk psychology"), a cognitive system "by which people organize their experiences in, knowledge about, and transactions with the social world."[60] In media studies, Antonio Gramsci's writings on common sense have been the most widely employed in examining mass media content. As a Marxist, Gramsci's interest in common sense is how it serves the process of ideological legitimation and maintenance of ruling class power, or hegemony, a process whereby the ruling class's ideas become normalized assumptions of how the world works. Although it is a particularly helpful approach for examining ideological processes at work in capitalist media systems, that is not the emphasis or approach taken here. I, like Horace Newcomb and Paul M. Hirsch, do not find such processes of ideological maintenance surprising because "that is what central storytelling systems do in all societies."[61] Clifford Geertz also examines common sense, but he approaches it as a "cultural system."[62] Geertz has developed perhaps the most useful typology for analyzing common sense in practice, one to which we return in chapter 6.

For the purposes of my argument here, however, Bruner's exploration of common sense as a primary cognitive system for processing social realities has more theoretical significance. He characterizes common sense as a "set of more or less connected, more or less normative descriptions about how human beings 'tick,' what our own and other minds are like, what one can expect situated action to be like, what are possible modes of life, how one commits oneself to them, and so on."[63] What interests me in regard to television, however, is his contention that the organizing principle of common sense is "narrative in nature rather than logical or categorical" or conceptual.[64] It is through narrative that we process "established canonical expectations and the mental management of deviations from such expectations."[65] And this is the crux of the matter: that narrative provides an efficient means through which we establish both the normative and its breach through the stories we tell each other, stories that ultimately link us together in a common culture. The primary currency of television is, of course, narrative—whether it is news, dramas, documentaries, talk shows, home shopping, sports, or weather. Television is heavily invested in leading viewers through the narratives of normal/abnormal, the expected/unexpected, the acceptable/unacceptable, and new political television is awash in such narratives as well.

To argue as I have that much of our current engagement with politics occurs textually is to recognize that part of the process of making meaning of political and social realities will be located in the common sense narratives that television offers. The diversity and array of those narratives matter, as do the voices that are allowed to "speak" within narratives. And those narratives only begin the discussion, which is then continued by audiences as they engage in politics discursively with others. Some of the studies presented

above begin to offer a glimpse of how television's narratives play an important role in citizens' engagement with and thinking about politics. As seen in
the evidence presented by Thelen, many citizens refused to believe the "stories" that journalists were telling about "Ollie-mania" (the supposed infatua-
tion of the viewing audiences with the charismatic Colonel Oliver North).
The narratives that journalists and politicians constructed violated the audience's common sense understandings of politics and the bedrock principles
that government was supposed to protect. Therefore, many citizens "spoke
back" to the power of media and government by creating their own narratives to set the record straight. Or, as was seen in the study by Delli Carpini
and Williams, the focus group participants on environmental issues found
the narratives of both fictional and nonfictional television programming
equally meaningful and equally significant as referential material in their
talking and thinking about politics. Both were narratives that provided an
easy means of identification and understanding of political issues in fundamentally human terms.[66]

To argue, however, that television narratives are awash in canonical
common-sense understandings that allow people to make sense of the deviations from those norms, we should be careful not to fall into the trap of
believing that television is as ideologically monolithic (or hegemonically
effective) as scholars and critics on both the left and the right have made it
out to be. Its narratives, discourses, and common-sense thinking become a
means through which social/political issues and ideological dilemmas are
worked through, allowing politics to take a less violent path than many societies experience.[67] As Bruner notes, "In human beings, with their astounding narrative gift, one of the principal forms of peacekeeping is the
human gift for presenting, dramatizing, and explicating the mitigating circumstances surrounding conflict-threatening breaches in the ordinariness
of life. The objective of such narrative is not to reconcile, not to legitimize,
not even to excuse, but rather to explicate."[68]

John Ellis makes a similar argument when he asserts that television produces the social performance of what in psychoanalysis is called "working-
through," a "process whereby material is not so much processed into a finished product as continually worried over until it is exhausted."[69] By
extension, the same is true for television, he maintains. It "attempts to define,
tries out explanations, creates narratives, talks over, makes intelligible, tries
to marginalize, harnesses speculation, tries to make fit and, very occasionally, anathematizes."[70] Both of these arguments relate to Newcomb and
Hirsch's conception of television as a "cultural forum." The multiplicity of
messages and meanings offered by television suggests that television's overall emphasis is "on process rather than product, on discussion rather than in-
doctrination, on contradiction and confusion rather than coherence."[71] They
contend that "television does not present firm ideological conclusions—

despite its formal conclusions—so much as it comments on ideological problems."[72] In short, a cultural forum is a place in which it is more important to raise questions than to answer them. To bring the argument full circle by returning to the common sense found in television narratives, social psychologist Michael Billig and colleagues argue that common sense is an important means through which publics think through and discuss deeper "ideological dilemmas" that often lie at the heart of public issues and events.[73] Billig maintains that it is because "a social group's stock of commonsensical beliefs contains contrary elements that argument, and thereby thought, is possible."[74] Here again, common sense is central to public thought, and to envision television as a place where such thinking occurs about politics is to recognize television's central role in the construction of public life.

It is through the narratives of television and popular culture that we give meaning to political action by debating, arguing, mulling over, and working through that which television provides. Television is a site of common sense applications to politics through its narratives. It is a site that people look to for narratives that fulfill this need, a place to engage and work through the divergence between norms and realities, a place to apply lived experience to the intellectual constructions of state and ideology. News "stories" are a common starting place in the process of television's working through of public issues. News, however, is only the first (incomplete) step because it offers "bits of stories" but few endings. Hence its offerings are incomplete and frustrating to a narratively impatient audience, Ellis argues. Audiences often turn to talk shows next because these shows provide "greater narrative content that news can't provide."[75]

In political communication research, news is and has been the most thoroughly examined area of television, and the analysis of common sense within news narratives was one of the primary points of investigation in early British cultural studies research. More recently, scholars have examined the common sense found in talk show narratives, mainly those of daytime audience participation programming (such as *Oprah* and *Donahue*). The focus has generally centered on talk that pits "experts" versus "laity" on personal and social issues.[76] My investigation (in chapters 5, 6, and 7) focuses on the common-sense narratives of new political talk shows, the ways in which this programming offers interpretations of politics that are different from that offered by both news and the pundit variety of political talk shows. These common-sense narratives—in humor, monologues, skits, and group discussions—are produced in shows that exist in relation and response to news and other political talk programming, the latter having lost its appeal for many in the viewing public as a means of supplying sufficient explanations of social reality. As Paolo Carpignano, Robin Andersen, Stanley Aronowitz, and William DiFazio contend, "The present crisis of the public sphere is the result of . . . a crisis of legitimacy of the news as a social institution in its role of dissemination of information about and interpretation of events (i.e. the social construction of public life)."[77] The arrival of alternative political programming more firmly grounded in popular cultural appeals that offer *different* narratives of public life is, I argue, an important development for citizen engagement with politics on television.

CONCLUSIONS: POPULAR MEDIA WITHIN A CIVIC CULTURE

This discussion began with an assessment of current critiques of television and its supposed role in public disengagement with politics and traditional political institutions. The case has been made that television is instead a quite active source for audience engagement with public life. Politics has increasingly become a discursive behavior for audiences and that conversation occurs through the articulation of their public and private lives and their media surround. The argument I am making is that we should rethink what engagement with politics means as a result. Thelen also contends that textual activity by citizens (which he notes has greatly increased over the past generation) is perhaps "a much better activity from which to imagine the future of political participation than is a declining activity such as voting or more episodic ones such as strikes, demonstrations, and riots."[78] Finally, Carpignano et al. make the argument best, perhaps, when they offer us a choice: we can think of the reconstitution of the public sphere in terms of revitalization of old political organizations and politics as state management; or "if we conceive of politics today as emanating from social, personal, and environmental concerns, consolidated in the circulation of discursive practices rather than in formal organizations, then a common place that formulates and propagates common senses and metaphors that govern our lives might be at the crossroads of a reconceptualization of collective practices."[79]

The argument here is also addressed to criticisms that the boundaries between politics and entertainment are increasingly blurred, and that the supposed rational thinking that should surround all matters political is becoming subsumed by the entertainment and celebrity values of television and popular culture. My contention, based on the arguments and evidence presented above, is that popular culture—with television as the dominant engine driving it—is our central social practice that does more than offer spectacle, amusement, and distraction (although it certainly provides a bounty of that as well). Popular culture is, as John Street, Lawrence Grossberg, and Simon Frith have all argued, the primary location of our affective commitments in public life, the means through which we articulate our emotions to the wider world.[80] Popular culture is where we link our interests and pleasures to our identities, where we tell stories that are accessible and emotionally meaningful. Popular culture is proximate. It humanizes, simplifies, and embodies complex issues, concepts, and ideas. And to paraphrase Bruner's points about narrative, popular culture (and its narratives) is well fit for reiterating social norms without being didactic, persuading without being confrontational, and teaching without being polemical.[81]

From the studies reviewed above, it is clear that citizens do not segregate their practices of citizenship into "information" over here, "entertainment" over there. Many manifestations of mediated politics occur through our relationships with popular culture, and it is with popular culture that many citizens are emotionally invested. As Peter Dahlgren notes in regard to the citizenry's needs from media, "Information is necessary, though not sufficient. It must be made meaningful and must be related to previous understandings in order to become knowledge."[82] My argument is that for political life to be meaningful, its presence in venues that we ritually attend to, understand, are comfortable and familiar with, and maintain feelings and commitments to should not necessarily be seen in a negative light. And as will be seen in subsequent chapters, the political-oriented entertainment shows of new political television carry the dual quality of accessible popular culture and meaningful political material. Didactic, confrontational, and polemical is plentifully served up by the John McLaughlins, Bill O'Reillys, and Pat Buchanans of mediated political talk. New political television, I contend, offers something else.

I should warn, however, against any misreading of my argument as simply another populist (and formulaic) reading of audiences and popular culture that has become quite prevalent in cultural studies of late. That is, one might be tempted to see here an effort to celebrate the audience activities around the "disreputable" medium of television (or the lowbrow practices of popular culture) as being complex, progressive, or liberatory, thereby saving both the audience and the medium from the scorn typically levied by academic and cultural elites. Certainly there is an impetus here to present evidence to address continuing misconceptions about citizens and their relationship to television and politics that still, at this late date, continue to dominate the field of political communication (at least in America) and the discipline of political science. To argue, however, that people's relationship to television and popular culture is more meaning-full, substantive, and publicly constitutional than is often given credit for is not to argue that watching television will "save" democracy or that the masses will necessarily be "empowered" without moving their feet off the coffee table. Rather, the point I wish to advance is the need for a reconceptualization of how our common democratic culture is shaped by popular media and the practices that surround it.

I return to this point in the concluding chapter where I evaluate the evidence presented throughout this book in relationship to what Dahlgren calls our "civic culture." There I explore how popular media (and new political television, in particular) contribute culturally to the rudimentary components that support democracy—cultural aspects of democratic life such as common values, knowledge formation, identities as citizens, affinities for others, and democratic practices, one of which is the role, place, and importance of political discussion. Popular culture can support these cultural components when both producers and audiences make or find programming or other cultural practices politically meaningful and engage them as such. In short, popular culture is just as capable of shaping and supporting a culture of citizenship as it is of shaping and supporting a culture of consumption. This book explores evidence of those possibilities.

II

PRODUCING NEW POLITICAL TALK

3

From Insiders to Outsiders: The Advent of New Political Television

The airing of political talk on television has always assumed one crucial point: that those doing the talking should have direct "insider" knowledge of what they are talking about. The assumption by television producers has been that "expertise" should be the defining characteristic of who gets to speak—either by politicians who are directly involved, their handlers or strategists, or the journalists and opinion columnists whose job it is to study and report on their activities. The assumption is built on the belief that such speech is designed primarily to inform or educate, not fulfill other functions of political communication. By maintaining such a standard, however, a whole series of logical outcomes follow: that the subjects, issues, and players that properly constitute politics are the self-evident product of this expertise; that audiences are only interested in hearing expert opinions on politics; and that other forms of political discourse do not merit airing in the public sphere that television provides.

Such assumptions of speakers and audiences are, most certainly, the product of a political culture with expectations of an informed citizenry, a culture that has held the conduct of rational political thought as the discursive ideal.[1] They are also the product of a time in which social scientists, journalists, and even philosophers had a more prominent place in the national political dialogue conducted in the press and through mass-circulated magazines and journals prior to the arrival of television. And as various histories of political talk on television remind us, this thinking is the product of the history of network news bureaus that developed the shows, as well as the role and place that journalists felt they occupied as arbiters of political discussion and opinion.[2]

Over three decades later, these assumptions have changed. Although talk by political experts continues to dominate both network and cable political programming,[3] the decade of the 1990s ushered onto the stage a series of new programming types and specific cable channels that explicitly offered new forms and approaches to political talk on television. In particular, that change has been associated with the addition of talk not by political insiders, but inclusive now of those who position themselves outside the conventional wisdom and sense making of political elites. These new voices and programming types challenge the assumptions of what constitutes knowledge, who gets to speak, what issues can be addressed, as well as what types of political talk audiences will find both informative *and* pleasurable.

This chapter charts the evolution by first examining political talk on television from the network era through the first generation of cable programming (to the late 1980s), and then exploring how a series of developments and changes in the economic, political, cultural, and technological realms of American society in the 1980s and early 1990s provided the fertile soil from which new political programming would grow. Included here is a discussion of these changes in television that resulted from increased competition that was brought on by cable, leading to new risk taking, new programming stylistics, and attempts at new relationships with audiences. The discussion then turns to the rise of new forms of political talk television, beginning with the populist talk radio-style imitators that arose on cable and leading eventually to a transformation of cable news channels into ideologically driven talk programming. The analysis then turns to humorous political talk shows, including a comparison with their competition during that time slot—that is, late-night comedy talk shows. I examine how these new programs position themselves as both alternatives to and critiques of the fakery in news programming, pundit shows, and other late-night talk shows. The chapter concludes with a discussion of the new role these programs play as alternative political voices, including the guests and topics they host and the political stances they assume.

PUNDIT TALK IN THE NETWORK ERA

For much of television's history, political talk programming[4] has grown from the roots of journalism, in particular the practices of interviewing and op-ed writing. The earliest manifestations of this on network television were the shows *Meet the Press* on NBC (1947) and *Face the Nation* on CBS (1954), where newspaper and broadcast journalists interviewed government officials and newsmakers of the day.[5] The names of these shows, of course, signal the press's understanding of their role as representatives of the public and public interest through their journalistic interrogational style. That tradition lives on today through these shows, but also through descendants such as *Nightline* and *The NewsHour with Jim Lehrer*. Another type of early political talk program is the journalist roundtable discussion, first developed in 1969 through *Agronsky and Company*, hosted by television and radio journalist Martin Agronsky, and broadcast on public television. The show derives from the op-ed journalistic tradition and featured four journalists and Agronsky offering their opinions of the week's news events. The show was based in the belief that, because journalists are the closest independent observers of actions occurring in the political arena, they would offer the most informed yet impartial opinion of what was *really* going on. *Agronsky* (later renamed *Inside Washington*) became the model upon which programs such as *Washington Week in Review* (1967 on PBS), *The McLaughlin Group* (1982 on PBS), and *Capital Gang* (1988 on CNN) were formulated.

It is from this type of programming that critics have derisively given the participants the name "pundits," derived from the ancient Sanskrit word meaning "learned man." But as the word made its way into the English language, it became not only a reference for someone who gives authoritative opinions, but is also used in "mocking the pretensions of those who nag politicians through public and widely circulated observations."[6] Rather than simply an annoying gadfly role, critics contend that pundit programs are, in essence, somewhat dangerous because these journalists tend to spout opinions on all sorts of issues and events that they generally have little knowledge of as reporters (hence, they aren't really expert thinkers, just expert talkers). As Dan Nimmo and James E. Combs contend, "They now constitute a source of opinion-formation and opinion-articulation, agenda-setting and agenda-evaluation, so vast as to make the United States a punditocracy: a nation where the mediation of opinion by important and highly visible media figures is paramount."[7]

The last type of political talk show is somewhat an amalgam of the first two, whereby one or two commentators hold a discussion (rather than an interview) with a guest, thus creating a context in which opinions are freely forthcoming, albeit connected to political actors of the day. The pioneer and, in many ways, defining show in this sub-genre is *Firing Line*, a syndicated program first offered by RKO in 1966, featuring the firebrand conservative and founder of the *National Review*, William F. Buckley Jr.[8] Programs of similar structure that have developed over the years include *Crossfire* (1982 on CNN) and, to some extent, *This Week with David Brinkley* (1981 on ABC). On *Firing Line*, Buckley took the concept of televised political debate seriously and would resort to all manner of rhetorical techniques (both fair and out-of-bounds) to win his encounters. Buckley's producer even conceived the show as "an intellectual version of Friday night at the fights."[9] Buckley's take-no-prisoners approach to political discourse, complete with name-calling, physical threats, interruptions, and put-downs, was the presentational model of televised political discourse from which many subsequent programs have drawn.

Indeed, although the typology of shows offered above is based on the structural features of the programming and the arrangement of the cast that conducts those discussions, a more fruitful approach might be to chart the lineage of political talk based on the ideological leanings and discursive style that these shows offer. In such a formulation, the logical progression moves from the pedantic style and postwar libertarian brand of conservatism offered by Buckley to the belligerent style and Reagan school of neo-conservatism in John McLaughlin, to the inanely blowhard style and rabid right-wing reactionary Bill O'Reilly, the current king of agonistic political talk on cable television. This reformulated lineage also recognizes that the *quality* of political talk has seen a marked devolution from the days of *Firing Line*, not to mention the ideological triumph of conservativism.[10] Buckley, whom most people (including his archenemies) concede possessed a high level of intelligence, has spawned O'Reilly, who almost singlehandedly has shown that a talk show host need know nothing about anything to hold forth on every issue in stunning ignorance and yet draw the largest audience in cable political talk (and be a best-selling author to boot!). And, of course, O'Reilly is simply one of many manifestations of political talk in the rotisserie league of programming now found on the cable channels Fox News, MSNBC, CNN, and CNBC.[11]

Although this review of the genre of pundit-based political talk is cursory, the detailed histories provided by Alan Hirsch, Eric Alterman, and Nimmo and Combs lead to three primary conclusions about the nature of these shows, their participants, and the talk that is offered there.[12] First, and perhaps most importantly, the independent and impartial observer of politics that the journalistic form assumes is, in fact, neither of those things. That is to say, although most pundits retain jobs as columnists for major newspapers and news magazine weeklies, their participation in televised political talk has clearly shown how closely connected to power they are. Indeed, several prominent pundits (or their wives) have been employed in various presidential administrations.[13] Yet they all are active participants in the political sphere, employ an epistemology often called "inside-the-beltway" thinking, and contribute to the conventional wisdom and general circulation of meanings of politics that emanate from the nation's capital. Perhaps more damning, these pundits are full-scale participants in the spreading of rumors, the settling of scores, and intrabureaucratic power struggles typical of Washington politics.[14] *MediaWeek* reporter Alicia Mundy notes the important role that Sunday morning talk shows play in Washington political maneuverings: "These shows aren't mere entertainment, nor are they simply commentary," she writes. "Today, politicians use these shows to make news and to make waves. They use them to send signals to their allies and to the opposition. And they use them to evaluate their own packaging and marketing efforts."[15] In short, these pundits are not commentators on the system—they and their shows *are* the system.

The second, and related, conclusion about television's pundits is that they are not just journalists, but celebrity elites in their own right. As pundit Robert Novak notes, "When I'm recognized now it is as a television celebrity. Not even as a television commentator!"[16] As such, they are guests in the Georgetown social circles and maintain personal friendships with politicians, including many a president. They not only command larger salaries than their non-televised peers but also parlay their celebrity status into enormous speaking fees on the lecture circuit.[17] In short, they are the visible face of political opinion, and as a result have a vested interest—as all celebrities do—in maintaining that image by staying within the bounds of the celebrity system that created them.[18]

The final and overriding conclusion that can be drawn from pundit television is that its reality belies the argument that those with high levels of political knowledge will offer the highest forms of rational political discourse. What pundit television has clearly shown is that more often than not, their public presentations are pure spectacle. As noted above, the rhetorical flourishes of Buckley have only grown into full-blown circuses on programs like *The McLaughlin Group*, perhaps the flagship show in this regard. Most pundits, regardless of the program on which they appear, have learned the lessons of what makes for good television. Calm, thoughtful, introspective, and compromising demeanors are not among them. Audiences also recognize the spectacle nature of these talk "shows," but the incestuousness of the participants and their banter ultimately limits its audience appeal beyond those who can both keep up with the demands of insider knowledge yet also stomach the bellicose displays of showmanship.[19]

In sum, then, what has become the dominant form of political talk on television does not adhere to the journalistic ideals of objectivity, dispassion, or rational thought from which it was supposedly born. What has developed in its stead are programs that feature celebrity commentators who are intimately connected to power, who participate in a circumscribed system of political thinking, and who construct a discursive spectacle with limited appeal beyond the political cognoscenti or political junkies. Although it has been argued that these programs probably do more in greasing the wheels of the establishment than in informing and educating an electorate, as far as television political talk is concerned, these programs have generally been the only game in town. In turn, the viewing and voting public has received the media's message: "*This* is politics—love it or leave it." Of course, what was shown through the tremendously low levels of voter turnout in the 1988 presidential and 1990 congressional elections was that people were, in fact, leaving it in droves.

Hence, as a series of changes in the political and economic climate began to take hold in the 1980s and early 1990s, television producers recognized the weaknesses in the system and began to offer new forms of political talk programming they believed audiences were interested in seeing. Any objections that these new forms of political talk programming would be illegitimate because of their using celebrity hosts, or allowing people who were not experts to talk, or producing an entertainment spectacle all seemed moot because of what pundit television itself had become. Before discussing that programming, however, we must understand the changes in politics, technology, culture, and the economics within the media industries that laid the groundwork for these new types of programs.

CONTEXTUAL CHANGES

The most significant factor in shaping politics and political culture in the 1980s was the election and popularity of Ronald Reagan.[20] As a Hollywood celebrity, he maintained the credentials to effectively communicate his outsider status and his conservative populist mantra that government is not part of the problem—rather, it *is* the problem. To a great extent, Reagan's popularity was not built on actual policies or programs that benefited the vast majority of Americans who supported him, but rather on his posturing against government as a negative force in American life.[21] By the 1988 presidential election, both Republican and Democratic candidates Pat Robertson and Jesse Jackson attempted to assume Reagan's populist mantle by running "outsider" campaigns.[22] Although unsuccessful in their electoral bids, the populist rhetoric they offered from both the far right and far left would appear again two years later when populist angst became a driving force in several "Throw the Rascals Out" campaigns in the midterm congressional elections.[23] Two years hence, such angst again found its embodiment in Ross Perot's outsider presidential campaign with his "common sense" approach to government and town hall meetings to find out what "the people" really wanted from government.[24] Perot also led the way in using popular, nonpolitical television talk shows as a primary means of communicating with the public. Indeed, his candidacy was a product of his appearance on *Larry King Live* in which he informed the audience that if the American people wanted to draft him to run, he was willing to finance that effort himself.[25] As the campaign progressed, all of the presidential candidates appeared on similar types of "populist" entertainment talk shows to communicate directly with "the people" as well as to avoid the more confrontational questioning that typically occurred in forums with the press.[26] Yet again, two years later many citizens signed up with Republicans who now joined the populist bandwagon by promising fail-safe legislative guarantees through written "contracts" with the public.[27]

A component of this populist upsurge was the language of "common sense." Citizens and politicians embraced common sense as the Holy Grail of the legitimacy crisis, a cure-all remedy that would supposedly bring sanity, clarity, and efficiency to out-of-control politicians and bureaucrats.[28] Vice President Al Gore sought to sell his efficiency-in-government report by dressing it up as a voting man's beer commercial—*Common Sense Government: Works Better and Costs Less*. Around the same time, lawyer Philip K. Howard produced a best seller called *The Death of Common Sense: How Law Is Suffocating America*, which, in turn, attracted fawning Democratic and Republican suitors at both the national and state levels who wished to align themselves with this popular manifesto.[29] The rhetoric of common sense also sought codification by becoming one of the ten commandments of the Republican Party's "Contract With America," including a piece of legislation advanced in Congress known as "The Common Sense Legal Reform Act of 1995."[30]

This same period also witnessed the fluidity between the fields of politics and media. The traditional revolving door between government and industry became much more high profile. Politicians who once garnered media attention while serving in some capacity as government officials or political candidates became media celebrities after departing government service by working for media corporations that attempted to exploit their celebrity name-value. Oliver North, Mario Cuomo, Ross Perot, Jesse Jackson, Jerry Brown, Susan Molinari, George Stephanopoulos, David Gergen, and Pat Buchanan, among others, all found work in some capacity as on-air personalities. This movement toward "politician as celebrity," however, was simply a continuation of the dwindling loss of public identification with political parties and widespread public emphasis on choosing among politicians as *individuals* whom they "get to know" through media exposure.[31] As public frustration with government increased, politicians distanced themselves from traditional political structures, posturing as political "outsiders" not beholden to any interest except the mandate of "the people."

In summarizing the changes in the political climate, then, the decade of the 1980s and early 1990s witnessed an intermixing of celebrity and politics, the appeal to commonsensical ways of talking and thinking about politics, and a concurrent upsurge in populist anti-politics by a public that was increasingly finding the political arena repugnant. Audiences therefore tuned in to politicians on entertainment talk shows precisely because these shows did *not* produce the traditional staid political talk they had grown accustomed to. Instead, audiences now found that they too were allowed to ask questions of the candidates, and that responses came in a language that was more accessible and commonsensical than the highly cloaked and guarded language of spin offered in other venues.[32]

In the technological realm, political anxiety mixed with social expectations and technological opportunities to produce a degree of populist hope. The 1990s saw the flowering of potentialities developed in the 1980s through the microcomputer and cable television revolutions. The Internet became a commercial, social, and political reality, especially for middle- and upper-class citizens at that time. Expectations of media-driven political change rose amid a rhetoric of technological progress, exemplified by claims of five hundred cable channels, electronic town hall meetings, worldwide communication in the global village, easy access to political information in the form of citizen-centered presidential debates, candidate appearances on phone-in talk shows, congressional e-mail addresses, and the ability to organize and identify with like-minded people in cyberspace.[33] The frontiers of space and time had seemingly been conquered, and the divisions between elite and mass discourse seemingly overcome. Problems associated with recalcitrant politicians and bureaucracies would disappear as people became empowered by new communication technologies to participate in the decisions that govern their lives (or at least to make better and easier choices from the menus provided).[34]

In the cultural realm, citizens waged ideological battles in what is often called the "culture wars."[35] Roughly speaking, the term refers to the prolonged disagreements between liberals and conservatives over issues such as sexual orientation, racial identity, physical access equality, media representations, religion, public morality, and gender relations. These battles have been conducted as much through social institutions or cultural patterns and behaviors (such as media, language, "lifestyle," academia, religion) as through formal politics. The battlegrounds are quite fluid, though, to the point where cultural battles can be waged in political forums (judicial rulings, impeachment hearings, etc.),[36] and political battles may be waged in cultural forums such as talk television. "Political correctness" became the term used by conservatives and moderates alike to derisively chide efforts by liberals and progressives to alter what were seen as harmful, stereotypical, or ideologically loaded practices in society. Political correctness mandated certain behaviors, critics claimed, and resistance to such efforts in a strongly individualistic American society appeared with great frequency in public life, including on television talk shows.

Also in the realm of popular culture came a general displacement of afternoon soap operas with syndicated, issue-oriented talk shows. Although these types of shows had their initial success through male-hosted programs such as *Donahue* and *Geraldo* in the 1980s, it was the success of Oprah Winfrey and a bevy of imitators such as Jenny Jones, Sally Jessy Raphael, and Ricki Lake that led to the enormous expansion of the genre in the early to mid-1990s.[37] As has been examined in numerous scholarly works, these shows typically discuss personal issues such as anorexia, teenage pregnancy, incest, homosexuality, and so on, and involve both experts and laity on stage with the host moderating. Eventually in each program, the audience participates in the discussion, and it is here that scholars have argued that laity has successfully offered challenges to institutionally based expertise.[38] These programs have since grown into what has been called "trash television," featuring guests who appear on the program to reveal bizarre sexual and personal peccadilloes, or who appear so they can "confront" other people in their lives, all for the camera to record and witness as exotic spectacle. The king and queen of trash television, many people widely acknowledge, are hosts Jerry Springer and Ricki Lake.[39]

In the economic realm of media industries, the wisdom of "the people" also became a value that producers realized could be commodified. Talk radio formats became the godsend of AM stations nationwide as listeners and participants revived a flailing industry with populist political talk. Talk radio host Rush Limbaugh led the way, but a bevy of conservative copycats were also spawned nationwide by Limbaugh's success, such as Ken Hamblin ("The Black Avenger"), G. Gordon Liddy, and Sean Hannity.[40] Trying to model the success of talk radio, as well as tap into the interactive capabilities brought on by the Internet craze, cable television entrepreneurs developed talk television channels and programming strategies that sought to mobilize populist angst by showcasing commonsense commentary of the average person and exploiting interactive technologies to intensify the connection with the viewing audience. CNN developed an hour-long daily program, *TalkBack Live* (1994); MSNBC's precursor was America's Talking (1994); Multi-Media/Gannett produced the Talk Channel (1994) (renamed NewsTalk Television in 1995); C-SPAN introduced its morning call-in show, *Washington Journal*; Republican party activists produced National Empowerment Television (1993; renamed America's Voice in 1998), a channel that actually billed itself as explicitly "populist." Around the same time, two comedians stepped forward with shows that featured entertaining political talk in new and unusual formats for both the political and entertainment genre: *Dennis Miller Live* appeared on HBO in 1994, and Comedy Central introduced *Politically Incorrect* in 1993, only to lose it to network television four years later.

In sum, then, by the early 1990s, an environment existed in which populist rhetoric and thinking had become a popular vehicle for addressing political anxiety, where "common sense" became a catchall solution to complex problems, and where political celebrity became the point of public identification with new types of politics that might provide a more appealing solution. This is a social environment where communication technologies offered hope and optimism for overcoming one-way flows of communication from distant forces of bureaucracy and control, thereby giving people greater voice, access, and choice. It is a cultural environment in which political struggles are increasingly played out in cultural forums such as talk shows, and it is an economic environment where media industries competitively struggle to create programs and channels that are cheap to produce, yet innovative and popular with audience tastes. Also important to note here is how interrelated these processes are: disillusionment in politics leads to hopeful answers in technology and new media; frustration with government finds an outlet in culture, including the primary currency in popular culture of "celebrity"; cultural wars become political wars (and vice versa), and hence, attractive content for conflict-driven media programming; technological convergence produces opportunities for political and economic exploitation; economic competition results in new forms of programming related to politics featuring technology.

In understanding the type of political programming that would develop from this context, it is important that we examine in some detail the television industry's specific response to the increased competition brought on by the rapidly expanded offerings made available by cable. That is, it bears asking: What specific measures did programmers take (in particular, for both new and existing cable channels) not only to mark themselves as appealing to audiences, but also to establish different *relationships* with audiences based on that appeal?

TELEVISUAL STYLE, AUDIENCES, AND "OUTSIDER" TALK

Two major things occurred in the postnetwork period of the late 1980s and early 1990s that speak to the issues at hand: the television industry's change in programming style to appeal to audiences in new and different ways, and the concomitant popularity of syndicated audience participation shows in afternoon programming and their effect in altering assumptions about such issues as authority, voice, knowledge, and participation in television's presentation of public issues. It is from these two major developments that new political television was formed, leading to a style of political programming inclusive of "outsider" political voices provided by both comedians and the nonexpert public itself.

The first of these developmental changes was produced as a result of the rise of competition to the network oligopoly from cable programmers. For the networks, consumers were now able to choose from a broad array of more narrowly defined options on cable for their viewing pleasures (sports, music, news, etc.). For new and existing cable channels, the challenge was to provide some level of interesting and attractive content that would draw viewers away from their former habits of attending to network programming, but also away from *other* cable competition. In the process, it was necessary to give the network a specific "brand image" in viewers' minds. The increased competition led one network executive in 1993 to state, "It's not business as usual anymore. We have got to find ways to recreate this business so that it will survive into the next decade."[41] In addition to this increased competition, the industry was also experiencing changing production factors such as advances in audio-visual technologies and changing costs of production, both allowing for newer presentational aesthetics and altered appeals to audiences.

John Thornton Caldwell offers perhaps the most thorough and illuminating analysis of the ways in which the industry responded. The means the networks used to fight for survival, he argues, involved an intensive program of innovation and stylistic development. The new look offered is what he calls "televisuality," an aesthetic tendency toward excessive style. "Television moved from a framework that approached broadcasting primarily as a form of word-based rhetoric and transmission," he notes, "to a visually based mythology, framework, and aesthetic based on extreme self-consciousness of style."[42] Style became the subject, the defining practice of television as a means of attaining a distinctive look in the battle for audience share. Excessive style, however, is more than simply a visual phenomenon. Instead, it becomes a means of developing a "look" by individualizing programs in viewers' minds via their distinctive appeal.

A driving force behind the need for this new exhibitionism was the changing relationship between audiences and the televisual product. "The individuation and semiotic heterogeneity evident in televisual excess," he argues, "means that such shows are from the start defined by, and pitched at, niche audiences who are flattered by claims of difference and distinction."[43] These new rules affect both viewers and industry, and the texts that exist between them. Viewers are positioned as savvy and self-conscious televisual consumers by the industry, while the texts "demand a more conscious form of viewer negotiation."[44]

Simultaneous with this reconfiguration of industry perspective was the increasing popularity and multiplicity of syndicated issue-oriented afternoon talk shows, often called audience participation programs. As noted above, an enormous body of scholarly work has been devoted to exploring these programs and their place in society. What merits our attention here are the conclusions these scholars make in two regards: first, how (through the inclusion of studio audience participation in creating these programs) these shows led the way for audiences to question what constituted "authority" and "expertise" in televised talk about issues of public concern, including questioning who has the right to speak and be heard about such issues; and second, how such programming has eroded the boundaries between the differing programming genres of talk (e.g., the "entertaining" and the "serious"). Paulo Carpignano, Robin Andersen, Stanley Aronowitz, and William DiFazio argue that audience participation programs "problematize the distinction between expert and audience, professional authority and layperson." For them, these shows "constitute a 'contested space' in which new discursive practices are developed in contrast to the traditional modes of political and ideological representation."[45] Through talk that often pits "experts" against "laity," these authors highlight the importance of the studio audiences' (and perhaps the viewing audiences' as well) rejection of the claims offered by authority figures:

> What is expressed is a refusal not of knowledge but of expertise. The talk show rejects the arrogance of a discourse that defines itself on the basis of its difference from common sense. In debate, the authority of the expert is replaced by the authority of a narrative informed by lived experience.[46]

Similarly, in their study of British and American talk shows, Sonia Livingstone and Peter Lunt make an analogous argument by expanding upon Jürgen Habermas's conception of a separation between the life-world and system-world, that is, the differences between the organic knowledge derived from lived lives and that of the specialized knowledge produced within the professionalized and institutionalized logic of "the system." They contend that these shows "adopt an anti-elitist position which implicitly draws on . . . alternative epistemological traditions, offering a revaluation of the life-world, repudiating criticisms of the ordinary person as incompetent or ignorant, questioning the deference traditionally due to experts through their separations from the life-world and their incorporation into the system, and asserting instead the worth of the 'common man.'"[47] Livingstone and Lunt find these altered patterns to be so substantive that they read into the British media at large a tendency for movement "away from critical exposition and commentary. Letting ordinary people speak for themselves is replacing critically conscious social realism."[48]

The second conclusion from this literature is that contemporary talk shows are a distinctive field of discourse composed of intergeneric and crossgeneric features where the boundaries between the "serious" and the "popular" or "entertaining" are increasingly blurred.[49] The reason this is possible, argues Wayne Munson, is that the talk show is a contingent and malleable form of programming—a hybrid, by definition. The talk show, he contends, "combines two communicative paradigms, and like the term itself, the 'talkshow' fuses and seems to reconcile two different, even contradictory, rhetorics. It links conversation, the interpersonal—the premodern oral tradition—with the mass-mediated spectacle born of modernity."[50] Within it, there is space for the creation of multiple points of audience identification, as well as the opportunity for programmers to "refresh" the televisual landscape. He argues,

> the talkshow mingles the "professional" or "expert" with the "amateur," the guest or participant who appears by virtue of particular personal experience or simple audience membership. It shrewdly combines the folk and the popular with the mass, the immediate and interpersonal with the mediated, in a productive dialectic that both reflects and constructs an image economy's "voracious need for change and innovation" and for "continually changing the rules, and replacing the scenery," as Andrew Ross puts it.[51]

The result of these changing and recombinatory forms is the fact that the audiences for such programming are increasingly "fragmented." Echoing Caldwell's claim that television producers sought to create new relationships with niche audiences who are flattered by claims of distinction, Andrew Tolson argues that there "is no longer the general 'popular' audience (targeted by mass advertising), but rather it is diversified into cults and cliques, characterized by different kinds of 'knowingness.'"[52]

In short, this literature illuminates features that would also become distinguishing characteristics of new political television. These features include the cross-generic construction of programming, the inclusion of "ordinary voices," the range of diverse positions presented, the challenge to "expert" authority, the informal conversational style, and the usage of a common vernacular and "common sense" thinking about issues and solutions that were traditionally approached through professional languages and knowledge. These features are important in that they offer a qualitatively different approach to the more paternalistic political discourse offered through pundit television. Combined with Caldwell's observations about stylistic excess in postnetwork television, programmers of the new populist brand of political television (discussed below) utilized angry political talk as a stylistic marker, a distinctive presentation of excess wrapped in the gadgetry and buzz of new communication technologies. Furthermore, viewers were flattered by a rhetoric that their voices mattered, and that America was waiting to hear what they had to say. A new relationship was built on viewer activity around the televisual text, rewarding the viewer as an "engaged" citizen as he or she helped construct the programming. Television's search for style, then, its search for a new and different look, actually opened up new modes of discourse and new forms of participation and presentation for political talk on television that had previously been ignored or disregarded.

VOX POP PROGRAMMING AND THE TRANSFORMATION OF CABLE NEWS

Cable television in the mid-1990s gave birth to a handful of programs and channels offering an eclectic array of programming featuring audience-centered political talk. NBC, Multi-Media/Gannett, CNN, C-SPAN, and the Free Congress Foundation all constructed programs or entire cable channels dedicated to offering an "outsider" political voice in the mode of talk radio.[53] As a cheap form of programming, these groups attempted to ride the waves of success not only of talk radio, but also of the populist rhetoric of the anti-politics/ anti-government groundswell and the buzz over new communication technologies. Indeed, cable programmers attempted to access these citizen/viewer dissatisfactions with politics *via* the promise of communication technologies, thereby allowing programmers to establish both stylistic and content changes relatively inexpensively while providing enormous potential for including its audience within the programming beyond talk radio's disembodied voices. Political commentary and opinions from viewing audiences could become part of the programming via e-mail, faxes, voice mail, phone calls, chat rooms, video-conferencing, and bulletin board systems. The stylish new programming also offered high-tech sets and gadgetry featuring fax machines, screen "crawls," computer screens, video kiosks in malls and shopping centers, and other visual displays of "the people's voice" in action.

As Caldwell argues, competition in the cable marketplace required these distinctive stylistic markers but also required an appeal for new and more significant relationships with viewers. The move to "the people's voice" in cable programming created different temporal and spatial relationships with viewing audiences as networks encouraged viewers to extend their participation in the program prior to, during, and after a particular show's airing by joining in discussions via chat rooms, bulletin boards, e-mail, and voice mail. In short, audiences were tired of elite-centered political and social discourse, cable network executives argued, and therefore were perceived as interested in consuming new forms of talk programming that included their own voices and concerns.

Efforts in this regard include NBC's attempt to exploit synergies between their broadcast and cable properties by creating America's Talking on July 4, 1994, a new channel dedicated to all-talk programming (which became MSNBC two years later). America's Talking (A-T) was NBC's effort to expand the limited talk television concept that it was featuring on CNBC during prime-time hours into an all-talk format. With talk radio's enormous popularity in mind, the network hired Roger Ailes, former Republican Party strategist and the executive producer of Rush Limbaugh's syndicated television program, to head both America's Talking and CNBC. As a result, Ailes brought the impulses he developed with Limbaugh to the new network, offering initial program lineups and an overall channel concept that mirrored the success Limbaugh was having with his "common man" persona and rage-against-the-liberal-system populism.

With programs like *Pork* (about government waste and corruption), *Bugged!* (billed as "primal scream therapy brought to you courtesy of the information superhighway"), and *Am I Nuts?* (about the stresses of everyday life), Ailes sought to construct the network as an outlet for the perceived frustrations viewers were supposedly experiencing with modern life.[54] He also emphasized that the network was "trying to represent real people."[55] A-T sought to position itself on the cutting edge of televisual difference by acting on the assumption that audiences don't passively watch television anymore but instead actively participate in constructing programming. Twelve of A-T's programs incorporated on-line bulletin boards, polling, electronic mail, and chat room services.[56] The linking of technology and populist politics was intended to flatter and involve a certain niche audience, thereby not waiting for an audience to appear, but in many ways attempting to create it.

The same populist impulse was seen in the programming of National Empowerment Television (NET), a small cable channel officially associated with the Free Congress Foundation—a conservative political organization founded by Republican party activist Paul Weyrich. NET launched on December 6, 1993, and was run as a tax-exempt, nonprofit entity. The primary purpose of the channel was not to make a profit, but to impact politics. Its mission was simple: empower people to hold (liberal) political elites accountable. That task would be achieved, they argued, first, by providing programming that would bypass the media elite, presenting their viewers "unbiased" and "truthful" information necessary to see the lies they were being told by mainstream media and elite politicians; and second, by providing the means—interactive call-in programming—through which Americans could "talk back to Washington" and thereby "put government on the defensive."[57] "Our bent is populist," proclaimed Burton Pines, vice chairman of the network. "America has a grievance against Washington. We will be on America's side, not Washington's side."[58] The network sought to empower its viewers (and achieve their loyalty) primarily through its programming, 80 percent of which incorporated viewer call-ins. But as a network that arose alongside the conservative populism of Newt Gingrich et al. and the "Republican Revolution" of 1994, the network found that it could not sustain itself as those forces subsided, and ultimately it declared bankruptcy in January 2000.

One final example of the move toward featuring "outsider" audience voices in cable programming came from CNN. In an effort to bolster its afternoon ratings when no news stories merited extensive coverage, the network introduced *TalkBack Live* on August 22, 1994. *TalkBack* was a one-hour public affairs talk show that aired in the heart of CNN's afternoon schedule (3:00 P.M. EST), and sought the traditional town hall meeting as its romantic corollary. Upon its launch, CNN argued that the program would create a national forum for dialogue, a place to build bridges and seek commonality, a place where publics could interact with policy makers who had power to "change things." Whereas America's Talking incorporated interactive technologies for both stylistic and populist purposes, *TalkBack* embraced a rhetoric of democratic utopianism—technology as a means of reviving democracy, providing access to power, and bringing the nation closer together. "The point is to re-create an old-time town meeting using the most advanced technology to create a connection that I think we lack," said Teya Ryan, the show's executive producer.[59] "People are interested not simply in what the experts have to say, but what their fellow Americans have to say," she noted elsewhere.[60]

Like America's Talking, *TalkBack* would employ numerous technological vehicles to incorporate the lay voice into the program, including phone calls, electronic mail, faxes, videoconferencing, and chat groups. The show's original host, Susan Rook, argued, "This is 'Crossfire' for real people."[61] The studio set was built to visually represent the interactive nature of the program (as well as effectively merge the spheres of business, consumption, and politics into one seamless whole). Constructed in the atrium lobby of CNN Center in downtown Atlanta, the set would seat up to 150 people, including tourists, shoppers, workers, and local residents. In addition to a live audience, the program integrated the voices and messages of viewers at home by including a table in the middle of the set with a ten-line telephone, a fax machine, and computer terminal. Producers off-screen would also integrate viewer opinions and questions via video remotes and on-line comments while allowing faxes to pop out of the machine on stage.[62]

As both the populist and techno-euphoric mood of the country receded substantially by the turn of the century, the overt rhetoric of angry voters, town hall meetings, alienation from Washington, and electronic democracy largely left with it. With *TalkBack Live*'s cancellation on March 7, 2003, only C-SPAN's morning call-in show, *Washington Journal*, has survived as a program solely dedicated to interactive viewer participation centered on politics.[63] What this discussion offers, however, is insight into how cable television programmers attempted to exploit the mood and context of the moment, and in turn challenged the normative conceptions of who gets to speak about politics on television and what will be spoken about. America's Talking, National Empowerment Television, and *TalkBack Live* altered the landscape by insisting that the audience was not simply to be spoken *to*, but also to be spoken *with*. The audience was welcomed into the conversation and flattered—not only for what they know, but also for their technological savvy and abilities to connect to information and share it with others. Television had finally asserted that politics isn't just what occurs inside the beltway but rather is also what people make of it in their daily experiences and activities of living. These programs and channels were venues, according to the producers, where citizens could express themselves, connect to power and to each other, and create political change. Each of these three encouraged, to various degrees, an "us versus them" approach in attracting disaffected audiences to political talk—a marked change from the pundits' assumption of a public as a singular "us."[64]

The legacy of this programming for new political television is twofold. First are the formal components of the programming that are active today in other talk shows. The outsider public voice is still present in political programming in various ways. For instance, *Crossfire* changed its format to include viewer e-mail, as well as beginning performing before (and fielding questions from) a studio audience that formerly did not exist. Many of the other talk programs on cable news networks (such as the popular *The O'Reilly Factor*) also feature viewer e-mail.

Perhaps the most substantial and lasting legacy of Vox Pop programming, however, has been the stunning success of Roger Ailes and his almost singlehanded transformation of the genre of cable news programming. When America's Talking became MSNBC in 1996 (Microsoft and NBC's effort to up the technological ante by further enhancing the linkages between television news and on-line viewer activity), Roger Ailes left the network to become programming chief at Fox News. Whereas Ailes had generally failed to capitalize on his efforts to feature conservative, populist, and bombastic rhetoric with *The Rush Limbaugh Show* and America's Talking, here he found success by cloaking it in the mantle of journalistic "objectivity." Featuring overtly conservative talk show hosts and programming and outright ideologically biased news reporting, the network nevertheless brands itself "Fair and Balanced." The network has also retained its alignment with "the people" from Ailes's Vox Pop days by using slogans such as "we report, you decide" in its promotional materials. In some ways, the network doesn't shy from the conservative label placed on it by critics because it argues that "the American people" believe the news media is liberal, and hence the network is therefore offering a corrective choice.[65]

Since 1996, Fox News, CNN, and MSNBC have been the leading networks featuring political talk programming on cable. In general, these "news" channels have experienced a weakening in the audiences for the hard news format of CNN, an enormous rise in the audiences for the opinionated talk programming of Fox News, and a complete about-face for the programming strategies employed at MSNBC in the wake of its dwindling viewership.[66] In short, what has occurred is that these "news" channels actually program more hours of talk shows than news.[67]

Waving American flag banners in the corner of the screen, Fox News became the cable news leader after the terrorist attacks of September 11, 2001. The political mood had changed from one of know-it-all viewers in a robust America to a public desperate for answers after one of the most puzzling and disturbing events in American history.[68] Fox News embraced the flag and its own patriotic hubris in establishing a connection with its viewers in America's "War on Terrorism," employing the same "us versus them" rhetoric of the Vox Pop days, only now with a different "enemy." The "people's voice," it seems, would be that of Bill O'Reilly, with his common-sense rhetoric and his use-and-abuse style with guests who just don't get it. Or perhaps that voice is Geraldo Rivera, the surrogate American qua Fox News reporter rummaging through the caves of Tora Bora, Afghanistan, with a pistol on his hip in search of Osama bin Laden! In sum, it may be talk television under the label of "news," but the excessive style of discursive spectacles (whether through lay or expert voices, screaming hosts, or roving reporters) and the alignment with and flattering of the viewing public (through e-mails

and studio audiences, ideological sensibility, or patriotic zeal) is still a fix-
ture in political talk programming on cable.

The arbitrary boundaries between experts and nonexperts are now much
more fluid, and the variety of ways in which programs intentionally recognize and flatter their audiences have greatly increased from the earlier model
of political talk programming. Whether the exaggerated claims of political
"empowerment" for viewers by "talking back" to power made by Vox Pop
producers in the mid-1990s were ever achieved is questionable. What did occur in the process, however, is a reformulation by television producers and
audiences of what counts as desirable and attractive political talk on television. What also occurred concurrent with Vox Pop programming was the appearance of two comedy-driven talk shows with politics at the center of the
discussions.[69]

HUMOROUS POLITICAL
TALK SHOWS AND LATE-NIGHT TELEVISION

Late-night network television is generally dominated by two types of programming: the local newscast of network affiliates, followed by the late-
night talk shows featuring David Letterman and Jay Leno, among others.[70]
The problem with this programming for three comedians—Bill Maher, Dennis Miller, and Jon Stewart—is that these forms of programming have lost all
relevance as either meaningful forums for public discourse and/or entertainment. Indeed, these comedians argue that the talk and comedy on the late-
night shows offer the public nothing but boring banter with celebrities pitching their latest project and politically irrelevant comedy from uninspired
hosts. The local and national broadcast and cable news is also deficient, offering "news" that is manipulative, trivial, and fatuous, so much so that reporters have turned reporting into entertainment. Each of these comedians,
over the course of the 1990s and early 2000s, set out to address these deficiencies by offering their own brand of politically humorous talk show as an-
tidote. Indeed, from what the record shows, their intention in crafting these
shows seems to have been as much an effort to address deficiencies in programming as it was to redress the lack of meaningful *political* talk available
to citizen-viewers. What has resulted, however, is the emergence of three politically engaged, aggressively iconoclastic, sharp-tongued, and sharp-witted
comedian-hosts who have offered truly original political programming that
addresses the fakery in public life as manifest in news and late-night television talk.

The three programs that led the way in the development of the humorous
political talk show are *Politically Incorrect with Bill Maher, Dennis Miller
Live,* and *The Daily Show with Jon Stewart.*[71] Each is discussed at length in

subsequent chapters, but here they are examined for what they share in common: their critique of the fakery in news, late-night television, and political rhetoric in general; and their crafting of a subgenre of late-night talk that shares certain distinctive characteristics that mark them as both political and entertaining.

A Response to Fakery

These three comedians, with their producers and writers, have defined themselves in opposition to their competition. That is to say, each of their shows was created (somewhat) as a response to the deficiencies of both the talk and humor offered in late-night television, as well as the fakery of television news reporting and the politics reported there. Indeed, fakery is the defining trait that all of these programs critique—from the frivolous and scripted chitchat that Letterman conducts with guests, to the toothless political jokes in Leno's monologues, to the feigned objectivity and rampant sensationalism of news programs, to the empty and misleading rhetoric of politicians that appear there. These comedians express a desire for honesty in public life, resulting most often in a take-it-or-leave-it criticism of the political and social landscape that they encounter and respond to in the course of each day or week. Hence, the contribution of Maher, Miller, and Stewart to new political television is this: They have intentionally set out to say what can't or isn't being said elsewhere on television.

Bill Maher has made it perfectly clear, from the beginning of his show's run until its cancellation by ABC, that the program was designed in response to the type of television that irritated him. "The genesis for this show," Maher noted in 1993, "comes in some ways from my frustration with doing talk shows over the past 10 years and always being shoved away from controversial material."[72] Therefore, when Maher pitched his program idea to producers, he says he "sold the idea that there wasn't anything that lived up to being a talk show. Talk shows had become boring, publicity-driven promotional shows with one guest at a time. They were missing the two biggest areas of humor: the connection of guests and controversial subjects."[73] Maher wanted a show in which guests would actually interact with each other, and that interaction would be based on things in life that actually matter—two features he felt were not present anywhere in the late-night talk show conversation.[74] "The original point of the show," he notes, "was to get out of people what they're like at a cocktail party. We want to have people talk about real things, but in an amusing way that's not forced."[75] And after being cancelled nine years later, Maher again offered a defense for why his program should be seen as an important contribution to public awareness of current affairs, as opposed simply to blurring the line between entertainment and politics. "Anyone who would make the choice to watch 'Politically Incorrect' was at least interested in something of substance. . . . I was doing a show pitted against two other purely entertainment shows that would not even attempt to tackle the subjects we were tackling."[76]

Maher is also critical of the type of humor offered by Leno and Letterman. Although Maher maintains that he has made his own share of "Bush is dumb" jokes, he nevertheless prides himself on also holding President George W. Bush's "feet to the fire on every single thing he's ever done. That's what Leno hasn't done." Maher contends that comedians need to plumb the depths of Bush's public deceits and propaganda ploys, but they don't. "That's what I want Jay Leno and the others to make fun of. But they won't. They make fun of him for mispronouncing a word."[77] Dennis Miller has been less overtly critical of his comedic peers, but he has made it clear that he considers the type of humor they offer monotonous. When his show debuted, he noted that he wanted to "put the spine of vitriol in that staggering rag doll known as comedy."[78] Although each program begins with a traditional comedic monologue (similar to his competition), it is his signature five-minute breathless exposition known as the "rant" that has won him acclaim as a political commentator. When asked if his comedy might get lost on some of his viewers as they struggle to make sense of what he calls his "arcane simile" approach to comedy, he says, "I think a high percentage of the people want to have to figure it out a little. . . . I'll just bet you that most lay people out there are upset that they're treated like such morons."[79] His head writer also notes that Miller's first syndicated talk show, the one that was cancelled in 1992, was "a little ahead of its time. . . . They hired him to be another Johnny Carson . . . and Dennis is a different type of comedian. He's a much edgier type of comic."[80] Miller's conception of political talk is aggressive and demanding for audiences, yet he recognized that this type of comedy is what was missing at the time.

Finally, Jon Stewart has also expressed his dismay over the artifice of public life—whether it is news reporting, political rhetoric, or entertainment talk. Indeed, *The Daily Show* directly parodies the news program by pretending to be one, complete with the fake anchor role played by Stewart, a team of faux correspondents and commentators, and the tongue-in-cheek moniker, "The Most Important Television Show—Ever!" As a parody of television news shows, it skewers the absurdity and contradictions that pass for "news." "We find a lot of material in . . . how the news has been entertainment-ized," he says. "You'd think news has a higher mandate than entertainment, but, apparently, it doesn't."[81] Head writer for *The Daily Show*, Ben Karlin, offers his opinion of how the show positions itself in the void of late-night programming: "[Our show is] not a straightforward talk show, so we don't have to be this thing that people turn to for comfort and direction. And it's not a news show, so it doesn't have too much of what is essentially this artifice of objectivity."[82] Because the program ridicules both politicians and journalists for being fakes, critics have charged it as being liberal. Stewart offers a telling response, al-

Fox News reporting with Jon Stewart as anchor and Stephen Colbert as reporter "on-location" on The Daily Show.

though "fakery" is not his word of choice: "The point of view of this show is we're passionately opposed to bullshit. Is that liberal or conservative?"[83]

This is the standard these programs define themselves against. They also share a level of similarity that helps define this type of humorous political talk as a subgenre of political talk programming.

Characteristics of New Political Television

The first defining feature shared by *Politically Incorrect with Bill Maher, Dennis Miller Live,* and *The Daily Show with Jon Stewart* is that they are entertainment shows that are unafraid to deal with politics directly or aggressively. Political subjects dominate the content of the shows, and through parody, conversation, or ranting, each places politics squarely in its comedic crosshairs. Johnny Carson believes that comedians can't be social commentators because seriousness and humor, in his view, are incompatible.[84] David Letterman intentionally chooses to remain apolitical in his comedy, noting that "I'd hate to think there were people in America saying, 'Well, hell, Letterman likes him; let's vote for the son of a bitch.'"[85] Maher, Stewart, and Miller, on the other hand, have taken advantage of the cable forums they operate in (or originated from) and have built shows around politics in all of its manifestations. Maher and Stewart frame their shows around issues and events that appear daily in the news, and hence provide running commentary on everything from the O. J. trial, Whitewater, the presidential sex scandal and impeachment, to the 9/11 terrorist attacks, homeland security, and the war in Iraq. Miller's discussion topics are more broad-based, allowing for a more wide-reaching rant, but nevertheless they are centered on issues such as race, Republicans, homosexuality, political correctness, freedom of speech, activism, funding for the arts, liberals, and the electoral system. None of the hosts claims an expertise in politics, and indeed, some even proclaim a level of nonsophistication on the subject. Miller, for example, says, "I am the definitive layman. If I see something that (ticks) me off, I have a childlike urge to just say it (ticks) me off, instead of trying to figure it out."[86] Moreover, when they speak, it is not with a voice that assumes insider knowledge. Instead, it derives from a commonsensical layman's version of understanding that comes from reading newspapers and watching television—just like many of their viewers.

A second feature for the programs by Miller and Stewart is the way the show is divided between political commentary and guest interview (although for Maher, these are somewhat combined by having his guests talk on the topic of his choosing, that is, politics). Both *Dennis Miller Live* and *The Daily Show* begin with their own brands of political commentary, and then segue halfway through the show into an interview with a guest that may or may not have anything to do with the preceding political critique. Sometimes the guest is related to the topic—for instance, Miller had Surgeon General Joycelyn Elders on the same show as his rant on teenage pregnancy, and Stewart has had Madeleine Albright on the show to discuss Middle East diplomacy. But again, this need not always be the case, for Stewart is just as likely to discuss the war in Iraq in the first part of the show, then bring on (as he says) "the girl from *Felicity*" for a fawning celebrity chat.[87] The point here is that these shows have no problem balancing politics and entertainment in the same half-hour of programming.

The third related feature of these programs regards the types of guests they host. At least for Maher and Stewart, their shows include celebrities as well as guests who are not household names (indeed, guests who can be outright obscure for some in the viewing and studio audience). Maher's show was perhaps the most pronounced in this regard for several reasons. The central premise of the show was to assemble a mélange of people from various walks of life (film and television, politics, sports, music, literature and journalism, and political/social activism) as well as of differing ideological stripes. In producing a show with four guests, five nights a week, over the course of nine years, *P.I.* almost always included obscure guests. The show even hosted a "citizen panelist" for part of its run, selecting a "Joe or Jane American" from various cities across the nation to participate in the discussions. Most of the guests, however, were public persons, but again, not necessarily someone who was simply a celebrity. Miller and Stewart have also hosted the occasionally obscure guest, such as *Harper's Magazine* editor Lewis Lapham (a person who is not known for his entertaining demeanor, nor a magazine that is typical table reading for the eighteen- to thirty-four-year-old demographic), a former UN weapons inspector, or a former official with the Federal Aviation Administration to discuss airport security. To be sure, the fact that these shows are about politics—not simply celebrity pop culture—leads to these guests' inclusion. The point here is that the show's hosts are unafraid to bring on guests who they think will provide an interesting take on public affairs, irrespective of the fact that the channel-surfing audience could vote with their changer not to stay with an unfamiliar face. As discussed in chapter 8, many in the audience actually enjoy the guest variety as well as hearing people with whom they are unfamiliar. They also like hearing the political opinions of celebrities whom they have never heard hold forth on political issues—sometimes to their shock and dismay and other times to their pleasant surprise.[88]

Fourth, these shows are distinctive in that the political discussions are conducted in front of a *live* studio audience (unlike almost all other political talk shows). Indeed, holding political discussions in the presence of audiences—who naturally laugh, jeer, cheer, applaud, and occasionally heckle both the hosts and guests—adds a powerful dynamic to the televised sense making of politics. Political oratory is participatory, and just because it is being televised does not negate the audience's natural impulse to respond to that which they feel strongly about. As such, no longer can political commentators and guests (especially those who are particularly partisan or ideologically driven) trot out inanities without also having to hear how these formulations play with the public. When Jon Stewart offers various video clips of government officials spouting ridiculous statements, or clips of manipulative news broadcasts, the audience doesn't even wait for Stewart to make a joke or to reference the clip; they are quite capable of knowing when and where to laugh, and generally do so with great exuberance.

The dynamics of how a live audience can affect televised political discourse can be seen very clearly on an episode of *Real Time with Bill Maher*. Maher held a conversation via satellite with Sandy Rios, president of the Concerned Women for America, to discuss President Bush's proposed constitutional amendment to ban gay marriages. Rios boldly proclaimed, "Bill, we have a crisis in our country. Even if you were in favor of gay marriage, we've got anarchy going on, especially in San Francisco," at which point the audience erupted in laughter at her fevered assertions. But she continued, "This is a breaking of law. This is lawlessness," only to be greeted again with a loud burst of laughter. Her only recourse at that point was to respond by saying, "I don't know why your audience is laughing [followed by more audience laughter]. If it were an issue they were against, they would be very upset about this."[89] Surely Rios followed the letter of her particular script despite the audience's wholesale rejection of her thinking. Nevertheless, the tenor and tone of the conversation (and that which viewing audiences at

home were presented with) was altered as a product of simply allowing citizens to witness and participate in (even if only through laughter) such televised political discourse.

The ways in which these shows mix their serious and humorous components comprise the fifth feature of similarity. Indeed, there really is no segregation of these features (such as serious rant, then humorous talk with a
celebrity). The humor, anger, amusement, dismay, and disagreement are all
mixed in the narrative flow each show creates. On *P.I.*, the guests may find
themselves yelling at each other at the tops of their lungs, only to have Maher or a fellow comedian remind everyone that perhaps they are taking
themselves too seriously by offering a pithy rejoinder. *P.I.*, in particular, tries
to include different guests who can provide both seriousness and humor to
the discussion. Miller's rants are not just diatribes or polemics. He makes his
political points *through* his humor, pointing out the contradictions and absurdities of a situation, while offering a smirking smile and outraged tone simultaneously. The rant allows him to thumb his nose at the rigid boundaries
of stand-up humor that have traditionally required the comedian to offer a
line and wait for the laugh. Instead, by being humorous and serious at the
same time, the comedian becomes an essayist, opening up the opportunity
to make points without the obligation to simultaneously score laughs within
a line or thought. And for Stewart's program, the parody is, by definition, a
combination of serious humor. The humor is delivered with a straight face
(or at least a repressed grin) until the audience catches on.

Yet by freely mixing humor with political talk, critics have tended to assume that the former trivializes the latter. For instance, one critic has argued,
"By providing a hideous burlesque of political debate, in which semi-literate
rock stars, stand-up comics and think-tank ideologues flogged one another's
so called opinions, *Politically Incorrect* did more to encourage stupidity than
an army of Tom Greens."[90] Wayne Munson, however, argues that talk shows
that employ such playfulness with "discursive boundaries and identities"
are threatening to "critics (who) are desperate for clear labels and stable
structures—in other words, for a representational 'purity' the talkshow will
not allow."[91] The executive producer of *P.I.*, Scott Carter, asserts that the
show's "format acknowledges the blurring of the line between news and entertainment," but he suggests that such lines are essentially meaningless to
most audiences.[92]

What this mixture has allowed for (the sixth common feature of these
shows) is the development by each comedian of a political persona built on
his particular type of humor. Yet having a politically opinionated persona
(something avoided by hosts such as Leno and Letterman) automatically re-
duces their audience appeal at the mass level (though not for the small and
paying audiences associated with cable viewing).[93] Critics have commented
on Miller's supposed "smugness factor," contending that "most of the time,

he seems mighty pleased with himself and his brand of high-IQ comedy."[94] Maher too has been charged with a know-it-all quality, or for being shrill and condescending to his guests, especially by nonfans (as demonstrated in on-line discussion forums, discussed in chapter 8). Some critics have also noticed how such posturing has played itself out with audiences to a level of positive outcomes. In regard to Miller, one journalist wrote, "Once, his comedy was tinged with a hipper-than-thou attitude; to some, Miller seemed to be smirking, setting himself above his audience. Now, he and the fans are on closer terms; he invites them into his exclusive little circle, and they respond eagerly."[95] If this journalist is correct, the crafted political persona as savvy but humorous commentator plays well with audiences who appreciate the cultish and cliquish distinction that such a relationship seemingly bestows.

Which leads to the seventh point: how these shows demand a level of sophistication or knowledge about both politics *and* popular culture. Critics often contend that these shows are the equivalent of a "Politics for Dummies" manual. Even Jay Leno contends that in political humor, "the audience has to know what you're talking about or else you'll be sunk. . . . You can't know more than anybody watching. And we've found that once you get past secretary of state—and even that is a stretch—no one knows what you're talking about."[96] These political comedians, through their performances to date, obviously disagree. Maher and Stewart quite often employ in their jokes less-than-common-name political figures that many viewers may not recognize, such as Russian Prime Minister Yevgeny Primakov, UN leader

Jon Stewart taking on Deputy Secretary of Defense Paul Wolfowitz.

Kofi Annan, Treasury Secretary Paul O'Neill, and Deputy Secretary of Defense Paul Wolfowitz. Miller is perhaps the most aggressive comic in drawing from a catalog of obscure news, literary, and pop culture figures to make a point. In one of his rants inveighing against the "death of common sense," for instance, he cries:

> Christ, we're so bogged down in procedure, we make Radar O'Reilly look like Henry David Thoreau. You couple that with a Blanche DuBois–like denial of personal responsibility for the crap in our lives, and it's no wonder we're in a malaise that makes a bout of Epstein-Barr seem like a Laker Girl doing the Watusi after four triple lattes with a Dexatrim chaser.[97]

Although some critics contend that these shows contribute to ignorance about current events in young people, Jon Stewart argues that to even understand his show, one has to retain some level of knowledge about what is going on in the world. "I honestly don't think that young people can avoid getting news," he says. "I mean, news and information surround you almost on a molecular level these days. . . . And if you don't inform yourself, or have some sense of what's going on, our show won't even make sense to you.[98] The point to be made here is that far from trafficking in idiocy, these shows actually demand a high level of viewer savvy about the world and a more conscious viewer negotiation of the text for sense to be made from it. Furthermore, these shows are less inclined to care if the viewer doesn't get the reference, for they provide the type of cliquish knowledge that cable generally trades in. If the audience is too slow, dumb, or ill informed to get it, then that is their loss and the joke is on them. The networks, of course, provide programming tailor-made for such audiences. For the audiences who do "get it," they are rewarded for their savvy and distinctiveness as such.

The last two points of commonality refer to these shows' brevity and their mildly populist appeal. All three of the shows are only thirty minutes in length (as opposed to Leno and Letterman, who often fill their time with meaningless banter between the host and band leader), therefore offering a taste of interesting and digestible conversation about politics while refusing to beat the audience over the head with redundant arguments. The result, as audience data show, is that this generally leaves them wanting more.[99] Also, all three comedians recognize their place as representative of other outsider voices, and hence maintain some populist feature in their program or in their thinking. Miller takes phone calls from viewers during the interview segment of his show; Maher allows "citizen panelists" to join the conversation from time-to-time; and Stewart says he speaks for the "politically disappointed" and "represents the distracted center."[100] In short, each of the three shows offers some level of respect for their audience, its opinions, and its time.

ALTERNATIVE POLITICAL TALK

Over the last decade, the presentation of political talk on television has changed. Although pundit talk still dominates both cable and network political programming, we have witnessed new forms of political talk that have taken advantage of their cable origins, home, or sensibilities to transform the genre and develop alternative approaches. For critics of humorous political talk, these shows have blurred the lines between serious and entertaining programming, and hence have made politics a frivolous matter. For these new talk hosts, however, the shows they produce offer a measure of honesty that combats the fakery that dominates both politics and entertainment in public life. Their programs allow for seriousness and humor to mix through the flow of conversation—the way that it does, they contend, everywhere in life *except* on television.

Yet that response to fakery is also a desire to call a spade a spade when it comes to government lies. That is, these new political television programs not only cover politics in humorous ways, but they also seek to illuminate the artifice of public discourse (by other talk shows, news, politicians) and those who refuse to hold those in power accountable (e.g., government officials, corporations, journalists). As discussed in chapter 5, these comedian-hosts discuss certain topics, make certain connections, and point out "realities" that they contend are plainly obvious but that the news media and pundit shows—as the consummate political insiders—either refuse to cover or tend to handle in very similar ways. For instance, here is a small sample of topics covered by *The Daily Show* in 2003: Iraq and Halliburton; the FCC's media ownership vote; Bush dodging questions about weapons of mass destruction; gay marriage; the new head of the Environmental Protection Agency; tax cuts for the rich; why white collar crime does pay; faith-based government aid; the California governor recall election; Texas congressional redistricting; and the role of media during wartime. Through subjects such as these, the comedian-hosts are not held simply to repeating the government's position on these matters. Instead, they doggedly attack those things that they find disturbing, puzzling, or outright lies and fabrications.

In sum, we can conclude several points about this move from political insiders to outsiders and the advent of new political television. Politics and culture are not separate spheres but are intimately interconnected. People are now allowed to talk about politics on television without being *in* politics. That is, people outside the political clubhouse are allowed to hold publicly televised conversations with and about those who *are* in politics. The language used in those conversations tends to be both politically basic and culturally obscure, which in essence turns the pundit/journalist formula on its head (i.e., politically obscure and culturally basic). The issues and events are not covered from the standard pundit/journalist approach, and the things said offer alternative perspectives from an outsider position. The shows are intended to uncover the fakery that dominates public life and politics. Finally, audiences have shown (by tuning in over the course of twelve years) that they want these new connections to politics and culture because such connections mirror their own political habits and cultural behaviors. To state it quite succinctly: new political television offers viewing audiences the ability to watch nonexperts discussing politics with comedian hosts who roast political distortions and fakery when they see it, yet who offer opinionated and thoughtful ruminations that aren't always designed to be taken *too* seriously. All of this is mixed with other cultural artifacts that the audience cares about and is invested in. As one reporter has noted, "These are not your father's late night talk shows."[101] Indeed. But on the other hand, neither are they your father's pundit talk shows.

4

The Rise and Fall of *Politically Incorrect*

> I enjoy telling the truth. The truth is not the best social calling card you can have. It doesn't make you popular.
>
> —Bill Maher

It would be hard to overstate the importance of the 1992 presidential campaign as a signal event in the development of new political television. As described in chapter 3, executives at many of the Vox Pop political talk shows and channels appearing on cable in 1993 and 1994 directly invoked the popularity of new forms of public talk in the 1992 campaign—the "straight talk" of the Ross Perot campaign and the candidate appearances on shows such as *Larry King Live, Donahue, Arsenio Hall,* and *Good Morning America*—as a reason why their program or channel would prove successful.[1] The popularity of candidate appearances on these shows signaled to television programmers that audiences were hungry for alternative forms of political talk.[2] The 1992 campaign included the public's questioning of the legitimacy of gatekeepers of traditional forums of political information and talk on television.[3] These entertainment talk shows, which incorporated interaction between audiences and the candidates, allowed people to circumvent elite gatekeepers by directly addressing the candidates with questions that were more pertinent to their interests.[4] Audiences seemingly did not care whether such venues were categorized by critics as "entertainment" or "serious." Instead, such traditional distinctions were both arbitrary and artificial to them, and cable programmers recognized this as they searched for a formula that would prove popular enough with audiences to put themselves on the map of the new cable landscape.

This chapter describes how the cable channel Comedy Central challenged the legitimacy of the traditional gatekeepers of political discourse by offering programming that intentionally blurred the lines between serious and entertaining programming. I examine the decisions leading up to their introduction of the political roundtable discussion show *Politically Incorrect* in 1993, and the decisions by the show's producers that made the program a hit for the comedy network. The discussion then follows *Politically Incorrect's* move to the broadcast network ABC, and the numerous aspects of that relationship that forebode its eventual demise as a result of the program essentially living up to its name. The chapter concludes with an analysis of Maher's political persona as comedian and political provocateur and what the story of *P.I.*'s rise and fall might ultimately mean for audiences who enjoy the blending of entertainment and politics on television.

"SAME WORLD, DIFFERENT TAKE": BRANDING A CABLE NETWORK

Comedy is arguably one of the most prominent and popular programming genres in television and has been since the medium's inception. From the success of Sid Caesar's *Your Show of Shows* and Milton Berle's *Texaco Star Theater* to the contemporary popularity of *Friends* and *The Simpsons*, comedic genres—variety shows, situation comedies, talk shows, comedy-dramas, and so on—have proved a mainstay on network television. The question for cable programming entrepreneurs, however, was whether such a central programming feature of network television could stand alone as a niche programming choice on cable. News, sports, religion, and music had proven successful as narrowcasted cable channels—why not comedy?

Two media companies believed the concept would work. On November 15, 1989, Time Warner, through its HBO subsidiary, launched The Comedy Channel, which featured original short comedy pieces (or "clips"), with a subscriber base of 4.2 million. On April 1, 1990 (April Fool's Day), Viacom launched HA! TV Comedy Network, a channel that primarily featured off-network programming (i.e., reruns of old network comedy shows) with four million subscribers.[5] Scott Carter, executive producer of *Politically Incorrect*, worked for HBO Downtown Productions at that time and produced two shows for The Comedy Channel. Carter describes the problem faced by these two networks: "By the end of the year of 1990, it was clear that neither of those services were making money and a lot of cable subscribers [cable system operators] didn't want to make a choice. They didn't want to offend Viacom, [and] they didn't want to offend HBO. So a lot of them just chose to not carry either service. The thought was that if they could get together, then it would become a successful cable franchise, which indeed has happened."[6]

On January 1, 1991, Comedy TV (later renamed Comedy Central) was born as a merger between these two competing channels in a fifty-fifty ownership agreement between Viacom and Time-Warner.[7] The question became, however, which of the two different programming philosophies would Comedy Central (CC) adopt—original programming, reruns, or both? As Carter put it, "There was the sort of spilling out of, well, 'what's the new channel going to be,' and it took a couple of years for a sense of vision to develop. . . . There was that effort . . . of moving to 'how do we react to what's going on so this doesn't seem to be twenty-four hours of reruns of *The Phil Silvers Show* or *Mary Tyler Moore* or something? You can get that anywhere. How is this different?'"

Comedy Central needed original programming, but situational comedies or comedy-dramas are also expensive to produce and, if the failure rate of network comedies is any indication, a risky financial undertaking. An alternative was to create programming by trying to find the comical within the everyday, or as network executives put it, they began a "quest to be more topical" by featuring programming based on news and political events.[8] Within a year of the network's launch, one of its first attempts was a controversial satirical treatment of President George H. W. Bush's State of the Union Address as it was being delivered. Titled "State of the Union—Undressed," a panel of "commentators" (read: comedians) offered their humorous opinions during the natural pauses and breaks for applause throughout the speech. Comedy Central's intention to broadcast the speech was met with stiff resistance by the three broadcast news networks and CNN, who administered the pool satellite feed of the speech from the House of Representatives Television and Radio Gallery. Intent on maintaining the boundaries between serious and entertainment media content, and in turn, the legitimacy of the former and frivolousness of the latter in the political arena, George Watson, ABC News' Washington bureau chief, noted, "We do not believe that the pool has any legal responsibility to provide news to non-news organizations. Doing so, particularly in this case, violates professional standards we respect."[9] With the threat of a lawsuit by CC (and the resulting bad publicity it would bring), the networks eventually consented to share the broadcast feed with the Comedy Channel network.

The broadcast was a success, as the network not only doubled its January ratings with the telecast but also garnered high-profile press coverage from the controversy with the broadcasters. By April, the network had decided to continue with its satirical treatment of politics by covering both the Democratic and Republican party nominating conventions that summer. Labeled "Indecision '92," CC aired two hours of coverage each of the four nights of the Democratic convention in New York and the Republican convention in Houston, double the time dedicated by the Big Three broadcast networks. Anchored by comedian Al Franken, the network sought to apply a "raised eye brow approach" that took advantage of the slow-moving proceedings while still reporting to viewers anything important that might happen.[10] Comedy Central's coverage of the conventions was an amazingly direct statement of what it considered the vacuous nature of both an empty political ritual and the mainstream news organization's "news coverage" of the event.[11] Executive producer of the convention coverage for CC, Billy Kimball, said it best by noting, "News has an interest in proving that the event is newsworthy. We have an interest in proving that it's comic,"[12] a statement that presages what would later become the network's slogan, "same world, different take."

More than that, however, Kimball's comments point to an increasingly common recognition both within and outside of media that "news" does not simply occur waiting to be discovered, but rather is *constructed* out of certain events by media personnel. But if news is a construct based on certain institutional relationships and ideological factors, so is comedy. Events can be endowed with great significance by calling a particular perspective on those events "news," Kimball seemingly argued, but CC could construct a humorous take on those same events and call it "comedy." The producers at CC believed that the comedic is no less legitimate than the news perspective, mainly because no actual "news" was occurring at the convention. CC's coverage of the conventions garnered favorable reviews in the press, commentary that the new network needed in its effort to establish a name and identity for itself.

But special events coverage was not enough to convince cable operators to include the channel in their lineup.[13] By early 1993, CC announced plans to spend $40 million that year to satisfy the demands of operators for more original programming. Included in that announcement were plans for a show called *Politically Incorrect*, initially billed as "a weekly McLaughlin Report-type show hosted by comedian Bill Maher."[14] Executives at the network were clamoring for a "signature show"—such as *Beavis & Butt-Head* on MTV or *Ren & Stimpy* on Nickelodeon—that would give the network an identity and get people talking about CC.[15] *Politically Incorrect* was an original twist on two existing talk show genres, the political pundit and entertainment-variety talk shows. But it developed a creative reformulation of both genres by capitalizing on weaknesses it saw within the primary feature of both forms: the "talk."

"THE MCLAUGHLIN GROUP ON ACID": *POLITICALLY INCORRECT*'S FORMATIVE YEARS

Politically Incorrect (*P.I.*) is the brainchild of the show's host, Bill Maher. Before pitching the idea for the show to HBO, Maher was a comedian who had worked the comedy circuit since around 1979.[16] He was a stand-up comic and emcee at the Catch-a-Rising-Star comedy club in New York in the early 1980s. He made appearances on *The Tonight Show* under both Johnny Carson and Jay Leno, appeared in several B-movie comedy flops, and even wrote a novel. Maher had not crafted his career as a "political comic" per se, but he had performed a substantial amount of political material during a 1992 HBO comedy special in which he starred. He also served as a roving reporter during CC's 1992 presidential election coverage and co-hosted an election night special on CC in 1992. According to Scott Carter, executive producer of *P.I.* from 1993–1999, the stand-up special and the election night special "made Comedy Central interested in perhaps doing a show with Bill. He had this idea for a while, so he presented [it] to them and they bought it."

Carter was on staff at HBO Downtown Productions at the time, and he accompanied Maher when Maher pitched the show to HBO. As Carter reports it, HBO bought the show "as is," without any modifications. Comedy Central ordered twenty-four episodes for the show's initial run. In a move that would later cost them, the network did not purchase the rights to the show. Rather, it was owned and produced through Brillstein-Grey Entertainment and HBO Downtown Productions, with the show being taped in HBO's studios in Manhattan.[17] As for why they picked up the show, Carter confirms that the executives at CC "were looking for some way to have a sense of the topical. They were looking for some way to be reacting to current events." Maher pitched a concept that would do just that, while staying true to his comedy roots.

For the initial run, Maher and Carter used the description "the McLaughlin Group on acid" for the show when it first appeared on television. According to Carter, that was simply an "easy way to describe it." Yet it was the name of the show itself—*Politically Incorrect*—that attracted more attention. Carter says that Maher came up with the title as a response to the climate of the times, where political correctness is "the condescending attitude towards anybody who might be perceived as having any kind of disability or disenfranchisement, that they should be coddled with euphemisms."[18] Maher describes it slightly differently: "I have always defined 'politically correct' as the elevation of sensitivity over truth. I think truth is more important."[19] Elsewhere he noted about the show's title, "People [have] misinterpreted 'politically incorrect' as shocking, which it sometimes can be. To me, it just means truthful—not liberal or conservative, but just keeping it real. It may be rude, but it doesn't mean it's not true."[20] The title of the show, then, was to signal Maher's philosophy that being truthful—despite who's feelings might get hurt—was his primary goal with the show; that, and being funny in the process.

The set design in the first season included broken Greco-Roman columns with the show's title etched into the broken structures. Carter explains, "We started out with it feeling like you were out doors and were on a portico or were outside at like the Parthenon or something, the Acropolis." During the first two seasons, broken democracy was the theme, certainly fitting into the populist, anti-politics rhetoric that had so much currency at that time. The show's format was a blending of two subgenres of television talk: the late-night comedy-talk

The first episode of Politically Incorrect *on Comedy Central, July 25, 1993.*

shows of the Leno and Letterman variety and the political discussion shows similar to *The McLaughlin Group* and *Capital Gang*. The program included Maher walking onto the stage to the applause of a live but small audience and opening with a comedic monologue. Maher would then introduce each guest, who was selected from different arenas of public life (celebrities, politicians, comedians, authors, musicians, journalists, activists, etc.). Maher and guests would then begin a discussion of political and social issues in both serious and humorous ways. The guests, therefore, were people who more typically appeared on Letterman, yet the issues discussed were more similar to those found on McLaughlin's program. "We're always living in this world in between the variety shows like what Jay and Dave do, and then the information shows like *Capital Gang* or *McLaughlin Group*," says Carter. "We're somewhere in between the two, but we have to come down more on the side of entertainment than of information."

This hybrid political-entertainment format, according to Maher, "more reflects real life."[21] That is, politics is not segregated from the concerns, interests, and pleasures of everyday life, or from the way people discuss political and social issues. To accentuate that fact, bringing in an assortment of guests from many walks of life embodies that discursively. "The key to this is the mixture and it's one of the things people love about it," Maher later noted. "It's the casting of four weirdly thrown together people."[22] The "casting" occurs as the booking staff "tries to fill four imaginary 'quadrants' with, respectively, a funny person, a famous 'face,' a conservative . . . and a wild card meant to offset the other three."[23] An example of a panel assembled in the first season includes Roseanne Arnold, Roger Clinton (the president's brother), Richard Viguerie (labeled as a "conservative spokesman"), and Alexandra Penney (editor-in-chief of *Self* magazine). "Every panel is a completely unique entity that takes on a life or death of its own," Maher notes.[24] And as we see when we examine audiences for the show, that assemblage is a large part of the pleasure that audiences find in watching the program— to the point where they routinely assemble their own "dream team" of oddly mixed people that they wish the producers would put on the air.

Comedy Central aired the shows weekly, beginning July 25, 1993, on Sunday evenings at 8:00 P.M. (EST). "[When] we did our first season," Carter explains, "we taped it in May and June of '93, and it didn't come on the air until July. So we couldn't do topical topics. We had to do evergreen topics." By that he means more broad-based political or social issues (such as welfare, taxation, or prostitution) than specific events or policy initiatives that occurred daily or weekly. Carter says that they felt they had actually "found" the show, in terms of the right look and feel, when on the first day of taping, "Bill is talking and Tom [Arnold] interrupted him with something and it made Bill laugh and everybody in the audience laughed, and it was what you like to see in your house when people are talking and having a good time." As discussed below, it is this casual repartee, this cocktail party atmosphere of conversation (even for the "seriousness" of politics) that the show was intentionally attempting to construct—something the show's creators believed that television used to offer, but no longer did. The irony, of course, is that in a time when cable television was slicing and dicing viewer tastes and interests (what the industry calls "narrowcasting") into specific channels and programming segments, *P.I.* was doing just the opposite, recognizing that casting a wide net could provide for interesting and engaging discussions.

Critical response to the program was fairly positive during the first season. Many commentators found it a breath of fresh air, markedly different from the pundit variety that dominates the genre and the artificially constructed entertainment talk shows. In the *San Francisco Chronicle*, for instance, a reporter wrote,

> If you want to get a quick take on what the comedy show "Politically Incorrect" is about get a look at the set, which looks like a collapsed Greek temple. It's a perfect commentary on the state of American democracy and an appropriate satire of the sets for those pompous Sunday morning political shows where various windbags gather each week to lie, spin, mislead, influence opinion and otherwise govern the country. . . . Oddly enough, some of the best social and political commentary on television can be found [on *P.I.*]. The talk is real— unlike entertainment chat shows, in which the "conversations" are setups, and unlike most political talk shows, in which people are constrained by the necessity of appearing dignified and impartial.[25]

One commentary, in particular, had an important effect on the producers and Maher. As Carter reports it, "There was an article in *Time* magazine about the show, and they sort of compared Bill with Dennis Miller. That sort of solidified Bill's sense that this is maybe where his career direction was going to be. This format was being heralded, and that was something he should not maybe tamper with too much." The article ran near the beginning of the show's second season, and lauded the political satire of Maher and Dennis Miller, whose HBO show had just premiered (1994):

> In an era when most comedians are too cool to care, here's an odd twist: the two best stand-up comics on TV are the ones who have ventured most boldly into the political arena. Not the easy-to-take, non-partisan "topicality" of Leno and Letterman, but informed, savvy, opinionated comedy about real issues. Miller and Maher are helping stand-up comedy escape from its contemporary cul-de-sac, where Jerry Seinfeld clones obsess about sex, TV and life's little annoyances. These two comics read the whole newspaper—not just the funny clippings their writers collect for them. . . . "We will strive," said Miller on his first show, "to be in the vanguard of the movement to irresponsibly blur the line between news and entertainment." Finally, two comedians who actually know the difference.[26]

Not all assessments were so favorable. Indeed, with a format that tended to feature people who were not "experts" in political matters, it attracted its fair share of scorn, typically from those who take their politics very seriously. "Do we really need a panel show in which stand-up comedians, minor former celebrities and the odd political and/or media operative sit around in a circle and say dumb things?" wrote the voice of insider politics, the *Washington Post*.[27] In typical condescending fashion, the left-wing journal *Mother Jones* was even less kind to the show and the people who would watch it: "The host of *Politically Incorrect* serves up warmed-over, celebrity enhanced pop politics to an uninformed audience. Just the way America likes it."[28] Not to be outdone, the right-wing *National Review* wrote, "The discussion can seem trivial and intellectually dishonest, [which] merely reflects the society from which the show has emerged."[29]

When Carter is asked whether *P.I.* offers citizens the equivalent of "candy" instead of the civic "vegetables" they *should* be consuming, Carter replies, "I think there's some validity to that. I don't think we've ever been pretending to be the vegetable show. That's not our job. In fact, I think that if the hard news people would do a better job of hard news, I think there would be a greater distinction between the two of us and more people would be going to watch the other shows." Carter readily admits that *P.I.* blurs the line between entertainment and news, yet contends that both he and the general public no longer find the distinctions between the two meaningful or legitimate. He argues,

We have a more legitimate stance [than the news programs]. In other words, when 1996 came around and we went to the convention in Chicago and San Diego, I felt like our coming there as an entertainment show had a more legitimate claim to being there than all of these news cameras and anchors and color commentators and all these other people who were pretending that news was occurring. The media keeps imagining there's this big distinction between the legitimate press and the tabloid press, or the tabloid press and the entertainment community, [but] it's all kind of one thing. The public, I don't think, makes any distinctions any more about it.

For Carter, *P.I.* more accurately represents where the American people are with both politics and television. In his view, voters and television audiences don't maintain rigid distinctions in regard to where issues might fall within the ideological spectrum, whether candidates belong to certain political parties, or whether they are watching a favorite or trustworthy television network. Those distinctions—markers that have been used traditionally to map the political and televisual landscape—have largely eroded or are simply long gone. "I don't know of anybody my age or younger who [maintains strict party loyalty]. I think that people go back and forth. A candidate is a candidate," he says. Whether Carter is correct in his assessment of audiences and voters is less important than the fact that he, as the producer of the show, finds these distinctions unimportant and irrelevant.

Politically Incorrect met CC's desire for topicality and irreverent humor, so the network placed a second order for new shows while the first season was still airing. For the second season, *P.I.* produced forty-five episodes but altered the taping schedule somewhat in a move to be more topical (that is, taping two shows a week instead of in one block over an entire month or two). During that time, experimentation resulted in a major change in the program. As Carter describes it, "We had long talked about how Leno and Letterman both come on at 11:35 P.M. What about a show that comes on at 11:30 and goes off the air at 11:35 and was just the monologue? So what we did was four episodes of a show called 'Just a Minute with Bill Maher,' where Maher would come out, tell six jokes, and then end by saying, 'Oh, we're out of time.'" The head of programming at CC liked it so much he suggested that they go to a nightly format. Another fortuitous "accident" occurred during the second season when the show was forced (through a studio booking error) to tape at a studio across town that seated 115 people (instead of the usual 40). After filming the two shows that day, Carter said, "We just realized there is a lot more electricity here. And so then we said all right, next season, third season, we want to get to a bigger place."

The second season also brought more critical recognition for the show, this time from within the television industry. Both Maher (as host) and the program won Cable Ace Awards (1994), and the result, according to Carter, is that the show got an extra bounce from the recognition. "That was a big deal in sort of giving us some credentials," he said, "and probably helped [guest] bookings a little bit."

The third season began, then, with a move to a nightly format, a larger audience, a higher profile, and more topical discussions. Comedy Central moved the program to an 11:00 P.M. (ET) nightly time slot and began to recognize the value of the show to their network. "This is the show we use to define ourselves," proclaimed Bob Kreek, Comedy Central's president and CEO. "It's probably our best show, and it has hit its stride this year."[30] These changes also created greater interest from celebrities who wanted to be on the hot new show. As noted earlier, the format requires celebrities to do more than simply plug their latest projects, which, it seems, was an appealing proposition for many. By making the discussions loose and wide ranging and more than simply a form of cloaked advertising, Maher contends that the show is "retro" in its return to an earlier form of talk television. Carter too suggests the program offers a certain form of repartee between guests and host that is pre-Carson, similar to earlier entertainment talk shows hosted by Jack Paar, Merv Griffin, and Dick Cavett. "I remember as a kid watching Dick Cavett," Carter notes,

> And there would be John Simon, the drama critic for the *New Yorker* magazine with Little Richard and Lester Maddox and Raquel Welch. I remember seeing Albert Schweitzer on *The Jack Paar Show* and I remember seeing Norman Mailer all the time, or Gore Vidal. And as a child growing up, a lot of my introduction to the world of literature was seeing [authors like] Tom Wolfe on a show, being intrigued to then go to the library or go to a book store and get works by them based upon how entertaining they had been when they were being interviewed on television.

Carter continues by arguing, "Increasingly, that [type of] person doesn't have a forum on talk variety shows now. Jay isn't really interested in authors and Dave really isn't interested in authors, and we still see our show as a place where that person is very welcome," noting appearances by Norman Mailer, Jay McInerney, John Irving, and Ray Bradbury as examples of their success in that regard.

To obtain such guests, all of the staff contributes their suggestions. Sometimes guests are invited because of specific topics Maher wants to discuss, and sometimes a topic will be set aside until a guest can be found. Potential guests are most often discovered by the staff's day-to-day interaction with other media. "One of the great things about this project," says Carter, "is I've never felt like I've got to dumb down when I wake up in the morning and come here. . . . We're always looking for who could be brilliant." Carter also notes that fan mail and viewer suggestions are often focused on guests they would like to see. "'Why don't you have Hulk Hogan on?' [fans might suggest]. . . . We're always trying to read everything and see everything to bring people from different disciplines on the show."

The show sought to add a bit of excitement as well as land guests who were difficult to get on the program by going on the road in the third season. *P.I.* first went to Washington, D.C., in 1995 where such big-name political guests as D.C. Mayor Marion Barry, playwright Harvey Fierstein, G. Gordon Liddy, Sam Donaldson, and Congressmen James Traficant, Bernie Sanders, and Bob Dornan appeared on the program. Three months later, the show taped in Los Angeles for a week and found a phenomenal response from celebrities clamoring to get on the program. Jay Leno, John Malkovich, Ray Bradbury, Garry Shandling, Dick Clark, Tim Allen, and Roseanne Arnold were all guests that week. As the trade press wrote at that time, the show "has become a favorite of celebrities, authors, comedians, politicians, lawyers and anyone else with an opinion because it allows guests to show who they are and what they believe in instead of promoting their latest projects."[31]

The third season proved highly successful and ended on November 30, 1995, after a run of 192 shows. Comedy Central signed a contract with HBO Downtown Productions for a fourth season, but by the fall of 1995, rumors were circulating that the program would move to the ABC network as a post-*Nightline* companion show.[32] The decision by *P.I.*'s producers to move the show's taping location in the fourth season to Los Angeles (January 1996), therefore, came as little surprise. The move to Los Angeles was something Maher desired. As he explained, "I've been trying to get home for years and years. I was like Odysseus. I've always wanted to be here, because this is where I live. I can't give you any more noble reason [for the move] other than I want to sleep in my own bed. And there's no reason not to do the show out here."[33]

Other than its location, little else with the show changed. The set design was altered, though, moving away from the stone-gray look, although retaining the Greco-Roman columns. The "rubble" of broken columns that dominated the first set was cleaned up, and the existing columns were now adorned with ivy. Adding a city skyline in the background and more comfortable-looking leather chairs also softened the set's look. The new set design seemed to suggest that guests were sitting in a study overlooking a patio and grounds with Maher adjudicating or refereeing a debate between two sides. By taping in Los Angeles, it was also easier to get celebrities as guests, yet harder to get politicos and intellectuals from the east coast. Hence, greater effort had to be made to convince them to be on the program.

In January 1996, the announcement was made that *P.I.* would be moving to ABC beginning January 1997. The one-year lead-time allowed ABC to attempt to gain clearance for the program from their affiliates as the local stations finished up existing contracts for syndicated programming. It also gave Comedy Central time to respond to losing its signature program. Comedy Central CEO Doug Herzog's response was to "get a replacement program in the pipeline and schedule it to follow *Politically Incorrect* so that Maher's audience would be exposed to it as early and often as possible before the marquee show moved on."[34] Comedy Central developed what would become its new flagship program, *The Daily Show*, featuring Craig Kilborn, as another effort at retaining its "topical" signature by focusing on a satirical reading of the day's news stories. The network placed the show in the 11:30 P.M. time slot immediately following *P.I.*

In the meantime, however, Herzog and CC continued to use *P.I.* in every way they could to achieve the network's continued goal of name recognition, brand identity, and increased subscriber levels. *P.I.* was still a highly valued workhorse for Comedy Central. The program was bringing in an audience of 280,000 households for the network, its highest rated original show at that time. The network also saw its subscriber base increase from 34 million in 1995 to 42 million in 1996, its most substantial annual increase up to that point.[35] Although increased carriage can't be attributed directly to the popularity of *P.I.*, many industry observers believe that having a hit program is very important in creating a demand for carriage by cable operators.[36]

Comedy Central repeated its 1992 success in covering the presidential nominating conventions by running *Indecision '96*. The most notable gag during CC's coverage of the conventions was the placement of the show's two hosts, liberal Al Franken and conservative Arianna Huffington, in bed together, symbolically commenting on the cozy relationship between politicians and lobbyists, sources and reporters.[37] Tony Fox, vice president of CC, explained the show's decision to cover the conventions again: "We're there to show that the [political] process is not above reproach and humor."[38] *P.I.* was shown live during the conventions and expanded to an hour each night. The program also held a live election night special that included a band, "The Presidents of the United States of America," and running commentary as the election results were reported.

After four seasons totaling 411 shows on CC, the show departed for ABC, but not before it had helped CC achieve its signature look as "a sharp political animal" while assisting the network to obtain carriage in an additional twenty million homes.[39] In its effort to attract audiences and carriage, the network had taken the risk to offer a show that defied typical genre categorization, and as a result, helped construct a truly original political animal in the process.

FROM CABLE TO NETWORK: THE MOVE TO ABC

ABC began broadcast of its new acquisition on January 1, 1997, with a "Greatest Hits" special from the previous four seasons of *P.I.*'s run on Comedy Central.[40] As if to announce to the nation just what this new type of show was all about, the special was co-hosted by Jeff Greenfield, a reporter for ABC News and frequent contributor to *Nightline*, and Yasmine Bleeth, a *Baywatch* babe. Brains and boobs, intellectuals and lookers—ABC seemingly had no problem with the blending of genres that *P.I.* had perfected on cable and now brought to network television. ABC had been out of the late-night entertainment programming race since 1991, and indeed had really never had a successful show during that time period.[41]

Although networks are not known for their cutting-edge programming, the risk in picking up *P.I.*—a show that billed itself as saying things that might ruffle feathers—seemed minimal. The program had a proven track record and a popular following with the eighteen-to-forty-nine-year-old demographic. As one industry publication put it, "The program would give ABC a shot at the younger, urban audience that makes late-night entertainment so attractive to advertisers."[42] Furthermore, the "topical" nature of *P.I.* seemed a good fit with *Nightline*. An unidentified source at ABC is quoted as saying, "If we followed *Nightline* [with *P.I.*], [audiences] would have already seen 30 minutes of serious stuff so they would be ready for some fun."[43] Maher agreed: "Soon after we went on [CC] I thought the perfect place for it would be after *Nightline*. I thought that's an entertainment sort of hour of the night and the other networks have on variety shows. ABC has *Nightline*, and why wouldn't they want a show that combines news and entertainment?"[44]

As for potential conflicts between the more racy content that cable often produces and the mass-audience, advertiser-conscious programming that networks provide, Maher was not worried about the switch at the time:

> I would be [concerned] if we were doing a pilot, and they didn't know what the heck was going on. But the show has already lost four Emmys. We've been around for a while. We've never had any language license different from the networks. The only thing different is the content—we deal with controversial issues in a frank and open way. If they take that away, there is no show.[45]

In the beginning, the differences between cable and network, according to Carter, were hardly noticeable: "It didn't necessarily result in a change in the way we did business. In fact, after about a month on ABC, it was no different than being on Comedy Central. We were in the same studios, same set, same people, same everything." What did change for *P.I.* was exposure. The audiences for the program were now, on average, up to ten times as large as the audience on CC. And the program proved to be a competitor in the late-night ratings race, at times beating Leno and Letterman in major markets where they competed head to head.[46]

Yet these rosy assessments from early in the show's run on the network hid more deep-seated problems that would continue to mark the relationship between *P.I.* and the network until the show's eventual demise. Despite the belief by Maher and "unnamed" others at ABC that the show would be a good companion to *Nightline*, that was evidently not the feeling of Ted Koppel, *Nightline*'s anchor. Koppel never once provided a lead-in to *P.I.* (that is, reminding viewers to stay tuned for the upcoming programming or highlighting the particular guests that would be appearing). Maher later complained bitterly, "You could never ask Ted Koppel to do anything. He never asked viewers to watch 'Politically Incorrect' after his show; instead, he'd tell them to go to nightline.com."[47] Sheila Griffiths, an associate producer with *P.I.* and now co-executive producer of *Real Time with Bill Maher*, believes that Koppel "just didn't feel like it was a fit. . . . He didn't feel like we were the right show for somebody that would follow him."[48] As for why, she can only speculate: "I think maybe [the reasons] were just more personal" than anything else.[49]

Koppel wasn't the only ABC employee to look down his nose at the show. Another telling incident occurred when Barbara Walters did a piece for *20/20* on the role of late-night comedians in the 2000 presidential election. Instead of interviewing Maher, a comedian from her own network with a very specific *political* persona, she chose instead to interview Jay Leno (from NBC) and Jon Stewart (from Comedy Central). Other lack of support is evidenced by the fact that when the network would conduct a press tour for its affiliates (where they trot out their stars and preview their programming to make sure their affiliates are excited about carriage and can sell the programming to advertisers in the local markets), Maher was not part of those image campaigns. As Griffiths confesses, "There were press tours that we would show up and there was no picture of Bill there." This lack of selling the program to affiliates certainly had its costs, as the program was continually plagued by the lack of live clearance from numerous affiliates in major markets.[50]

Clearance is the process where affiliates "clear" their schedule for network-supplied programming. Affiliates, by law, retain control over the decision of when and when not to accept network programming. During prime time, that is rarely an issue. But when it comes to late-night programming, many affiliates believe they can make more money by running popular off-net syndicated programming (e.g., "reruns") such as *Seinfeld* or *Friends* than by carrying network programming through which they receive low amounts of remuneration from the network (and in some cases, lower advertising dollars). Since ABC had really never been successful in late-night programming after *Nightline*, many affiliates either had contractual relations for syndicated material at that time or they found *P.I.* an unattractive alternative. Some affiliates would delay the broadcast an additional thirty minutes (sometimes even an hour) while they ran syndicated programming. But since *P.I.* appeared at 12:05 A.M. on the East Coast, every delay was very costly in terms of ratings. Hence, having network support in selling the show to affiliates was crucial, yet in this instance, not very forthcoming.[51]

In lieu of such support, the show took it upon itself to attempt to obtain clearance in major markets through a particularly crafty technique. From the show's early beginnings, the producers had received volumes of viewer correspondence requesting that they feature an "average Joe" (not just a celebrity) as a panelist. The producers, therefore, decided to fulfill this request by holding auditions for "citizen panelists" at the local ABC affiliate's studio in major cities across the nation—cities that often were not cleared live.[52] Griffiths coordinated and conducted this project by holding the auditions on Saturday mornings, while Maher would often arrange for a stand-up comedy gig that evening in that particular market. Both Griffiths and Maher, then, would appear at the affiliate for the tryouts, pick a local citizen, garner news coverage from the local broadcast and print media (who are always hungry for a story connecting celebrities to the city), and then meet with the affiliate's executives. Sometimes it worked (such as in Detroit and Atlanta); other times, it didn't (such as in Chicago).

Finally, the relationship with ABC was generally plagued by the lack of support from any particular individual within the network. ABC executive Ted Harbert was responsible for bringing the show to ABC, but he eventually left the network. Marilyn Wilson was also with late night at ABC, but she ended up joining the staff at *P.I.* Therefore, Griffiths contends, there was no one at the network who carried the torch for *P.I.* on a daily basis.[53] In sum, then, ABC was glad to import a program with a proven track record from cable. But perhaps as a result of that imported history, the network did not seem particularly invested in making sure the show was successful. I can only speculate that this was perhaps the result of the fact that no particular individual had too much to gain or lose (an enormously important driving force in Hollywood) as a result of the show's success or failure. The show was simply on its own to sink or swim.[54]

That is not to say, however, that ABC was not involved with the programming. Like any current affairs program, *P.I.* was a place where audiences tuned in for discussion when major events occurred. The show, therefore, had a field day with topics such as the Columbine High School shootings, the death of Princess Diana, the 2000 presidential election debacle, Congressman Gary Condit's suspicion of murder, and as discussed in chapters 6 and 7, the Clinton sex scandal and impeachment. But in slow news times, the network pressured the program to produce what the producers call "stunt shows"—thematic topics designed to attract viewers. For instance, *P.I.* produced "Love Week" to coincide with Valentine's Day, where the primary issues of discussion were gender relations. Other programming stunts also coincided with sweeps periods, such as going on the road for a week at a time to Las Vegas, Washington (for Black History Month), London, to Arizona for a week's worth of shows in a prison, and to Brooklyn for "Mob Week" featuring gangsters as panelists (to leech off of the popularity of *The Sopranos*). According to Griffiths, such shows did in fact provide major "bumps" (or increases) in the ratings but ultimately did not garner new viewers over the long run. Therefore, she notes, such shows "ended up serving no purpose."[55]

Politically Incorrect *taping in Washington, D.C., in 2000.*

The citizen panelist feature was another way of "keeping the show fresh," as Scott Carter calls these efforts. When asked why he thought viewers requested this feature so often, Carter responds, "We just had somebody on for the first time yesterday (Alec Baldwin) . . . who said, 'yeah, I was yelling at the TV set and then I thought, I should just be on [the show].' . . . I think everyone has a sense of that [when] they watch the show. I think people talk back to the TV set."[56] But the citizen panelist feature was also related to how the show positions itself against other forms of political talk television. That is to say, the show further activated the producers' belief that Washington insiders and talk show pundits are out of touch with how "regular" people think and talk about politics. As Carter notes,

> Bill is becoming increasingly frustrated by the picture that the media gives to America. The mirror that the media holds up is a mirror so reflected by privilege and a certain level of jadedness that we sought to find other ways to get more of what we think is a more accurate section [of America]. . . . Very often you'll see pundits on shows where they are all kind of talking to each other and you know what they're saying doesn't really reflect the country.

Yet having citizen panelists on the program created problems for the staff members responsible for booking celebrity guests. As Griffiths notes, "Publicists didn't necessarily want their clients on with just an average Joe" because the citizens "had nothing to lose."[57] Griffiths explains that the citizen panelists were "not like a politician who needs to get reelected or an actress that needed to get her next job, or even a pundit or an author who have something to risk if they go on a show like *Politically Incorrect*." As a result, many of the citizen panelists let it all hang out, because "the more 'out there' they were, the more attention they got." And as she notes, "Some of them were really, really 'out there.'" Hence, some publicists found such encounters dangerous and tried to prevent them.

Then again, some publicists found both Maher and the show's format in and of itself just as threatening. The *Los Angeles Times* quoted an unnamed publicist as saying, "'You've got to have the right person' to do the show—someone who isn't afraid to mix it up with Maher or overly concerned about saying something that might boomerang back at them."[58] Griffiths also notes the publicists' dilemma:

> *Politically Incorrect* was very loose; it was . . . the six topics we're going to talk about, [and] a lot of times they're political things. So [as a publicist] you're taking a risk because you don't . . . want your client looking stupid. And it's unscripted, so you may think [they're] coming down to talk about global warming so you can do research and then all of a sudden global warming turns into something completely different.

But if celebrities were fearful of noncelebrities because they didn't know how to play the game by the unwritten rules of celebrity culture, a similar situation existed between politicians and celebrities. That is, in an unscripted show, celebrities could not be counted upon not to violate the unwritten rules of politics, which is that politicians can't afford to be ambushed on television. *P.I.* was successful in getting certain risk-taking members of Congress to appear, including regular participation from Representatives Billy Tauzin, Dana Rohrabacher, Bob Dornan, Barney Frank, and city and state politicians such as San Francisco Mayor Willie Brown and former Governor Ann Richards. But the program was rarely safe for senators or presidential candidates, who seemingly had more to lose from encounters that they couldn't control. According to Griffiths, "Bill doesn't hold back, unlike Jay Leno or Letterman. That's very scripted. You pretty much know when you walk out and sit down that 'you'll say this and I'll say this, and then we'll do this, and then the segment will be over.'" On *P.I.*, however, "Bill is going to be true to who he is. And he's not going to throw softballs," Griffiths notes.

She uses Maher's new program, *Real Time*, as an example of how controlled interactions make a difference in getting certain guests. *Real Time* features a satellite hookup, and Maher regularly interviews higher profile politicians in a one-on-one exchange. Maher had recently interviewed Democratic presidential candidate Wesley Clark, and as Griffiths suggests, Clark "would probably never

Maher interviewing California governor Gray Davis via satellite on Real Time
with Bill Maher, *2003.*

do *Politically Incorrect* because he [would have] to share the floor with three
other people. He's running for president, so you don't know if you're going to
be on a panel with somebody who's going to say something to you about some
policy you made five years ago. It's just too unprotected." Griffiths notes that
"initially, when *P.I.* first premiered, it was very easy to get . . . a senator on with
a celebrity, but then as time went on, all it takes is one celebrity to say one bad
thing to one politician and [then] it was very difficult to get any politician on our
show." In sum, *P.I.'s* uncontrolled and unscripted dialogue is what made the
program exciting, interesting, and as Griffiths says, "that's why it's funny." But
even under such conditions, the public persons appearing on the program always recognized that there was a risk or danger involved. Therefore, many of
them worked to minimize that risk whenever possible—some by avoiding it altogether. Instead of feeling shunned by such avoidances, Maher, as one might
expect, says that he wears that "as a badge of honor because they know they're
not going to get their ass kissed. That's what the other talk shows do."[59]

"THE LAST STRAW": SEPTEMBER 11

Maher[60] has noted on numerous occasions that his calling card is his desire to
speak the truth—damned be the consequences. He refuses to kiss up to
celebrities or politicians, and he insists that Americans are too sensitive to deal

with certain realities that they would rather ignore. As one might imagine with such a philosophy, it was simply a matter of time before he ran into trouble with his comments, especially given the larger audience and the tremendous amount of power advertisers have in network television (as opposed to the much weaker role they play in cable). Maher had courted controversy on ABC on several occasions, including calling former first lady Barbara Bush a "bitch," offending Catholics with what they considered anti-Catholic remarks, comparing retarded children to dogs, and making supposedly disparaging remarks about President Reagan.[61] And in several instances, he went so far as to offer an apology or clarification of his statements.

Maher and his producers were completely unprepared, however, for the firestorm that erupted over his remarks following the terrorist attacks of September 11, 2001. On Monday, September 17, 2001, Maher hosted Arianna Huffington (political commentator), Dinesh D'Souza (foreign policy analyst for the Reagan administration), and Alan Meenan (pastor of the First Presbyterian Church of Hollywood) for the first broadcast to air after the attacks. During the conversation, the following exchange occurred:

> *D'Souza:* Bill, there's another piece of political correctness I want to mention. And although I think Bush has been doing a great job, one of the themes we hear constantly is that the people who did this are cowards.
> *Maher:* Not true.
> *D'Souza:* Not true. Look at what they did. First of all, you have a whole bunch of guys who are willing to give their life. None of 'em backed out. All of them slammed themselves into pieces of concrete.
> *Maher:* Exactly.
> *D'Souza:* These are warriors. And we have to realize that the principles of our way of life are in conflict with people in the world. And so—I mean, I'm all for understanding the sociological causes of this, but we should not blame the victim. Americans shouldn't blame themselves because other people want to bomb them.
> *Maher:* But also, we should—we have been the cowards lobbing cruise missiles from 2,000 miles away. That's cowardly. Staying in the airplane when it hits the building, say what you want about it, it's not cowardly. You're right.
> *Huffington:* You make such an important point. When you talk about the American idea and the American way of life, all, you know, worth dying for. But let us not forget how many innocent civilians we killed when we bombed Yugoslavia to rubble, because we did not want to have a single American soldier die. And now we have over 5,000 innocent civilians die because we were cowardly when it came to our military personnel. And that goes across the board to Iraq, many parts of the country where we bombed innocent civilians.[62]

A conservative Christian radio talk-show host from Houston (KSEV), Dan Patrick, heard the remarks that evening, and went on his show the next morning and "urged his listeners to call Sears and FedEx (they were the two commercials he remembered seeing after the offending segment) and demand that they stop advertising on such a virulently un-patriotic show," as the *Los Angeles Times* reported the events.[63] Calls were indeed placed, and by Wednesday, both Sears and FedEx had dropped their advertising.[64] At that point, a media-related panic had ensued, and when the dust settled, seventeen ABC affiliates had dropped the program temporarily (nine permanently) and many major advertisers refused to sign on as sponsors. Maher, then, became the first victim of those who play a one-upmanship game in the patriotic fervor that often accompanies such national tragedies (witness Fox News). Despite the fact that Arianna Huffington had made similar comments, as had Susan Sontag writing in the *New Yorker* the following week, Maher became the scapegoat for all public voices who appeared unpatriotic.[65] Maher apologized for his remarks, and then spent much of the next two weeks appearing on numerous radio and television talk shows in an effort to explain himself.

The following Wednesday (September 26), the White House got into the act when a reporter asked White House spokesman Ari Fleischer for the president's reactions to Maher's remarks. In relating Maher's comments to Fleischer, the reporter inaccurately described them as: "Members of our armed forces who deal with missiles are cowards while the armed terrorists who killed 6,000 unarmed are not cowards."[66] Acting on that information, Fleischer responded by saying, "It's a terrible thing to say; and it's unfortunate" and that "the reminder is to all Americans that they need to watch what they say, watch what they do, and that this is not a time for remarks like that. It never is."[67] The executive producer of *P.I.* at the time, Marilyn Wilson, calmly said in response, "It would be unfair of me to comment on Ari's comments because the question posed to him was misrepresented."[68] A little over a year later, however, Maher was less than happy with the White House's involvement in the controversy.

> When I was being scolded by the White House [press] secretary, I was thinking what he said was creepier than anything I ever said. I was thinking, "Well, no. We love this country because we don't need to watch what we say." In Iraq, you have to watch what you say. In many societies, you have to watch what you say, including some democracies like our friends in Egypt.[69]

Within the last two years, however, Griffiths reports that Maher has actually defended Fleischer and contends that Fleischer was only trying to say that "people are sensitive now and you need to watch what you say and do because people are sensitive" (suggesting an alternative reading to the authoritarian intentions that are easily assumed in the Bush administration's statement).

Griffiths describes the program's dissolving relationship with the network following the remarks as a series of succeeding waves. "The first wave," she notes, "was [the thought] that we were just going to get cancelled because the network was upset with Bill; that they just . . . have had it. But they kind of stood up and supported the show. But then the second wave was, well, they couldn't get advertisers to advertise in the show; everybody was pulling out." As the ruckus finally settled and it seemed that Maher would stay on the air, the network, however, stepped up its monitoring efforts, again related to advertising. "After 9/11 was the only time we were ever getting specific calls [from the network]," Griffiths notes, "about you can't say this in the monologue because it's going to piss so and so off and we can't afford to lose them." In the third wave, she says, "There was just sort of a distance. Before, it felt like the network was very involved and wanted to know who the guests were going to be, [but then] we just sort of stopped hearing from anybody at the network." In the meantime, the act of performing the show simply became less fun for Maher. As Griffiths describes it, "Just every day he came in the office and it was something else—'you can't do this' or 'you can't do that' or 'you should be careful,' [but] he can't be that. And I think it just wasn't fun for him anymore." As for how Maher was changed by the whole affair, Griffiths notes, "I think it was a year of, you know, 'you screwed up.' . . . It's terrible to think the entire country hates you."

The staff of *P.I.* knew the handwriting was on the wall when a colleague from CBS (who also worked in the same building where *P.I.* is taped) informed them that ABC was courting David Letterman as a replacement for *Nightline* (and by implication, *P.I.* as well). They knew at that moment that the show was over, despite the fact that they had another year on their contract. "It was over within two to three months," Griffiths notes. As for whether the show was cancelled because of Maher's 9/11 remarks, she replies, "They didn't want to be the network that was limiting freedom of speech; they were never going to say that. . . . They came out and they supported the show, and then basically they sort of let it wither on the vine and claimed it was ratings. But it was never ratings; our ratings never slipped."

With ABC owning the rights to the program, the show's last broadcast on June 28, 2002, was its ending. Nevertheless, Maher and staff had proven successful in producing a remarkable show (given the overall concept) that ran for three years on cable and twice that long on network television. On February 21, 2003, Maher returned to cable television (HBO) with a reincarnated yet modified version of the *P.I.* formula. *Real Time with Bill Maher* ran into the fall of 2003 and began its second season in January 2004. Although the new show incorporates numerous changes—including extending the time to forty-five to fifty minutes, airing live, an opening monologue, a "rant" (à la Dennis Miller) called "New Rules," and a satellite hookup to interview politicians—it is essentially the same concept as *P.I.* That is, Maher continues talking and arguing politics with a mixture of celebrity and political guests using his signature no-holds-barred approach. And, of course, the new show has once again attracted critics who find that the mixing of celebrity and politics does not produce the type of discourse or pleasure that they yearn for

Maher arguing with guests during the second to last episode of Politically Incorrect, *June 28, 2002.*

(which, when push comes to shove, is what it really boils down to).[70] Being back on cable also means that Maher doesn't have to worry about jittery advertisers when the going gets tough. Should Maher prove himself "politically incorrect" again, subscribers could, of course, cancel their subscription to HBO. But with the prospect of simultaneously canceling their access to *The Sopranos* and *G-String Divas*, subscribers are more likely to resort to the next best thing—simply turning off the programming that offends them.

MAKING CIVICS "COOL"

Reflecting back on the events that led to his network demise, Maher notes, "What happened to me on ABC was an indication of what happens when you say something . . . at a time like that, when people were so sensitive."[71] Elsewhere he again reiterated his poor timing: "Timing is everything—the thing that got the Smothers Brothers thrown off the air 30 years ago was saying Vietnam was a terrible waste. A couple of years later, almost everybody recognized it was the truth." As noted earlier, speaking the "truth" (as he sees it) is vitally important to Maher and, in his mind, is what *P.I.* was all about. Sheila Griffiths agrees, noting her pride in the fact that Maher's comedic peer, Jon Stewart, "was asked in an interview 'who do you admire the most,' [and] he said 'Bill Maher because he's the only one on television that's telling the truth.'" But Griffiths admits that Maher tends to operate "without a net" and, hence, isn't always well loved as a result. She believes he pushes his point "to a place that usually gets a visceral reaction," and as a result, "people either love him or hate him." And according to her, "He's alright [with the fact that] people hate him as long as it makes people stand up and . . . have an opinion one side or the other. 'Fine I pissed you off, but why did I piss you off? What's your opinion on it?' . . . I think he likes the fact that he makes people think."

Griffiths's characterization of Maher's persona, then, is as a political provocateur—pushing buttons, saying exactly what he thinks, and *asking* for engagement. Maher agrees with this assessment when he notes, "I think what I'm always trying to do is say something that hasn't been said before at all and which people are thinking but . . . nobody else will say," yet done in "a way that's funny and enlightening."[72] And that is a key point to understanding Maher and the intended role for the show—comedy is always central to his stated mission as an entertainer. "I attempt to primarily [offer] an entertainment and comedy show. . . . What people remember, no matter how many interesting points are made, [is] when you really knock 'em dead with comedy." It is this blending, then, of comedy and informative conversation that Maher sees as his mission and that which he provides for the viewing audience.

But just because it's funny doesn't mean it can't also be provocative. "The only way you know you're really doing the job is if you occasionally get booed or at least hear a little gasp," Maher says. He relates a story that makes this point but also exemplifies what he sees as the relationship that must exist between comedy and enlightenment:

> I started an editorial at the end of the show this week about the Super Bowl not taking advocacy ads, and the point was that they do take advocacy ads and what they advocate is drinking beer and eating fried food until you explode. And I heard a little gasp in the audience, and I said, they have a "don't-get-AIDS" ad but AIDS is not on the list of the top fifteen things that kill people. But food is. And I heard this kind of like, 'Oh . . . like Bill, don't let facts get in the way of our prejudices'. . . . And then we went on to make it . . . very funny. I think it was well received and people were laughing, and we had a lot of funny jokes about food, and I think the message got across.[73]

For Maher and his producers, this necessary relationship between humor and the seriousness of the issues he discusses is not because humor is disarming (although one could certainly make that argument). Instead, as Griffiths notes, "People are lazy. They don't want to actually watch the news or read the papers. So [if] the only way that we can inform people is through entertainment [or] some sort of a hybrid entertainment/news show like the one we're doing now or like the one Jon Stewart does, well then fine." Maher concurs when he argues, "If you're going to enlighten people in this day and age, it has to be like a pill in a dog's food; you have to slip it in amid the jokes and the entertainment and sometimes the celebrities, because otherwise, they're just not going to bother to listen."[74] As we see in chapter 8, however, the qualitative evidence I have uncovered on audiences does not support this characterization of those who actually watch and enjoy Maher's program (although it does fit with the myth that young people get all of their news from late-night talk shows). Audience desires to see such linkages between information and comedy arise from different sources or needs than their lack of interest in or attention to more erudite sources of information. Therefore, perhaps this is simply a justification that Maher and his producers have developed in response to the years of criticism for offering a hybrid program that critics rarely acknowledge as "informative."[75]

Both Maher and Griffiths have also noted their desire to make civics "cool." When *P.I.* first appeared on ABC, Maher was quoted as saying, "It would all be worth it if this show could in some way help make an interest in current affairs cool."[76] More recently, Griffiths has said that the mantra of *P.I.* and now *Real Time* is that "it's good to try and make it hip to be informed. . . . You should be able to talk a little bit about what's going on in the world, even just a little bit." Critics of new political television, as one might expect, vehemently disagree with any claim to being able to achieve this. Andrew Ferguson, writing in *The Weekly Standard*, posits his position this way: "God knows I hate to sound uncool, but there's a slight problem here. 'An interest in current affairs' isn't cool—cannot be cool, in fact. An active curiosity about the world of public affairs demands that you take things seriously, or at least semi-seriously, and seriousness in our ironic age is the very antithesis of the cool sensibility."[77]

And so, the fault lines are yet again present between those who do and those who don't see politics and popular culture as mutually exclusive domains. But perhaps both of these camps are incorrect in their assumptions about the typical citizen-viewer. Perhaps viewers don't really care what other people think (or even know) about the type of television they watch or that they even possess information about current affairs (as Maher and Griffiths seem to suggest). Just because young (and older) citizens watch doesn't mean they are driven to do so by their need for approval from other people. Likewise, perhaps people's desire to be informed and "serious" about the state of the world (or oneself, for that matter) doesn't mean that they don't simultaneously desire to laugh at the foibles of the human condition. As seen in later chapters, irony can be (and often is) very serious. But we need not offer conjectures or assumptions here about how "people" think because ultimately the evidence is in the mix. That is to say, the guests that *P.I.* hosted on the show are evidence enough. From rapper Coolio, singer Toby Keith, actor Tim Robbins, and athlete Charles Barkley to author Ray Bradbury, professor Lani Guinier, journalist Cokie Roberts, and Congressman Barney Frank—they all bring with them a myriad of competencies, experiences, knowledge, and sense-making skills that *represent* "the people" in some form or fashion.[78] At some level, they all exhibit abilities to hear and spread information, hold serious and humorous conversations, approach political life with earnestness and skepticism, and find some value in attempting to do so.[79] What *P.I.* did was showcase these abilities in action. At times, the program could be hilarious, upsetting, frustrating, enlightening, marvelous, and simply pathetic. But that, of course, is the world of television as well as the world that television represents.

CONCLUSIONS

The story of the rise and fall of *Politically Incorrect* offers numerous explanations for how and why new political television has appeared, as well as the different positions and roles that cable and network television play in offering the viewing public political programming. The upstart cable network Comedy Central used politics as a means of branding the network, that is, helping identify it in the eyes of viewers. In turn, such identification would increase demand for this new programming and hence also increase pressure on cable system operators to carry the network. Comedy Central also needed original programming that was inexpensive to produce, so various forms of humorous talk about politics—including *Politically Incorrect*—was a logical way to go.

The comedic vision of Maher was also important in that he recognized that television rarely offered conversations that mattered. He sought to reinvent the talk show in ways that would integrate people's interest in the important issues of the day with their interest in the *people* holding the discussions. He recognized that politics is important and serious, but also outrageous and ridiculous and hence deserves the jokes and spittle that publics might want to exact on it. He therefore merged several subgenres of talk, and in the process, called into question the validity of those he sought to replace. Highlighting the populist politics that was popular at the time, both Maher and Comedy Central challenged the notion that only "experts" (e.g., journalists and policy wonks) had the right to talk about politics on television, and both overtly recognized that politics is as much theater as anything else. Yet Maher's comedic vision also led him to recognize that much humor (as well as education) can occur by calling a spade a spade. That is, Maher's primary concern is to illuminate the truth that everybody "knows" but refuses to admit or say. Along with his comedy, these features comprise the primary ingredients in his political persona. As such, it is the recipe that has produced both his successes and his failures.

P.I.'s move to network television also exemplifies why a broadcasting network would take risks in offering politically aggressive programming, yet also why the network would shed that programming after it had served its purposes.[80] ABC had never been successful in the type of late-night programming that would attract younger, more urban audiences. *P.I.* represented a proven hit with such audiences. ABC recognized that if (or when) the show was finally cancelled, the network would have finally proven its ability to attract this profitable demographic, thereby establishing a relationship with major advertisers and local affiliates for this time slot in the process. And indeed, when *P.I.* was finally cancelled, the network brought on a "safe" comedian who isn't too edgy or discomforting (Jimmy Kimmel) in the traditional talk show vein. Although the network initially thought *P.I.* might fit with its existing news programming, the news personnel at the network were offended by the implications of their close proximity to a show that might threaten their own legitimacy as the rightful (and sole) arbiters of politics.

Finally, the story of *Politically Incorrect* shows yet again the power of advertisers in determining what Americans see on their television screens. Whereas cable television is largely financed by means other than advertising, commercial sponsorship is the only thing that really matters in the world of broadcasting. As Maher himself notes, "Television, far from being an art medium [or] . . . an entertainment medium, really it's a selling medium. It's a medium to get across the advertiser's message and the networks don't really care . . . what the product is as long as the toothpaste gets sold."[81] When the product is political talk that breaks the mold that broadcasters and the mass audience generally feel comfortable with, it is only a matter of time before the one who pays the piper calls the tune. New political television, as a result, is largely the product of a cable television environment and the institutional structures and audience relationships that produce, support, and sustain it.

III

HUMOR, OUTRAGE, AND COMMON SENSE IN POPULAR POLITICAL DISCOURSE

5

The Comedian–Talk Show Host as Political Commentator: Dennis Miller, Bill Maher, and Jon Stewart

> I just don't feel Johnny Carson should become a social commentator. . . . If you're a comedian, your job is to make people laugh. You cannot be both serious and funny.
>
> —Johnny Carson, host of *The Tonight Show*

> It's like they've handed over the reins of commentary and reporting to comedians because we're the only ones who can make sense of it; because our currency is one of insanity.
>
> —Madeleine Smithberg, co-executive producer, *The Daily Show*

In February 2000, at the beginning of the presidential primary season, a poll from the Pew Research Center for the People and the Press reported that 47 percent of people under thirty years old were "informed at least occasionally" about the presidential campaign by late-night talk shows.[1] For many reporters, this statistic—which really only reveals that young people are watching late-night television (what advertisers expect) and are picking up *something* they've not yet heard about pre-primary campaigns—had become a threat to both democracy and to their profession. When seen in concert with other data (such as declining newspaper readership by young people), the statistic takes on greater importance, and indeed is easily transformed into myth. So, for instance, in seeking some explanation for this supposed phenomenon in an interview with Jon Stewart, host of *The Daily Show*, CNN's Judy Woodruff offered the following bastardization of the statistic: "We hear more and more that your show and shows like your show are the places that young people are getting their news."[2] Because Stewart runs a fake *news* show (not just a late-night comedy show), he is often asked to answer for the crime, as if he is doubly at fault. In answering the charge, Stewart didn't miss a beat with the rejoinder, "I apologize for that. Who do I apologize to?"

As with much social scientific data employed by broader publics, the accuracy of the actual statistic can often be of less concern than its social utility. That is to say, a statistic such as this gains great currency in social discourse because it "confirms" that which we *want* to believe.[3] In this instance, it seemingly verifies our fears of civic ignorance, youth disengagement from politics, couch potato kids, the entertainmentization of politics, and perhaps even the cynicism that supposedly grips our society.[4] There is little concern here for scrutinizing the actual phenomenon being criticized, that is, late-night shows themselves. These shows are simply assumed to possess or create the traits that have now been identified and proven as a "cause." But again, the statistic upon which this myth is based is almost meaningless from the start because terms such as *informed* and *occasionally* receive no specificity for the respondent or for those later reading the results. With no electoral contests having even been held by the time the question was asked, perhaps late-night talk shows should be applauded for at least addressing the upcoming campaign instead of spending that time discussing Jennifer Lopez's rear end or other celebrity matters of pressing concern.[5]

Nevertheless, by September 2000, the concern over the increasingly significant role that late-night comedians were supposedly having as commentators on politics (perhaps because audiences were increasingly tuning in to these shows as the campaign became ever more bizarre)[6] grew to a fevered pitch when Marshall Sella, writing for the *New York Times Magazine*, wrote an eight-thousand-word cover article titled "The Most Trusted Source for Campaign News (well, almost): The Power and Prejudice of Political Comedy."[7] Again, taking the Pew study as a jumping-off point, Sella's major emphasis was to uncover the political (read, "liberal") leanings of the talk show hosts and their writers. Another supposedly disturbing point Sella advanced was that increasingly comedians were being seen by the public as *legitimate* political commentators.

We should ask, however, what exactly is so disturbing about humorists participating in political discourse? Are they illegitimate because they are as interested in making us laugh as they are in making a political point? Is it that their humor is reductive or that they trade in caricatures of politicians and the political environment? Or perhaps that their politics are "cloaked" under the shroud of jest?; that the audience is laughing over "serious" matters?; that politics is being degraded because of its dalliances with amusement and entertainment? Sella and other critics would presumably answer "yes" to these questions. Indeed, as the epigraph above notes, Johnny Carson, who more than any other individual solidified the definition of America's late-night television talk show genre, is representative of those who believe in the strict separation of laughter and serious thought. Yet Americans also generally retain an appreciation for figures such as Mark Twain and Will Rogers for keeping politics honest through their satire and humor. Why do the current equivalents of this tradition scare us? Because they appear on television, and hence reach millions of Americans nightly?

Any student of politics should be aware of the role of humor in the conduct of politics.[8] Furthermore, the conception that politics *is* entertainment, and that it is composed of many of the same rhetorical tactics, narrative dramas, and overall appeals to and relationship with its audience (e.g., voters) as the "official" show business industry, is again somewhat of a commonplace.[9] Even the concept of the "wise fool" and his relationship to power and the ruling classes has been a popular literary device for centuries, perhaps finding its most memorable manifestation in *King Lear*. The wise fool plays a metaphorically important role in political dramas, as one scholar has noted, because "the idea of the wisdom of the fool always stands in contrast to the knowledge of the learned or the 'wisdom' of the worldly. In this respect, the oxymoron, 'wise fool,' is inherently reversible; for whenever it is acknowledged that the fool is wise, it is also suggested, expressly or tacitly, that the wise are foolish."[10] As such, the wise fool exemplifies the important role that humor can play in safely advancing what is often devastatingly honest (and sometimes personally risky) critiques of power.

In the last decade, a new breed of comedian talk show host has appeared on television, and perhaps confirming the fears expressed above, they have indeed become popular commentators on politics through their role as wise fools who talk back to power in ways rarely found in television political talk. They have revived the art of humorous political critique, yet expanded it by merging it with other features of late-night talk—one of which is the crafting of a celebrity television persona (in this instance, one that is explicitly *political*). And through the various successes of their shows (obtaining solid ratings, receiving numerous awards, forming strong fan bases, among others), they have increasingly come to be seen as political commentators by fans and others within the television industry.[11] Outside of his own show, Bill Maher, for instance, regularly appears on various pundit talk shows such as Fox News's *The O'Reilly Factor*, MSNBC's *Hardball with Chris Matthews* and *Scarborough Country*, and CNN's *Wolf Blitzer Reports*, *Crossfire*, and *Larry King Live*.[12] Jon Stewart, too, is increasingly called on for commentary outside his own program, including most recently being interviewed by NBC News and Tom Brokaw after the president's State of the Union address in 2004. And clips from their shows often run within news programs, the network morning talk shows, and even on the Sunday morning pundit programs.[13] Certainly these news programs are trying to leech off the entertaining approach these commentators can provide to the serious business of politics for their own ratings. Yet, these comedians aren't being called upon simply to crack jokes but, in-stead, to offer an opinionated comment.[14]

To recognize how they have become political commentators, we must un-derstand the context in which they have constructed their personas, that is, the political events and political climate to which they respond. As the epi-graph above by Madeleine Smithberg contends, this is partly the result of a set of events in which audiences have turned to comedians in their need to locate some sanity amid the confusing and bizarre conditions that have come to dominate the political landscape in America. If the talking heads of pun-dit television and news were ineffective in providing answers through their serious discourse to console the populace, the parody, satire, and wit mixed with seriousness of the wise fools has perhaps offered an alternative (or bet-ter) means for making sense of political life. Sociologist Michael Mulkay con-tends that the basic feature of "serious" discourse is its assumption that we occupy a "one, known-in-common world," and that "ambiguity, inconsis-tency, contradiction and interpretive diversity" are problems that serious dis-course tries to remove or reduce because these are impediments to finding a common social worldview.[15] But the problem exists, as he notes, in that "coherence and uniformity are not inherent characteristics of the social world." Indeed, as current events would have it, finding coherence and uni-formity in the playing out of culture wars or wars against terrorism are well nigh impossible. Similarly, using serious discourse to establish social or po-litical consensus in interpretively ambiguous events such as a presidential sex scandal or terrorist attacks becomes a daunting task. As a result, "Hu-mour occurs because mundane, serious discourse simply cannot cope with its own interpretive multiplicity." In turn, by employing humor, "the con-straints of serious interaction have been removed, and . . . a whole range of new interpretive possibilities has been made briefly accessible. . . . The oner-ous duty of maintaining a unitary world-view has been replaced by the joy-ous creation of multiple realities.[16] In a postmodern world in which multiple realities (offered by politicians, the news media, and others) are thrust upon citizens who desperately want to make sense of that world, the availability of humorous discourse as a means of making sense of politics and events is perhaps an attractive alternative for such cognitive resolution.

What follows is an examination of three comedians in their roles as polit-ical commentators. The discussion in chapter 3 outlines the ways in which the programs by Dennis Miller, Bill Maher, and Jon Stewart share similar fea-tures yet also differ from pundit and late-night talk shows (and indeed, are a response to deficiencies in both). Here the investigation centers on how their individual political personas are crafted through a combination of their per-sonal perspectives and approaches to politics, the structuring of their pro-grams, and their engagement with significant events in the social and politi-cal realms. I argue that each comedian has crafted a particular political persona: Dennis Miller as Mad Prophet of the Airwaves, Bill Maher as Shadow President, and Jon Stewart as Court Jester. The discussion concludes by examining ways in which these comedian-hosts reflect the confusing postmodern conditions to which they react while simultaneously offering a decidedly modernist response.

We should note, however, that as show business performers, the personas they create might be temporary and change over time.[17] The personas described here represent their presentations of self for a significant period of time. Yet all three comedians were changed by the tragedy of 9/11. Miller has recently reemerged on television with another program, yet in the interim seemingly experienced, as one reporter put it, a right-wing "conversion" that has "led to zealotry" and "seems to have cost him his satiric instincts." As a result, he no longer offers the "savage commentaries about social hypocrisy" that he once did where "no one was safe."[18] Maher, after essentially being fired by ABC for his comments after 9/11, also reemerged with a new show, although not as a Shadow President. Now he seems to be more of an aggressive Presidential Gadfly. And Stewart, whose wise fool instincts were always present, grew into the Court Jester persona described here explicitly as a result of 9/11 and the government and media actions that followed in its aftermath. The discussion that follows attempts to illuminate the identifiable, nonneutral constructions of these televisual political personas, irrespective

Dennis Miller interviewing Governor Arnold Schwarzenegger on Miller's new program on CNBC in 2004.

of their actual or potential morphed nature over time. The important point to highlight is the fact that television comedians and talk show hosts have constructed *political* personas that are the basis for their public image and fan base, an image that has emerged as a product of the historical times in which they live and work as commentators. We should therefore expect those personas to change as a result.

DENNIS MILLER AS MAD PROPHET OF THE AIRWAVES

As the "Weekend Update" anchor for *Saturday Night Live* from 1986 to 1991, Dennis Miller established himself in the public eye as the brash and sharp-tongued, if not somewhat smug, interpreter of the week's news highlights. After leaving *SNL*, Miller became a syndicated late-night talk show host in 1992–1993, although the show was cancelled after six short months. It was not until 1994, when he launched the half-hour *Dennis Miller Live* on HBO, that the comedian found both the right venue (subscription cable) and the right formula for his greatest success. *Dennis Miller Live* opens with a traditional monologue, includes a guest interview, accepts viewer phone calls (seemingly to verify the "liveness" of the show), and ends with a brief run-through of the week's headlines a la his shtick on "Weekend Update." But it is Miller's signature five-minute "rant," as it is called, sandwiched between the monologue and the guest interview, that primarily established him as a political commentator. It was also a significant factor in the show's winning five Emmy Awards for comedy writing as well as providing material that Miller turned into four best-selling books.

The rant is a long-winded but smartly written screed based on Miller's frustrations with society and politics. Focusing on only one topic per episode, the rant has dealt with myriad subjects over the show's nine years (1994–2002) and 251 episodes—from the war on drugs, affirmative action, the Religious Right, freedom of speech, and political correctness to the death of eccentricity, homosexuality, buying a house, fame, equality of the sexes, and network newscasts. As a once-weekly program (although rebroadcast by HBO throughout the week), the topics for comment and discussion are broader political and social issues than the daily events or news that comprise *Politically Incorrect* or *The Daily Show* (both broadcast five nights a week). Therefore, Miller's engagement with politics is at this expansive level, removing his commentary from a focus on micro-events to the larger sweeps of political life, giving the rant a more prophetic quality as a result.

With the stage fully lit, Miller segues into the rant from his monologue by stating, "Now I don't want to get off on a rant here, but . . . ," cuing the stage lighting to simultaneously darken with only a spotlight on the star. This effect, combined with the "mad as hell" motif of the rants, reminds the viewer of the Howard Beal "Mad Prophet of the Airwaves" character from the 1975 film, *Network*. Indeed, the rant is composed of many of the same types of social and political criticisms Beal levied against the corruption and hypocrisy of institutional elites, as well as the ever-widening madness and frustrations of modern existence. For example, Miller's take on elites begins, "Now I don't want to get off on a rant here, but it seems that the special interest groups have narrowed the stripes of Old Glory into a democracy-for-sale computer bar code. Do you realize it's almost as easy to buy a politician these days as it is to buy a semiautomatic rifle?"[19] When focusing his attention on what he sees as a declining state of civility in America, he concludes another rant by stating emphatically:

> Civility is acknowledging that we don't live in a solipsistic universe. We do share this planet with each other, and we should strive to coexist in some sort of civilized, respectful manner. And so to all of you out there who don't cover your mouth, and who don't have the money ready when you get to the tollbooth . . . if you don't want to join in this noble pursuit of good manners we are all cordially invited to, *please* . . . go fuck yourself. (Original emphasis)[20]

As a topical comedian, a primary target of his caustic wit is the political world—one that Miller does not hold in high regard. "Politics is a fool's game, and it's played by pompous men," he contends. "It's a freak midway, that's what politics is. It's a bunch of guys in cages screaming and looking for your touch."[21] And although Miller has no problem fulminating on the stupidity of politicians, he contends his own level of knowledge concerning politics is "rudimentary. . . . enough to get me through comedically, but if anybody asked me the backup question about tax rebates or health care, I'd be as lost as anybody."[22] His lack of knowledge, however, does not prevent him from taking a public role as a political commentator. He is similar to Will Rogers in this regard, with Rogers proudly proclaiming that his knowledge of politics was solely derived from reading newspapers.[23]

Furthermore, Miller doesn't consider himself a Democrat or a Republican but a "pragmatist."[24] Indeed, it is his baldly stated and honest formulations based on a commonsense approach to political problems that he markets. In inveighing against the legal system, he rants, "Nobody can go into the jury room anymore and achieve a good solid Code of Hammurabi hard-on because good old-fashioned common sense and a primal notion of right and wrong have been supplanted by lawyer's tricks and haberdashery."[25] As one critic noted about Miller, his "solutions to everyday problems—wrapped in his disarming humor—are not very complicated: Throw the bums out of government. Get the bad guys before they get us. Do unto others as you would have done unto you."[26] Miller echoes this characterization in describing himself: "There's right and wrong for me. I'm not deeply evolved with multilayers about things."[27] For Miller and his audience, the political novice is still allowed to comment and have a voice about politics in the public forum provided by television. But why? For the same reasons that audiences appreciated Will Rogers and Mark Twain—for their commonsense formulations based on basic principles and values, combined with an accessible level of intelligence. As Charles Schutz puts it, part of the popular appeal of these "comic sages" (as he categorizes them) was based upon "the assumption that (their) comic intelligence is a reflection of, or at best, a refinement of popular intelligence."[28]

Yet Miller builds upon this basic level of political intelligence by also crafting himself as a savvy and intellectual guy who offers a mix of literary and cultural references that expects a similar level of sophistication and knowledge from the audience. In his "Tips for Investing in a Bullshit Market" rant, he demonstrates his intellectual nimbleness: "For one thing, remember that day-trading dilettante prick neighbor of yours—the guy who threw a few lucky darts at the NASDAQ wheel and showed up at every party for the next year in his Lincoln Navigator, downed a few too many glasses of Turning Leaf Chardonnay, and got all self-important, going on and on like he was Warren Buffett with a soul-patch talking about P/E ratios and small-cap funds' place in the Keynesean oeuvre . . . ?"[29] In making sense of the political landscape, however, he will invoke Homer Simpson more often than Homer. That is to say, his main point of reference is usually popular culture. In explaining the battles between the Republican Party and Bill Clinton in the 1990s, for instance, he makes his point by invoking a popular children's cartoon, a Hollywood movie, and a television show from the 1960s:

> But you've got to feel sorry for the Republicans. They're constantly painting fake tunnels on the sides of cliff walls, only to see President Clinton somehow beep beep right through them. See, Clinton is like the bad guy in *Terminator 2: Judgment Day,* able to assume the shape and voice of his enemies to get what he needs. He appropriated Republican ideas, added a little dash of his inimitable dewy-eyed "Bubba" magic, and presto! The next thing you know, ol' Jed's a millionaire.[30]

This level of referential dexterity is different, of course, from that used by political humorists such as Twain and Rogers. The common currency here is popular culture, which is not the folk wisdom of old. Instead, it requires its own degree of knowledge and sophistication, and an overall increased level of viewer negotiation with the multiple significations assembled from various sectors of one's public and private life. In his history of political humor, Charles Schutz has suggested that satirical journalists such as Russell Baker and Art Buchwald are the direct descendants of the comic sages, yet such satirists are distinctive in that "their humor demands from their audiences considerable political knowledge and subtle imagination." And making a point to which we return later, he notes, "It would seem that their appeal is necessarily to a qualitatively different citizenship from that of the comic sages."[31] Here too, Miller's use of pop culture as the base from which his humor is built suggests that modern citizens who attend to this form of political talk are expected to be savvy enough to "get it" at the levels of both seriousness and entertainment.

Miller is also a distinctive political commentator, for unlike the eight-hundred-pound gorilla of political ranting in the modern era, Rush Limbaugh, he is not afraid to offend the audience that loves him. For instance, in arguing what should be done to deal with the power of special interest groups in American democracy, Miller says: "All kidding aside, folks, we have to figure out a way of stopping a small minority of highly organized zealots from beating the shit out of the rest of us just because we're all apathetic fuck-ups."[32] Also in contradistinction to Limbaugh and television's pundits, Miller does not assert he has found *the* truth that must be accepted lest the empire fall. At the end of each rant, he instead invites the audience to freely reject him, his potty mouth, and his smarter-than-thou posturing with the tag line, "Of course, that's just my opinion. I could be wrong." As he notes in the first published volume of rants, "These rants are sometimes lacerated for being flimsy. I'm fine with that. I don't want to change your mind. I just want to make you laugh."[33] One of the keys to political humor as a means of political commentary, as we see again below with Maher and Stewart, is that it lacks the didacticism that political rhetoric and argumentation can easily be saturated with (especially elsewhere in the media). With many critics noting that the current era of politics has seen a marked coarsening of public life and harshness of political rhetoric (often attributed to talk radio and its ilk), a case can be made that Miller's take-it-or-leave-it-but-laugh-nonetheless approach to political commentary is a welcomed respite for his audiences.

Because Miller seems just as interested in getting a laugh as in making a political point, perhaps a good question to pose at this point is whether he is one of those mythological forces of cynicism that television supposedly proffers to (indeed, "creates" in) young citizens.[34] Although the vitriol and expletive-laced commentary might highlight negative aspects of the rants, Miller is as interested in stating what is right with America as what is wrong. In his rant on "Liberals—A Dying Breed?" he concludes by arguing:

> But as bloated as liberal politics has become, it grew from lean and noble roots . . . the battle for human rights, right here in this country. We can't afford to forget that. . . . So, as far as the nuts-and-bolts legislative details are concerned, liberalism is most probably dead. . . . But when it comes to the ongoing battle over reshaping this ethereal thing we've dubbed the American spirit, well, liberalism had better be very much alive and breathing fire, or we have truly lost our way as a nation.[35]

Or, Miller is as likely to mix cynical assessments with hopeful pleas to not give up on democracy. In discussing the Religious Right, he says, "I know we don't like to vote—marking your ballot nowadays is like choosing between the 3 A.M. showing of *Beastmaster* on Showtime and the 3 A.M. showing of *Beastmaster 2* on Cinemax. But the less we involve ourselves in the political process, the more special interest groups and fanatics move in. So vote."[36] Schutz argues that "political comedy and satire have something of both a cynical and tolerant outlook on man and his failings."[37] And although most political humorists, like the people themselves, are antipolitical, Schutz ultimately concludes that political humor participates in what he calls "positive negativity," that "its very nay saying maintains and strengthens politics."[38]

What Miller offers the audience, then, is himself as an intelligent but humorous commentator on politics who is unafraid to state openly and honestly how and why he thinks the world is, in his words, fucked up. In the process, he stands both traditional talk show comedy and political punditry on their heads. Although he begins each program with a tip of his hat to the traditional late-night comedy format—an opening monologue composed of one-liner, call-and-response type laugh lines à la Leno and Letterman—he quickly ventures into his signature verbal essay that doesn't wait for the audience to laugh, doesn't care if it offends, isn't assured that the audience will get it, and isn't afraid to be politically direct and committed. He treats his audience with respect by assuming they *will* get it, and that they too are a mix of the disappointed yet hopeful citizens who care nonetheless. The expletive-laced commentary links the language of contemporary stand-up comedy found in comedy clubs and on cable television with the late-night talk show (thanks to his show being on subscription cable) but suggests that both late-night comedy and political punditry could benefit from the real and honest language that curse words seemingly afford in communicating with some audiences. Perhaps some viewers find this crass, but in the search for sanity in a social/political world he thinks has gone haywire, the use of four-letter words may be called for in linking passion with reason.

Miller, like his comic sage predecessors before the creation of television, turns traditional punditry on its head by contending that as a political commentator, he need not be a master of every subject; that his common sense understandings of right and wrong are all the currency he needs to point out political and social idiocy when he sees it. Politics is not just a special preserve for those who traffic in insider knowledge and employ a specialized language. Instead, Miller has enough sense to get the big picture and then translate that into a popular vernacular that audiences understand.[39] As he uses them, the pop culture references are what produce both comedy and clarity, for culture more than politics is ultimately what the audience really knows and understands. Popular culture, Lawrence Grossberg argues, is where our affective investments are in late modern culture, the major points of location on our "mattering maps."[40] Miller's literary references are just to keep it honest, as well as to remind the viewer who is actually driving the bus here. Finally, the "truth" offered is neither singular nor forced down the viewer's throat. Instead, it is just an opinion, one that viewers are invited to take or leave. Which is perhaps Miller's defining accomplishment as a comedic political commentator—he assumes that audience members care enough about public life to tune in, are smart enough to know what he is talking about to laugh, will make the connections between the intertwined spheres of public and private life, and in the end, will make up their own minds.

BILL MAHER AS SHADOW PRESIDENT

In 1997, Bill Maher was asked how he would rate the Clinton presidency. He responded, "He's the right president for these times because he's full of shit and we're full of shit."[41] When later asked to clarify this statement, Maher argued, "We claim we want one thing but we really don't. Or we claim we want two things that are diametrically opposed, like cutting taxes and saving entitlements."[42] For Maher, the duplicitous Clinton is the perfect representative for such a polity. What his statement shows is the central dialectic in Maher's understanding of contemporary politics and culture. That is, Maher sees a fundamental tension in public discourse and thinking between this nation's ideals and the realities of life that don't match those ideals, a glowing falsehood that obscures the underlying truth. In numerous statements over the years, he has focused on three distinct areas that deserve special criticism, all of which can be seen in the comments and issues he tackled on his program: a politically correct culture, confused and dishonest voters, and an out-of-touch Washington establishment. Maher's frustration with this tension between ideals and realities is central to the construction of Maher's persona as political commentator during the Clinton years. For in each instance, these three areas are central to Maher's social and political criticism. They are also primary components of public discussion that ensued over the Clinton scandal and impeachment (as we see in chapters 6 and 7). Hence, they also helped comprise the show's direction and ultimate "meaning" during that event.

First, Maher has identified honesty in public discourse as the prime concern of his show. Political correctness, he argues, is an affront to honesty, a public masquerade that ignores reality. In turn, political incorrectness means "honesty, pure and simple. It's the opposite of being political, which means being full of shit."[43] Discussing the title of his program that he periodically had to explain, Maher noted,

> Politically incorrect means not flinching from saying what actually is, as opposed to stating what should be and then castigating anyone who points out the discrepancy. Which is what the politically correct do. They purposefully blur the line between aspiration and reality. Like in Orwell, an opinion that is "official" gets stated so much, we forget what is actually true.[44]

In an interview two years earlier, Maher maintained much the same position: "What's offensive to me are lies. They offend me, not truth. That's the problem with politically correct thinking. It's not thinking. It is the elevation of sensitivity over truth."[45]

For many of the early years of the show, political correctness, as played out in the culture wars between liberals and conservatives, was a primary target for group discussions on the show. But as the Clinton impeachment-sex imbroglio heated up, Maher repeatedly argued that the Republican assault on the president was part of the larger political correctness campaigns that had dominated the 1990s. Average people and politicians alike have affairs and lie about it, he argued, but that doesn't mean we should impeach a president because he does what everyone else is doing. Having an adulterous president is all too human yet is certainly not politically correct.

The second means of blurring the lines between ideals and reality, according to Maher, occurs when voters maintain the ideal that politicians should be infallible in their behavior, yet they know that politicians aren't. As he notes, "In general, I'm supportive of politicians. We ask them to do the impossible, because we speak out of both sides of our mouths. When they tell us the truth, we reject them. When they don't, we lambaste them for lying."[46] His frustration is with the duplicitous nature of the American people who maintain an idealistic perception of what politicians should be, knowing quite well that those demands are not realistic. In the case of President Clinton, this became a central issue in the debates over the president's actions, as many guests squared off with Maher over the should-versus-does of Clinton's private/public behavior. Maher consistently held that it is none of our business what the president does in his private life, but when the public finds out, we expect him to be something that he isn't or shouldn't have to try to be.

In turn, Maher thinks the American public deserves what it gets. "It's always been the position of our show that the people aren't blamed enough, and it would help them if they were. People need to be called on their own bullshit. . . . The people want to be lied to. They want the guy who can lie to them in the smoothest way."[47] According to Maher, these public demands create politicians who seem robotic, almost nonhuman, and hence are offensive to him because they are walking lies. This desire for honesty led Maher to proclaim Governor Jesse Ventura of Minnesota "the most important politician in America . . . because he is the first one who is not a robot, not a suit, who doesn't wear a tie and doesn't watch his language. He's the anti–Al Gore. He's not some guy who's beaten down all the rough edges and all the things that might offend anybody until he's a big pile of bland mush."[48] For Maher, Clinton was very much a flesh and blood politician. And although he often criticized Clinton for being a smooth-talking politician in the early years of both of their runs on the national stage, he turned out to be more sympathetic as Clinton's personal liabilities became the central point of public criticism despite a strong economy, a balanced budget, and solid foreign policy initiatives. During the scandal, Maher became more offended by the public's castigating the president for being fallible than by Clinton's lying in a smooth way about those fallibilities.

Third, Maher also retains a degree of populist frustration with the Washington establishment, which includes politicians and the handmaiden news media that he believes are out of touch with reality.[49] The establishment retains some ideal of how politics and political discourse is supposed to work that is disconnected from how people really talk about politics, he contends. One of those ideals is the strict separation between "serious" political discussion and Maher's "entertainment" variety. And the Washington elites have let Maher know they don't like his show. Maher responds by saying, "I tend to think many people in Washington live in their own little world and like it that way. Their view of talking politics is *The McLaughlin Group* or *Inside Washington*. They all piss in the same pot. They all have the same Beltway mentality, and I am on the outside of the tent pissing in, and they don't like that."[50]

As case in point, the *Weekly Standard*, a conservative journal of opinion published in Washington, ran an article titled "Politically Incompetent" which argued, "In the cool world of *Politically Incorrect*, the values of show biz must trump the values of politics: argument, appeals to history, the mustering of facts. Since everyone's opinion is inherently as valuable as everyone else's, the effort that goes into constructing an informed opinion—reading a book, say, or even a newspaper—is superfluous, a mug's game, a diversion for dorks. The bimbo from *Baywatch* will top the pocket-protector geek from D.C. every time."[51] Maher's response to the article was, "As usual, I have to say, people inside the Beltway don't get what the rest of America is all about."[52] He retains his populist stance that the "elites only" sign for political discourse needs to come down: "The concept of this show is that we live in a democracy, so everyone's opinion is equal. If everyone has a vote, why shouldn't everyone have an opinion?"[53]

The Weekly Standard's pretensions about the virtues of reasoning that belong to the political class in Washington—rational argument, appeals to history, and mustering of facts, all "ideals" rarely met in the best forums for public deliberation—also came under fire during the Clinton-Lewinsky scandal. For Maher, and indeed, for much of the country, the scandal clearly exhibited the arrogance of political and media elites who felt their "mustering of facts" would yield some deeper insight or different results than what the people had already discerned or ignored.[54] As Maher contends, the public's desire to move beyond the scandal "is a really good instance of the electorate being ahead of the people who are supposed to be leading them."[55] But again, the Washington establishment ignores "the people," if not completely misunderstands them, Maher argues.

This disjunction, then, between elite political ideals and the political reality experienced by the polity in regard to the Clinton-Lewinsky scandal became a major part of the cultural-political dialectic that played itself out for over a year on *Politically Incorrect*. But due to the nature of that scandal as a high-water mark in the culture wars, the other two disjunctions between ideals and reality described above—politically correct culture and duplicitous voters—were also closely intertwined in these discussions. Indeed, the show depends on guests bringing these dialectics, these internalized conflicting notions to bear in their debates, creating the agonistic discourse that can live up to the show's name. This perceived disjunction at the center of Maher's political and social critique became a featured component of his monologues and comic skits, the topics he chose to debate with panelists, and the commonsense thinking he attempted to mobilize. As he used the scandal to wage this war—and because of his strident defense of Clinton—his persona became, his head writer suggests, a "Shadow President."

At the beginning of *Politically Incorrect*'s second year on ABC, executive producer Scott Carter decided it was time for a change in the show's opening visual sequence as well as its set design. Although the producers had described the show as a "cocktail party," it had never tried to capture that "feel" in its graphics or set design, depending instead on the theme of a broken democracy. The new look, however, would announce the party with great flourish. As Carter recounts, "If we're the party, then the open should be Bill's getting ready for a party. So we see the cufflinks and the tie (in the opening visuals). There's a lot of this coming out of not only news shows and talk shows from the '60s, but also *Playboy after Dark*. . . . Actually, the inspiration (for the new set design) was the Playboy Mansion. There's a place at the Playboy Mansion that has sort of columns and glass windows looking out over the aviary that seemed to me like, okay, well, what I want to convey with this new set is Playboy Mansion Oval Office."[56]

Whether this was fortuitous foreshadowing or just clever hindsight, *P.I.*'s change in look and feel (which was made less than a month prior to public revelations of the affair) would capture the essence of the ensuing presidential political scandal. The discussions on *P.I.*, like all political talk shows on television at that time, centered on the affairs of President Clinton's real life Playboy Mansion Oval Office, and they offered a range of opinions, discursive complexities, and a positioning between the public and private spheres rarely found on the pundit shows. The program also incorporated Maher's enunciation of a defense of Clinton's actions rarely found on television.

On Monday, August 17, 1998, the night Clinton addressed the nation with an apology and explanation of his court testimony and the affair, Maher opened the show with a comedy skit based on the day's events. With Maher standing at a podium with the presidential seal attached, he pretended to be the president by making the following statement:

> My fellow Americans, I have just spent six hours doing a very difficult, almost impossible thing—explaining sex to Ken Starr. I have answered all of his questions. Now I have one of my own. Did this really happen? Did I really work my ass off my whole life to become leader of the free world only to be lashed to the stake of adultery by a grand inquisitor who nobody ever voted for?[57]

The skit continued, with Maher stating in very bald terms what the president should have said, but in very atypical "presidential" language. Chris Kelly, head writer for *Politically Incorrect*, noted that this "was a statement that Bill really wanted to make." Indeed, many of the lines were summaries of arguments Maher had been making in panel discussions about the scandal over the previous seven months. Kelly maintains that the speech represented a "Bill Maher Shadow Presidency." He suggests that Maher's public role throughout the Clinton-Lewinsky scandal and impeachment process was comparable to Norman Mailer's during the Kennedy years. In 1963, Mailer published a collection of essays under the title, *The Presidential Papers*. As Kelly describes it, Mailer "decided that the overarching theme was that . . . certainly his work during the Kennedy years would say as much to future historians as anything Kennedy had written, as though somehow he was just as much President." Kelly notes, "Our conservative guests come on and accuse Bill of that all the time—of, 'you're just like the President because you're projecting these things on the President'—the ideas, especially the idea of 'I'm doing this job, [now] leave me alone.'"

Critic James Wolcott seems to agree when he argues that Maher "has assumed the characteristics of the Presidency that has defined his show, and morphed into a junior, compact Bill Clinton," and that he "expresses a Clinton-without-apologies—a Clinton unbound."[58] The skit quoted above is most certainly a prime example of Wolcott's point, although other examples abound. Whereas Clinton can't speak openly of his past indiscretions with women, Maher cavorts with Clinton's paramours by having them on his show.[59] Whereas Clinton is labeled a sex addict for his blundering private acts gone public, Maher intentionally makes his own private acts public by admitting to masturbating in his dressing room, having bound volumes of *Playboy* magazine on his bookshelves, dating bimbos, and being a frequent guest at the Playboy Mansion. Whereas Clinton doesn't inhale, Maher freely admits he does. Whereas Clinton pretends to respect the institution of marriage while ignoring its demands through his dalliances with women other than his wife, Maher forswears the institution of marriage entirely. Maher is the publicly sanctified id to Clinton's ego (especially given Maher's aggressive support of the president on all these accounts).[60] Walter Kaiser corroborates this

Freudian analysis of Maher by observing that the wise fool, in literary history, has traditionally filled a similar role. The fool, he notes,

> embodies the untrammeled expression of the id. Lacking any vestige of a super-ego, the fool surrenders shamelessly to his bodily appetites and natural desires, and he is regularly characterized by his hunger, thirst, lust, and obsession with obscenities. . . . He is the pleasure principle personified. His enemy, the super-ego, represents all the ordered conventions and civilizing rationality of society which he finds both incomprehensible and intolerably repressive.[61]

This yin-yang relationship, however, extends well beyond the libido. Whereas Clinton is led by his political position to spin and color the facts, Maher's public role on *P.I.* is to tell it bluntly as he sees it. And whereas Clinton "feels the pain" of the American people, Maher states the unhappy truth about why it hurts. "Are we such a bunch of babies that we can't say what is true?" he argues.[62] The president is a politician who says what is expedient and necessary to retain his hold on power. The Shadow President states the truth knowing that his secret sharer can't. In fact, his honesty is his value. This Shadow President addresses the people in a language they understand. Maher is also Clinton's alter ego.

Maher suggests that he is not the president's peer, or even equal to the president. "I really object when people treat the president like he's their peer," Maher notes. "He is not their peer. . . . He's someone with great accomplishments who in some ways deserves great slack."[63] But Maher seems to recognize his shadow presence in the gallery of public opinion. In a 1999 interview, when asked if Clinton might appear on *P.I.* after he leaves office, Maher confessed that he hoped they could talk.[64] Maher noted, "I'd like to think he might say, 'Hey, I appreciated the support during that rough period, that little tough time I had. I appreciated you saying some of the things I couldn't say myself.' The night of the famous speech to the nation, August 17th, *I made the speech he couldn't make.* It ended with the words, 'She blew me—fuck you'" (emphasis added).[65] Presidential words indeed! The point to be taken from this analysis is the coterminous relationship between the two. Clinton helps define Maher, providing Maher with the material to voice his disgust with issues in the culture wars he is constantly waging battles against. Similarly, Maher helps define Clinton by giving voice to a commonsensical understanding of Clinton as the fallible hero, an Odysseus who has lost his way and makes the wrong choices because he's just a mortal.

The scandal became a site through which publics formulated broader social and cultural meaning than journalists and newscasters entertained. Maher, as talk show host and Shadow President, enunciated these issues in a language and form quite unusual in television political discourse. Maher embodied the hyperreal "politician" of the modern era in order to make him real, to resolve the tensions between a constructed façade of political life and its seedy, all-too-human underbelly. In the process, Maher constructed a new role for the talk show host. He is not content simply to sit back and reflect on politicians and political events, or to wait for his guests to make his points for him. Instead, he inserts *himself* into the audience's understanding and consciousness of politics—dramatically, rhetorically, and psychologically. This is a much more powerful position than late-night television has generally allowed. Chevy Chase, of course, "embodied" Gerald Ford through his parodies, but those were comedic skits (e.g., acting) not accompanied by serious, impassioned pleas in discursive exchanges with people who earnestly disagreed. Maher instead moves fluidly between the seemingly nonexistent boundaries of his role as subjective embodiment, rhetorical defender, playful antagonist, entertainer, celebrity, and host. It is here where we see most clearly the ways in which the definitions of the late-night talk show host and political commentator have been altered.

JON STEWART AS COURT JESTER

As host of *The Daily Show*, the news parody on Comedy Central, Jon Stewart took over the "anchor" job in 1999 from departing host Craig Kilborn, another defection from Comedy Central to a job in the major leagues of network television.[66] The humor and general direction of the program under Kilborn is now generally seen as being somewhat juvenile and mean-spirited, even by its staff.[67] But Stewart took over at a very opportune time—just before the 2000 presidential election. *The Daily Show's* (*TDS*) coverage of the election through its *Indecision 2000*—including sending faux news "correspondents" to the two political party conventions—continued Comedy Central's interest in mining the political for laughs (dating back to the network's election coverage from 1992). For the first time, however, the show began to enjoy some level of "respectability" as a legitimate commentator on politics.[68] When *TDS's* correspondents received press passes to cover the Republican National Convention, Bill Hilary, the executive vice president of Comedy Central, exclaimed in surprise, "People are taking us seriously, even though we're a comedy show. For the first time, they're saying '*The Daily Show*' has a place in social commentary." Stewart, on the other hand, was less amazed about his supposed new role: "The whole point of our show is that we're a fake news organization. What's more appropriate than going to a fake news event? Everybody knows it's a trade show."[69] This "legitimate" commentator's effort here was to signal to his audience that what had formerly been a meaningful political ritual had long lost its legitimacy as such, that it was part of the fakery of public life that he so detests.

As the campaign became increasingly bizarre—a robotic Al Gore trying on multiple fake personas, for instance, culminating in his Olympian effort to display some level of genuine humanness by French kissing his wife at the moment of his nomination, and George W. Bush's "subliminable" advertisements and gaffe-laden remarks when moving off script—the fake news show was handed a wealth of material with which to work satirically. Behind the scenes, however, the show's writers were not necessarily amused with what the public was being offered in the election. *TDS*'s head writer Ben Karlin, former editor of *The Onion*, noted his utter amazement at any claim to legitimacy and respectability by candidate Bush: "He's an ideal puppet, as though there's a hidden ghost-machine running *this thing*. It's so obvious he's wrong for the job in every way" (emphasis added).[70] Frustrations such as these is where their jokes often come from, notes Stewart—that is, "seeing things that make you cringe, and wanting to turn that into something that will make you laugh."[71] The election, then, became prime fodder for their comedic efforts. And although the network had used the moniker *Indecision* in its coverage of previous presidential elections, the naming could not have been more appropriate for the surreal outcome that would follow. With concurrent legitimate and illegitimate ballots (e.g., Florida), winners (e.g., the electoral college versus the popular vote), and outcomes (e.g., the five-to-four Supreme Court decision determined along strict party lines), "reality" increasingly became difficult to define or locate as the absurdities of the process seemed ever more constructed, arbitrary, and chaotic.

Hence, a fake news show became, at times, a legitimate substitute and/or supplement to its "fake" but all-too-real cousins on the other cable channels. The show's co-executive producer, Madeleine Smithberg, would later reflect on the show's fortuitous positioning: "Everything (in the campaign) became so absurd that the absurd people became the actual pundits. Jon Stewart is now a kind of recognized, viable pundit."[72] Although Smithberg might have overstated her case at that point, Stewart and *TDS* nevertheless emerged from the 2000 election with an air of respectability from a bewildered and punch-drunk audience who found that the court jester in the corner was making more sense than the traditional institutional voices that typically command center stage and interpretive authority on television.

As bizarre as the 2000 election was, it would be the 9/11 terrorist attacks, the domestic and military response to those attacks by Congress and the Bush administration, and the resulting coverage of those actions by the twenty-four-hour cable news networks that would solidify Stewart's Court Jester persona. Two things, in fact, emerged from the government and news networks' responses that ignited the programming on *TDS*: the sensationalistic, entertainment-driven, and pandering nature of news reporting, and the manipulation, distortions, and outright lying by the Bush administration. First, over the last decade, the nature of what constituted news and news reporting had changed as a result of the fierce competition among cable news outlets, namely Fox News, CNN, MSNBC, and CNBC.[73] Those changes became even more pronounced with the crisis in the American psyche that resulted from the 9/11 attacks. The overly patriotic and sentimental packaging of its music, titles, and graphics that CNN first developed in the Gulf War of 1991 was merged with the louder-brighter-faster graphics and sounds that Fox Sports had developed in its coverage of the NFL, now honed into a televisual spectacle unlike anything seen in the history of television journalism. Fox News, in particular, darted to the front of the ratings pack with its overt flag-waving and patriotic pandering, yet somehow found the gumption to promote itself as a "fair and balanced" alternative to the "liberal media" that was supposedly CNN. Stewart was dismayed. In regard to cable news reporting he says, "They've so destroyed the fine credibility or the fiber that was the trust between the people and what they're hearing on the air."[74] Not only had the reporting become a prime example of the excessive style highlighted by John Thornton Caldwell's notion of televisuality, but it is a viable illustration of Jean Baudrillard's argument that publics are offered simulated reality, even hyperreality—imagery that is realer than real.[75] *The Daily Show* took it as its patriotic duty, so to speak, to parody and ridicule these constructed falsities.

A second set of circumstances that greatly affected *TDS*'s content and direction was the Bush administration's "war on terror" that was conducted at both the domestic and international levels. From dubious claims and preposterous actions by government officials that affected civil liberties domestically, to the administration's unilateral decision to invade Iraq in pursuit of nonexistent weapons of mass destruction and a "regime change," Stewart and *TDS*'s writers took it upon themselves to persistently poke holes in the government's legitimizing claims. Communications scholar Susan Douglas, writing for *The Nation*, characterized *TDS*'s response to the administration as such: "Stewart's on-air persona is that of the outraged individual who, comparing official pronouncements with his own basic common sense, simply cannot believe what he—and all of us—are expected to swallow. The approach of Stewart and his 'reporters' is not to attack Bush policies as ideologically problematic; instead, they expose them as utterly absurd, as nonsense, deranged."[76] Indeed, Stewart was dumbfounded by the Bush administration's willingness to assert boldface lies and expect the public to believe them. He argues,

> This administration, more than any other I've ever seen, is gaslighting us! Literally, it's raining on us, it's cloudy, and they go, "And on this sunny day"—No, it's not sunny. And they say, "Uh—this sunny day," and then you look at the backdrop they've got and it says *sunny* and they say, "See, sunny?" It's just a lie. They just don't acknowledge it. And by not acknowledging it, what they say becomes true![77]

Such lies only give Stewart and his writers their mandate. "What we try to do," he notes, "is point out the artifice of things, that there's a guy behind the curtain pulling levers."[78]

Jon Stewart as anchor of The Daily Show.

Stewart's approach, then, to the political environment he encounters and the political commentary he creates is not to engage in an enraged yet bemused rant à la Miller or to construct elaborate counterarguments à la Maher. Instead, he simply asserts a smirking disbelief by using a smile, a raised eyebrow, and his antagonists' own words to ridicule and question through quips and video clips. For example, in one particularly damning video montage, *TDS* constructed a "debate" between President George W. Bush and Governor George W. Bush over U.S. foreign policy and the war in Iraq. That is, they spliced together statements made by the president juxtaposed by conflicting statements made several years earlier by the governor when he was running for president. Stewart introduces the debate by stating, "It's been difficult to have an honest discussion about the direction President Bush is taking this country. In fact, when you combine the new mandate that criticizing the commander-in-chief is off limits in wartime with last year's official disbanding of the Democratic Party, well, we're left at an all-time low in the good old fashioned honest debate category." He then assumes the role of moderator, with the first question directed to President Bush, followed by the president's and governor's "responses":

Stewart: Why is the United States of America using its power to change governments in foreign countries?

President Bush: We must stand up for our security and for the permanent rights and the hopes of mankind. The United States of America will make that stand.

Governor Bush: I'm not so sure the role of the United States is to go around the world saying this is the way its gotta be.

Stewart: Mr. President, let me just get specific. Why are we in Iraq?

President Bush: We will be changing the regime of Iraq for the good of the Iraqi people.

Governor Bush: If we're an arrogant nation, they'll resent us. I think one way for us to end up being viewed as the ugly American is for us to go around the world saying, "We do it this way, so should you."

The Daily Show *offering video evidence of contradictory statements by candidate Bush and President Bush.*

Stewart: Mr. President, is the idea simply to build a new country that we like better?

President Bush: We will tear down the apparatus of terror and we will help you to build a new Iraq that is prosperous and free.

Governor Bush: I don't think our troops should be used for what is called nation building.[79]

In an effort to ridicule the shoddy work of journalists and the news media (and their complicity in ideological manipulations), Stewart also regularly assumes the straight man role as he deploys his faux reporters "on location" for "live reports" from around the globe. In one exchange between Stewart and his correspondent in the field, Stephen Colbert, they discuss the U.S. military's march into Baghdad. With Stewart sitting at his desk and the caption "Tug of War" over his shoulder, he says to Colbert, "The job is done and now thankfully, hopefully, we can move on to the task of helping to rebuild Iraq." The camera cuts to Colbert standing in front of an image of a toppled statue of Saddam Hussein (supposedly on location). Colbert replies, "Rebuild? What are you talking about, Jon. We won! Rebuilding is for losers. It's time to party! Then it's off to Syria for the next invasion."

Many times, Stewart simply assumes the role of narrator and critic of various news clips, offering questions and commentary to express his utter disbelief in what the audience has just seen or heard. In one segment, for instance, Stewart shows a clip of Secretary of Defense Donald Rumsfeld's press conference of March 28, 2003, where the secretary announced Pentagon warnings to Syria and Iran for actions that the U.S. government found threatening to military efforts in the Iraq war.

Rumsfeld (on news clip): Military supplies have been crossing the border from Syria into Iraq. We consider such trafficking as hostile acts, and will hold the Syrian government accountable.

Stewart: Did you see what he just did there? We're in the middle of a war, and he's starting another war! We're already fighting Iraq, and he's like, "And oh, by the way, Syria? You want a piece?"

Rumsfeld (on news clip): The Badr Corps is trained, equipped and directed by Iran's Islamic Revolutionary Guard, and we will hold the Iranian government responsible for their actions.

Stewart: He's taking on all comers! You know, there is nothing like a cantankerous old man who takes a "Hey you kids, get off my lawn" approach to foreign policy. The guy is literally, like drunk, swinging a broken bottle at people. [Said drunkenly] "Hey, Netherlands, you looking at me?"[80]

In short, through his privileged position as fake news anchor on a fake news show, Stewart gets to play the fool by using the words of those in power against them, revealing "truth" by a simple reformulation of their statements. Stewart, then, becomes the court jester, cleverly positioned on the public stage to question what the rulers have just said through his "harmless" reassessment of what they (and their stenographers to power) have configured reality to be.

Stewart greatly resists any interpretation that this is somehow cynical, and therefore dangerous for American democracy. "It's so interesting to me that people talk about late-night comedy being cynical," he notes. "What's more cynical than forming an ideological news network like Fox and calling it 'fair and balanced'? What we do, I almost think, is adorable in its idealism. It's quaint."[81] And he has a point. The court jester actually does *care*, for otherwise the jester wouldn't be standing around contributing to the conversation as things around him fall apart. The jester is paradoxically noncommittal yet idealistic in his implicit hope that perhaps someone with the power to affect change will eventually wake up as a result of his truthful yet camouflaged ribbing.

The propaganda offered by Fox News (and perhaps other cable news networks), on the other hand, is very dangerous. Propaganda "substitutes opinion for facts" and is so powerfully effective (and affective), Daniel Boorstin reminds us, because it "is an appealing falsehood (that) feeds on our willingness to be inflamed."[82] Eric Alterman's discussion of the punditocracy that dominates political talk on cable news is especially instructive here. In making his case for why such discourse is dangerous for democracy, he looks back to the writings of Walter Lippmann, whose description of a "pseudo-environment," or a false political consciousness that is the combined product of journalistic speculation/opinion and an inattentive public, seems particularly apt in describing the state of news reporting that *TDS* is critiquing. As Alterman describes it,

> This pseudo-environment consisted not of imperfect representations of truth but of "reports, rumors and guesses" about it. Thus, the entire reference for political thought and action had become, in Lippmann's view, "what somebody asserts, not what actually is." People under the influence of this pseudo-environment, Lippmann warned, "lost their grip upon the relevant facts of their environment" and thus became the "inevitable victims of agitation and propaganda."[83]

In its less erudite, but more comical way, this is exactly the point that Stewart and *TDS* are trying to make—a news media that isn't doing its job will participate in manipulating the citizenry that it should be protecting through its watchdog role as the fourth estate. As Stewart contends about CNN reporting, the person who supposedly checks facts for the show "is just the one going, 'You know what I heard?' That's what they should call CNN—'You Know What I Heard?' I don't even know if they've got an acronym for that."[84] *TDS*, on the other hand, attempts to lead people to think again about the type and quality of information they are being given, by whom, and for what purposes. "When we spot silliness, we say so out loud," Stewart notes. "We're out to stop that political trend of repeating things again and again until people are forced to believe them."[85]

Head writer Karlin also notes, "We air complaints, then make them funny and not didactic for the show."[86] The show's desire not to be didactic, however, does not mean that it is beneath Stewart to point out when someone is full of crap. After the show received a Peabody Award for its excellence, Stewart put the award in perspective by analogizing its role in social commentary: "You know how at Club Med there are the people who get up and learn the goofy dances, and the ones who stand in the back of the room and make fun of them? Well, we got the award for standing in the back of the room and making fun."[87] Indeed, *TDS* is an "island of respite," as he puts it, for those who simply can't take the pageantry and charades of public life at face value. Stewart and company are the metaphorical bad boys in the back of the room lobbing spitballs. They are this generation's *Mad Magazine*, taking no prisoners, and offering up shades of gray in a world increasingly painted in the easy to understand tones of black and white.[88]

Stewart recognizes exactly where his commentary exists on the national stage—what it does and doesn't contribute to public discourse, and why it is not threatening—all in relation to where real power lies.

> It's like when people say about jokes, 'Where do you draw the line?' Well, why don't people ask that to corporate heads? Why don't they ask that to people that do things that impact people's lives in an enormously explicit way. What we do is implicit. It is in the ether. The national anthem is an amazing song. Did it win any wars? No, but it adds an atmosphere and a flavour and it adds to a national dialogue. Jokes don't destroy things. They don't kill anybody. They're just atmospheric.[89]

Yet Stewart also sees his role as more than just a background singer. Indeed, he sees himself as a stand-in for a section of the viewing public he calls the "politically disappointed." "I represent the distracted center," he contends.[90]

> My comedy is not the comedy of the neurotic. It comes from the center. But it comes from feeling displaced from society because you're in the center. We're

the group of fairness, common sense, and moderation. We're clearly the disenfranchised center . . . because we're not in charge.[91]

Who *is* in charge are Democrats and Republicans, as well as liberal and conservative interest groups, lobbyists, and think tanks that Stewart generally disdains. "Liberals and conservatives," he argues, "are two gangs who have intimidated rational, normal thinking beings into not having a voice on television or in the culture. Liberals and conservatives are paradigms that mean nothing to anyone other than the media."[92] Stewart exhibits a level of frustration with the activist wings and dominant voices of American politics that the public, in his view, feels disconnected from and manipulated by.[93] "The disenfranchised center," he continues, "is upset that the extremes control the agenda in disproportionate ways because the extremes care more, they're passionate. Whereas the disenfranchised center doesn't give a shit if gay people get married—it would neither stop them nor stand up for them."[94]

The program Stewart produces and the persona he then projects are addressed to this supposed constituency of partisan conscientious objectors. "Our audience can watch without feeling like we're grabbing them by the lapels and shouting, 'This is the truth!' in their faces," he notes. "Our show is about *not knowing what the truth is*" (emphasis added).[95] In a televised marketplace of ideas that almost never allows for the casual shopper who doesn't want a political opinion rammed down her throat, Stewart's approach certainly offers something refreshingly different. As *New York Times* columnist Frank Rich put it: "The relief that a viewer can take away from *The Daily Show* has less to do with its specific point of view than with its unfailingly polite but firm refusal to subscribe to anyone else's program."[96]

Stewart and his merry band of writers and correspondents recognize their special place in television talk. Stewart and *TDS* staff feel liberated from the constraints that other news and talk shows work under, and they realize that they can actually "say what (they) think" and "be a little bit more honest" as a result.[97] When Stewart was asked why that is the case, and why he hasn't experienced the same persecution from the patriotism police that others who criticized the Iraq war suffered (such as the Dixie Chicks, Martin Sheen, and Susan Sarandon), he responds, "It's expected that I'm going to make fun of things."[98] Jon Stewart's persona, like Bill Maher's, has been heavily influenced by the times in which the show is produced. And just as *Politically Incorrect* seemed the perfect vehicle for alternative public discussions and snickering about a political witch hunt that involved sex, *The Daily Show* also proved to be the appropriate vehicle for criticizing political mayhem when such criticisms could easily be considered unpatriotic. Indeed, Maher's brand of puncturing holes in political rhetoric was deemed "unpatriotic" by the White House and advertisers when he questioned the accuracy

The Daily Show *news team (from l–r), Stephen Colbert, Ed Helms, Jon Stewart, Rob Corddry, and Samantha Bee.*

of presidential rhetoric, whereas Stewart's parody-driven show could get away with harsh criticisms because they were cloaked in the jester's jests.

In summary, then, the court jester recognizes his special license to speak and understands that he will probably keep his head when others' will roll. And while Stewart's honesty is his ultimate value, this wise fool also believes he speaks for other Americans who have been shunted aside by those who play politics for keeps. As some critics have noted, Stewart projects an "Everyman" quality in his persona, and as such, perhaps his desire to speak for the displaced, distracted, and disenfranchised center is the source of that trait. As Stewart points out, "There are times when it's not about making a joke, it's about having to acknowledge what is going on, so you can feel like you're still in the same world as everyone else."[99] Which, of course, is the ultimate irony of the fool—he offers his insanity as the best means for staying sane.

POSTMODERN CONDITIONS AND THE COMEDIC RESPONSE

What has been offered up to this point is a description of three comedians who have crafted their personas as political commentators in the midst of rather strange political times. Indeed, the tensions inherent in those times and the media spectacles that accompanied them have been a central source for their humorous commentary. But as the last quote by Stewart suggests, their response isn't just about making a joke, but about offering something else. Bill Maher enunciated similar feelings in an interview on *The Late Late Show with Tom Snyder* when he noted, "There are days when the issues actually depress me. The guests don't stay with me [in his memory]. I can't remember who [was] on, but when I drive home at night, I think, this is not just a show; this really stinks, and this is really going on, and it's not getting better."[100] There is an overriding sense here that although these are two entertainers, they are also citizens working through their frustrations with the primary focus of their professional lives as comedians: politics.

This effort to maintain sanity by locating others—those who express their bewildered kinship through their laughter—is not simply the worn-out citizen's response to vicious political battles or elusive yet dangerous threats to security. As postmodern theorists have pointed out, our living in a highly mediated world makes it difficult to distinguish at times between the real and the simulated, the authentic and the artificial, the meaningful and the superficial. Some postmodern theorists contend that these mediated simulations have come to constitute reality itself. Although I find such claims exaggerated, it is undeniable that our lives are flooded with the circulation of signs—political, commercial, religious, cultural, and personal. And in regard to political life, this swirl of images and symbols (or texts) may be the only "reality" of politics or political events we acquire or maintain.

The condition of postmodernity, argues David Harvey, is the product of late capitalism, with its celebration of difference, choice, variety, experience, pleasure, flexibility, spectacle, ephemerality, and so on.[101] Baudrillard contends that these celebrations, this circularity of signs, produces a stream of solicitation for us to "constitute ourselves as subjects, to liberate, to express ourselves at any price, to vote, to produce, to decide, to speak, to participate, to play the game."[102] Yet as Lawrence Grossberg argues, we are finding that maintaining any affective commitment to the given formulations is problematic. Echoing the argument that late capitalism has produced a legitimacy crisis in western societies responsible for such disaffection, he contends,

> Postmodernity, then, points to a crisis in our ability to locate any meaning as a possible and appropriate source for an impassioned commitment. It is a crisis, not of faith, but of the relationship between faith and commonsense, a dissolution of what we might call the "anchoring effect" that articulates meaning and affect. It is not that nothing matters—for something has to matter—but that we can find no way of choosing, or of finding something to warrant our investment.[103]

Yet one would think that in a post-impeachment, post-9/11 world, such investments and rehabilitation of faith and commitment would come more easily.

In the swirl of simulation, rhetoric, manipulations, initiatives, and charges and countercharges outlined above, however, such conversions are not quickly forthcoming. For instance, how is the public to distinguish between the images and realities—mediated by our own faith yet common sense—in the following situations that Maher, Miller, and Stewart, as political commentators, responded to?

- The image of a Democratic president who reached new lows in personal conduct versus the reality of his sanctimonious Republican persecutors with similar lapses in personal judgment.
- A common sense understanding that the majority vote wins a presidential election, versus faith in a constitution that contains antiquated procedures for conducting such elections.
- The reality of a decisive yet violent right-wing response to terrorism versus the images of impotent yet peaceful left-wing protests.
- Faith in the images of embedded journalists reporting on American troops in Iraq versus the reality of Fox News in bed with government propaganda.
- The images of Geraldo Rivera crawling through the caves of Tora Bora on what looks like a fake Hollywood set versus a fake New York television set on *The Daily Show* exploiting the reality of Rivera's techniques.
- Images of military destruction and death, or the corporate reality of Halliburton's postwar contracts to rebuild from that destruction.
- The reality of a silver-spoon president who avoided Vietnam versus the images of dead working-class soldiers in Iraq whose funerals he won't attend.
- Imagery of a Top Gun president who produced a "Mission Accomplished" or the reality of his presidential handlers creating a photo-op for his reelection.

The answer for Baudrillard is that members of the public know they "do not have to make a decision about themselves and the world" because they have engaged in a conscious strategy of "transference of responsibility" onto the political and information classes. The public is engaged, he argues, in "a strategy toward others not of appropriation but, on the contrary, of expulsion, of philosophers and people in power, an expulsion of the obligation of being responsible, of enduring philosophical, moral, and political categories."[104] He calls this the implosion of the social, and as Steven Best and Douglas Kellner summarize his point, "The social thus disappears and with it distinctions implode between classes, political ideologies, cultural forms, and between media semiurgy and the real itself."[105]

What these postmodern theorists offer, then, are descriptions of ways in which our three comedians-hosts-commentators are, in some respects, representative postmodern citizens. None of the three identifies with conventional partisan categories or ideological positions because, as Stewart argues, the categories of liberal and conservative have lost their meanings. Instead, they are political *bricoleurs,* mixing, matching, and splicing together their political feelings and conceptions in a composite fashion that is rarely aligned with the inherited structures and meanings of their parents' generation.[106] They are contumacious in their response to the given structures, refusing to subscribe to anyone else's program or to abide by the rigid ideological positions of support or rejection in the various wars that are waged. Their politics are nondidactic, with Stewart saying he's not sure what the truth is, while Miller invites the viewer to ignore his truth revelations entirely. Stewart says he represents the disenfranchised center, expressing his belief that the masses are tired of the solicitation for their political passions. Politics is controlled by the passionate extremes, he says, whereas the center "doesn't give a shit." Maher says the public is not cynical enough, while Miller's assessment of the public's democratic investments is deftly asked and answered when he notes, "Why are Americans so disinterested in politics? Because we can be. Democracy is voluntary."[107] Miller, Maher, and Stewart are seemingly representatives of Baudrillard's conception of a strategically imploded society, for as Baudrillard contends, our "deepest desire is perhaps to give the responsibility for one's desire to someone else."[108]

But to label them "postmodernists" is perhaps an overwrought yet common attempt to characterize the smartly smug humor of late-night television.[109] A postmodern theorist such as Grossberg goes too far, I contend, in his attempt to describe the strategies people employ to rectify the disconnect between meaning and affect. For instance, he says, "Within this logic, cultural practices refuse to make judgments or even to involve themselves in the world." Labeling this strategy "authentic inauthenticity," he says people attempt to "anaesthetize" the world: "It starts by assuming a distance from the other which allows it to refuse any claim or demand which might be made of it. This 'hip' attitude is a kind of ironic nihilism in which distance is offered as the only reasonable relation to a reality which is no longer reasonable."[110]

Yet as we have seen above, these comedian-hosts are quintessential modernists in that they aren't leading us toward separation, but rather offering intimate views of the emperor (and empire) without clothes. They are committed to breaking the spell of the hyperreal through their comedy precisely because they still believe that something "real" exists. Maher, for instance, sees a disconnect between ideals and reality that is created through politically correct language and thinking, as well as in the constructed personas of politicians who have been crafted (by themselves and by others) to be "realer than real." His own persona as the Shadow President is an effort to personify the president in order to *make him real*. For Stewart, there is also a hidden truth (not just simulations or versions of the truth, as postmodernists would have it) behind the government lies and media spectacles. He may not know what that truth is, but he knows that whatever or wherever it is is obscured by institutional mendacity. Included here is also the implicit assumption that more authentic news/information *can* be achieved. And for Maher and Stewart, they are committed to stopping the political trend of politicians and media repeating things over and over until these things become reality, until people are "forced to believe them."

Charles Schutz argues that political "humor dwells on the contradiction between appearance and reality."[111] Although writing before postmodern theory, his observation of how political humor works becomes even more prescient when one understands that postmodern conditions make humor especially ripe for political critique. The gap between appearance and reality is where irony and satire do their work. But if such contradictions are already present in culture and politics, or are already at play in the field of media images and political rhetoric, then the comedians' work is half done before it's begun. Grossberg, as we have noticed, argues that it is increasingly difficult to have faith in things or places that actually matter, "so that one can actually make a commitment to it and invest oneself in it."[112] But this is where political humor inserts itself, stepping into the gap between faith and common sense. It doesn't ask for an investment in parties, ideologies, leaders, institutions, history, programs, responses, initiatives, and so on. It is an *affective* response to an entanglement of "choices" that may have no appropriate rational response (as in the current situations noted above). I concur with Mulkay when he notes that the realm of humor

> serves as a constant sign of the failures, inadequacies and limitations of our serious world and of the pattern of language-use by means of which we produce that world. The multiplicity of the humorous domain, even though it is restricted by its surrounding context, reminds us that the world in which we live is not exhausted by any one set of meanings.[113]

In short, I argue, we laugh because laughter provides the affective response that *can* connect us to substantive meanings that have really not strayed too far.

As such, I endorse Schutz's conception of the "positive negativity" of political humor in this regard. Political humor helps us recognize the norms and values that we as a polity hold in common.[114] He argues, "To a great extent, the successful reception of the humor depends on its audience's agreement on the standard. Then comic rationality reminds of common values; it does not declare revolutionary standard of politics."[115] Political humor, then, is innately conservative and serves social stability.[116] One way it does this is by "counteracting the ideological fanaticism of contemporary politics":

The dogmatism of ideology is fully serious, but imposing it would destroy the flexibility of politics whereby the pluralism of society is accommodated. And the pluralism guarantees a sympathetic audience for the political ridicule or invective against others' ideological politics.[117]

Furthermore, he argues, "Comic rationality is nondogmatic, but in its negative response to political excess it serves to restore equilibrium to politics."[118] In short, Schutz's insights suggest that political humor maintains a healthy negative and, perhaps at times, cynical outlook on politics, but it is balanced with a measure of idealism about our common political values that are challenged by the inanity it skewers. Indeed, some forms of political humor are just as "likely to be informed by some disappointed idealism" as cynicism.[119] Here again we see the modernist tendencies of Stewart, who believes he represents the "politically disappointed" and that his show is "adorable in its idealism." Or Dennis Miller, who lambastes politicians, elections, and the political process one minute, and then encourages viewers to resist the colonization of politics by corrupt capitalist interests and ideological fanatics by voting, despite the lack of good choices.

Finally, the modernist tendencies of these comedian-hosts are seen in the "Everyman" qualities of their personas. Stewart says he represents the disenfranchised center, the people of moderation and common sense. Maher says he represents the reality of people's thoughts and feelings, the things that people actually think but are afraid to say. And Miller represents the passion, frustration, and bemused tendencies that are manifest in his populist invocation, "I'm mad as hell, and I'm not gonna take it anymore."[120] As Everyman, they are not political experts, they speak a common vernacular with the public, they don't belong to the political class, and they are all watchers of the same news, messages, and images that the audience also operates from in making sense of daily political realities. In short, they are proxies for the people themselves. Schutz's history of political humor reveals that these populist qualities are typical for political comedians, whose popular appeal is often "based on the assumption that (their) comic intelligence is a reflection of, or at best, a refinement of popular intelligence."[121] Furthermore, people tend to see these comics "as themselves, only more so. To be exact, the people worship themselves in typical democratic fashion."[122]

But how can the people see themselves when these comedians are not simply the writers or radio personalities of disembodied media forms utilized by Twain and Rogers? These are television "personalities," stars and celebrities who are plugged into a different systematic relationship with their audience than the comic sages of old. In his study of celebrity, David Marshall also contends that celebrities are stand-ins for the viewing audience. Celebrities, including talk show hosts, are "both a proxy for someone else and an actor in the public sphere. . . . From this proxy, the celebrity's agency is the

humanization of institutions, the simplification of complex meaning structures, and a principal site of a public voice of power and influence."[123] They
take on these qualities because they "are also embodiments of the social categories in which people are placed and through which they have to make
sense of their lives, and indeed through which we make our lives—categories of class, gender, ethnicity, religion, sexual orientation, and so on."[124]
Marshall is correct here, but omitted from his list is a category that doesn't
differentiate us from one another (as cultural studies tends to do) but instead
unites us in our commonality (which political science simply assumes). That
is, I argue that these categories also include people as political beings, democratic citizens who believe, at some level, in their continued representation
and involvement in the processes of self-governance and the "will of the
people." Just as celebrity articulates products with consumption (including
consumption of the celebrity sign itself), celebrities with strong political personas (such as these talk show hosts) can also articulate impassioned rhetorical constructions and political commentary with deeper values and beliefs
that citizens maintain as Americans.

CONCLUSION

This leads us back, then, to the issues that began this discussion. It is no great
revelation that television matters in the lives of citizens, including young
people (and others) who watch late-night television. As Grossberg argues,
popular culture is increasingly where we make our affective investments in
life, where we plot the locations on our "mattering maps." It is also no great
surprise that celebrities are a compositional feature on those maps, including celebrity talk show hosts. Yet as Marshall notes, audiences aren't just
awestruck with the shimmer of the stars; they see themselves through these
public proxies. Miller, Maher, and Stewart take this a step further by crafting
personas built on paradoxes: smart and savvy yet an everyman; speaking
common sense through a common vernacular about politics, yet retaining
uncommon knowledge of trivial or arcane cultural references; being both a
cynic and an idealist, a postmodern yet thoroughly modern man. As public
life has become so confusing, wrapped in the simulations and hyperreality
of the media/politics spectacle, these comedian-hosts are the embodiment of
the multiple realities to which they attempt to offer insight and clarity.

The result, as Schutz suggested with the satirical journalists of the 1960s and
1970s, is a televisual "appeal to a qualitatively different citizenship" than that
offered by the comic sages or talk shows hosts before. The comedian-host as
political commentator offers audiences the means for connecting their interest in public life—their knowledge of both current events and popular
culture—through a language capable of entertaining multiple realities. As

Mulkay notes, "The interpretive openness of humour seems more accurately to reflect or reproduce or allow for multiple realities of the social world" than that offered in the realm of serious discourse.[125] These comedian-hosts offer the possibilities for truth and contingency, meaning and ambiguity, hope and disappointment, belief and irony, amusement and bewilderment. They speak to a citizenship where we monitor the landscape of both politics and culture for things that engage us or concern us, where we employ multiple vocabularies, consume myriad images, juggle multiple personas, feel multiple fears and desires, and in the end are still constituted as citizens *and* a viewing public.

When institutions such as the news media or government fail to offer meaningful avenues for cognitive resolution to postmodern realities—or, perhaps more accurately, are leading participants in constructing the cognitive dissidence in the first place—a space exists whereby the comedian-host as wise fool can fill in the gap between our traditional faith in these institutions and our commonsense knowledge that things are dreadfully amiss. The wise fool is licensed to speak back to power, to question the ideological fanaticisms that produce presidential impeachments, senseless killing of civilians through terrorist attacks, unilateral military invasions, and efforts to suspend civil liberties. The wise fool is idealistic in his belief that truth exists and that his wisdom can bring that to light.

Each comedian-host's persona is also the product of the times and the events to which he has responded on the public stage. The form and type of humorous narratives that define their approach to politics and entertainment has been a result of those times. Using Northrop Frye's Aristotelian approach to dramatic genres, Leah R. Vande Berg, Lawrence A. Wenner, and Bruce E. Gronbeck argue that dramatic narratives have an appropriate time and place. Using Frye's metaphor of nature's seasons, they contend that

> Comedies are summer, the season of foolishness, guile, and the bringing down of braggadocio bureaucrats and avaricious old men, a time even to critique social norms and acceptable behavior; tragedies inhabit the coolness of autumn, in situations where individuals through pride or other dangerous motivations bring about their own fall from station or fall from grace; and ironic literature is winter, where the world is subjected to Kafkaesque tyrannies and hidden dictators, where the human spirit all but dies—in hopes of being reborn in spring.[126]

Perhaps it is simply a coincidence, but we see the same progression in the humorous narratives utilized by Miller, Maher, and Stewart. Reflecting Frye's conception of summer, Miller and Maher offered their ridiculing humor in the era of sexual scandal and culture wars, when Americans were given the opportunity to laugh at the foolishness and hypocrisy of leaders and various social norms played out in the political arena. The autumn tragedy of 9/11 was America's fall from grace, when Americans learned that we were no longer the shining city on the hill but were, in fact, hated as a proud and arrogant nation —a painful realization. At that point, neither comedy nor brash truthfulness seemed appropriate, as Maher experienced in his own autumnal fall from grace. Finally, in what seems to be now a winter season, the tyrannies of the Bush administration became fodder for the ironic narratives told by Stewart and *TDS*. The wars abroad and the lies at home flagged both the American spirit and the "disappointed middle" America that the ironic Stewart has attempted to speak to and for. The political persona that the comedian-host has constructed has depended on the types of dramatic narratives that *could* be told given the historical context of political seasons. In other words, the historical context creates a dramatic season, which, in turn, influences what kind of wise fool speaks for that season as well as what narratives the wise fool tells.

The reformulation of the talk show host as political commentator, then, means that the comedian is no longer simply delivering cheap laughs and throwaway one-liner humor that offers comfort or distraction from our daily lives. Instead, as the programs by Miller, Maher, and Stewart attest, the humorist as engaged and enraged, amused and bemused political commentator has been revived in a time when the fool seems so wise and so desperately needed. And instead of fostering cynicism, as critics of late-night humor maintain, Miller, Maher, and Stewart are in many ways responding to it by their satirical comic vision designed not to seduce their audience but provoke it. They comprise a new breed of comedians in an old tradition of political humor and constitute a new form of political talk show host fostered by cable against the traditional mainstream mindset of network programmers.

6

The Common Sense of Nonsense:
Parody and Political Critique

In late January 1998, when allegations arose that President Clinton had an affair with White House intern Monica Lewinsky, Clinton made a public statement in which he aggressively denied any sexual relations with Lewinsky. Wagging his finger at journalists and their cameras, he proclaimed, "I did not have sexual relations with that woman—Ms. Lewinsky!" Eight months later, when the president admitted that indeed he had some liaisons with her, reporters and pundits were quick to point out the irony. Isn't it ironic, they argued, that this president, who had previously lied to the public about extramarital sexual relations before being elected, would not only lie again, but also chide the public (by wagging his finger) for asking if it had happened again? Isn't it ironic, they noted, that a president under investigation for lying about his sexual advances on a woman in an Arkansas hotel room would lie again about his unbridled sexual exploits within the White House? Isn't it ironic, they contended, that the chief law enforcement officer would break the law by lying to a court of law in an attempt to save his own neck?

James Ettema and Theodore Glasser argue that the use of irony in journalism is an important and often an effective way in which reporters can insert a moral language into their reporting while still respecting the conventions of objectivity. "Often," they argue, "such technical terms as *illegal, unethical,* or *unprofessional* seem insufficient to engage the public's interest in the misconduct that has been uncovered. Then journalists may turn to a rhetoric of irony that reveals the misconduct to be not only technically wrong but terribly wrong—a true moral outrage." The utility of a rhetoric of irony, they argue, is that it "does not merely operate within the constraints imposed by the conventions of journalistic objectivity; it *transfigures* those conventions into a moralistic vocabulary for condemnation of the villains to whom we have foolishly entrusted our public affairs."[1] They conclude, however, by arguing that although irony "effectively undermines one position—the villain's—while unequivocally supporting another—the wised-up victim's, irony can work as a corrective only when writer and reader share a clearly articulated moral vocabulary."[2]

But the Clinton-Lewinsky scandal did not allow for a clearly articulated moral vocabulary. Although many citizens and journalists alike found both Clinton's sexual affair with a young woman in the White House and his lying about it repugnant, they differed in their beliefs that such moral transgressions were outrageous enough to merit Clinton's removal from office. Journalistic irony generally failed to inflame public passions as a result. Instead, citizens found the situation (including Clinton's persecution by Republican moralizers) somewhat ludicrous, and therefore worthy of laughter and derision. Ettema and Glasser (writing before this scandal) join other social critics in bemoaning the fact that such a moral vocabulary has begun to "lose its coherence and expressive power." They warn of the danger when citizens might disallow the press to speak *to* and *for* the citizenry as guardians of their best interests. Instead, they contend that citizens have increasingly become captives of "the theatrics of derision, reversal, and parody" (one assumes through television).[3] The authors conclude their discussion by arguing, "when, at last, the ironies of victims and villains can generate no indignation but only derision, investigative journalism will have no vocabulary with which to discuss the true and the good or to express human solidarity. Then any possibility for a role in the defense of democratic values will be at an end."[4]

This argument should lead us to ask: Since when did the theatrics of derision, reversal, and parody lose its power as a tool of popular political critique? Could it be that a public, operating from a different set of political conceptions or sense, might *not* relinquish their critical faculties to journalists, politicians, pollsters, and social scientists, and instead make their own conclusions about the affair—conclusions that might lead them not to moral outrage, but to celebrated parody?[5] Or could it be that common sense did lead to moral outrage, but against a *different* set of political elites than the ones that journalistic irony was supposed to highlight as morally deficient?

The best means for answering these questions is to directly examine parody as a means of political critique. Only by uncovering the power of parody can we assess why it is perhaps an equal or more effective means for expressions of public discontentment with the behavior of political elites. Indeed, as discussed in previous chapters, *The Daily Show with Jon Stewart* is essentially one big parody of television news reporting. But in the process of parodying a media form, the show also harshly (but humorously) criticizes the arrogance, ineptitude, and dishonesty of the political leaders on whom it "reports." Therefore, we should analyze how parody works its comedic charm while simultaneously producing damning political indictments. In that regard, one parodic skit from *Politically Incorrect* is examined here in detail. On August 17, 1998, the night of President Clinton's televised public apology following his grand jury testimony earlier that day, Bill Maher opened the program with the following parodic performance, assuming the role of "president" himself.

"MY FELLOW AMERICANS"

If you own a TV—and since you're watching this, I assume you do—you know that President Clinton spent the day testifying before the grand jury. You've also heard the President's post-testimony address. But this is the statement I think he should have made.

[Maher walks up to a podium with the presidential seal attached]
My fellow Americans, I have just spent six hours doing a very difficult, almost impossible thing—explaining sex to Ken Starr.

I have answered all of his questions. Now I have one of my own. Did this really happen?

Did I really work my ass off my whole life to become leader of the free world only to be lashed to the stake of adultery by a grand inquisitor who nobody ever voted for?

I balance the budget. I preside over an unimpeachable era of peace and prosperity, but then you want to take me down for fibbing about diddling an intern in a thrown-out civil case by a woman whose gripe was she saw my weenie in the disco era?

Are you people kidding me? And now you want an apology? I don't think so.

But I'll tell you what I am sorry about—I'm sorry that for the service I do around here 24-7, the tail I did manage to get wasn't better.

I ain't Marv Albert over here, all right? And while we're at it, let's cut out this crap about this not being about sex. If I hear that one more time, there's going to be a stain on somebody's clothes and it's gonna be blood.

Look, I'm sorry Ken Starr can't get laid. I'm sorry wives don't like giving oral sex. I'm sorry I'm a flesh-and-blood human being in need of some affection and release in what some might consider a high-stress job.

And by the way, next time one of our embassies explodes or the Asian markets need a little hand-holding, remember who thought it was more important that I spend my time telling a jury about my penis.

Oh, I forgot, it's not about sex. Yeah, right, it's about lying. Well, grow up. People lie about sex. And nobody else in the world lapses into a police state over it. Of course if you empower a special persecutor to stray into sexual behavior, you will create perjury crimes. But come on, what guy hasn't lied about doing a fat chick?

If that makes me a criminal, take me away right now. But I also go as a victim of treason, because what else is it when an unconstitutional fourth branch of government conspires by endless legal harassment to overthrow a president twice elected by the people, the real and only real source of political legitimacy?

And so, as I go off to prison, I thank the people for the 70% approval rating. And to those many others who feel their curiosity about my personal life has blossomed into a right, who feel that the fate of the Republic is so dependent on me fessing up, let me, as a final gesture of grace, give you what you want.

You want the truth? You want to know what I really think? Well, here it is. She blew me. Fuck you![6]

Maher's skit seems a clear example of parody, although some may want to suggest this is satire.[7] This is a parody—although an interesting twist on parodic performances—because of the relationship of Maher's reformulated words to Clinton's original. Mikhail Bakhtin maintained that parody includes a "double-voiced word," or "utterance that [is] designed to be interpreted as the expression of two speakers."[8] As Gary Saul Morson summarizes Bakhtin,

> The author of a double-voiced word appropriates the utterance of another *as* the utterance of another and uses it "for his own purposes by inserting a new semantic orientation into a word which already has—and retains—its own orientation." The audience of a double-voiced word is therefore meant to hear both a version of the original utterance as the embodiment of its speaker's point of view (or "semantic position") and the second speaker's evaluation of that utterance from a different point of view.[9]

There are two aspects of Maher's "address" that make it an unusual parody, the first of which is the limited number of actual words used by "the president" in his address. The most direct utterance is the opening, "My fellow Americans." Beyond that, we are left with many words that belong in a presidential speech (*embassies, republic, branch of government, balanced budget, peace and prosperity*), or words that are familiar to the particular context in which the president speaks (*jury, perjury, special prosecutor*), but words that are not the actual words used by the president. Nevertheless, the utterance as a whole is to be interpreted as the expression of two speakers— a public, formal, political Clinton, and a private, unbound by ritual and political decorum "Clinton/Maher."

The second feature of Maher's speech that makes it unusual is the actual target of his disagreement. Again, working from a Bakhtinian perspective, Morson argues that

> a parodic utterance is one of open disagreement. The second utterance represents the first in order to discredit it, and so introduces a "semantic direction" which subverts that of the original. In this way the parodied utterance "becomes the arena of conflict between two voices . . . the voices here are not only detached and distanced, they are hostilely counterposed"—counterposed, moreover, with the second voice clearly representing a higher *"semantic authority"* than the first. The audience of the conflict knows for sure with whom it is expected to agree (emphasis added).[10]

Maher's disagreement in the parody, of course, is not with Clinton per se. Although Maher suggests these are words that Clinton *should* have spoken, he fully realizes that public figures are not allowed to speak such words—not because they are liars or can't speak "the truth," but because politics is a rhetorical pageant, a political theater that plays by different rules than vernacular discourse. Instead, Maher's disagreement is with the farcical, surreal situation that brought the president to make the address in the first place (as Maher notes, "Did this really happen?")—the forces that would have the "leader of the free world" speak publicly about his penis on videotape. The open disagreement is not with the first utterance, but with the *context* of the first utterance—the forces that make the first utterance necessary.

Morson stresses the importance of context when he argues, "Parody aims to discredit an act of speech by redirecting attention from its text to a compromising context. That is, while the parodist's ironic quotation marks frame the linguistic form of the original utterance, they also direct attention to the occasion . . . of its uttering. The parodist thereby aims to reveal the otherwise covert aspects of that occasion, including the unstated motives and assumptions of both the speaker and the assumed and presumably sympathetic audience."[11] From Morson's perspective, we recognize that the unstated motives in Clinton's address are to save his hide from the political fires raging around him. What Maher parodies, however, is not the president's motives (which a Republican parodist such as Rush Limbaugh might have done), but rather, the fact that the president isn't allowed to scoff at the occasion of its uttering, the affront to common sense and proportionality that Maher is frustrated with.

Maher uses several common parodic techniques, such as exaggeration ("I'm sorry Ken Starr can't get laid") and understatement (I'm just a "human being in need of some affection and release"). But Morson also notes "an especially common technique (in parody) is the introduction of an element—an incident in the plot, let us say, or an unexpected choice of words—that is incongruous with the tone or generic conventions of the original. In this case, readers are implicitly invited to discover the new point of view from which the incursion was made, and a new structure that would resolve the incongruity."[12] This, of course, is a prime means through which Maher's parody establishes its humor. He uses a whole series of conventions the audience does not expect from a politician. For instance, he employs a vernacular discourse such as "tail," "doing a fat chick," "work my ass off," "24-7," "diddling an intern," and "she blew me; fuck you."[13] Maher's politician also transgresses unwritten rules of politics, such as questioning the logic or will of one's constituents ("I don't think so," and "Are you people kidding me?"), stating imperatives to constituents ("grow up," "cut out this crap"), or using condescending descriptions (for example, characterizing international diplomacy as "hand holding"). Mary Douglas argues, "A joke is a play upon form.

It brings into relation disparate elements in such a way that one accepted pattern is challenged by the appearance of another which in some way was hidden in the first."[14] We do not expect the juxtaposition and subversion and hence find it humorous. She also notes, however, "The social dimension enters at all levels into the perception of a joke."[15] Again, we would never expect these words from the president.

Nor do we expect the president to say what he actually thinks about his political enemies. In this instance, the "president" says what some people thought was the case—he was being harassed for lying about behavior that people typically lie about with great frequency (e.g., sexual affairs). The words are unexpected and unusual—hence, humorous—but also a relief, offering the opportunity, as Freud would argue, for the subconscious to be released or unrestrained through laughter. According to Douglas's summation of Freud's theories on joking, "At all times we are expending energy in monitoring our subconscious so as to ensure that our conscious perceptions come through a filtering control. The joke, because it breaks down the control, gives the monitoring system a holiday. . . . For a moment the unconscious is allowed to bubble up without restraint, hence the sense of enjoyment and freedom."[16] In short, by altering the codes normally used to construct a political address, Maher as parodist offers a new "semantic orientation" that is quite subversive.[17] That new orientation is achieved by identifying and attacking the conventions that structure political discourse. Morson notes, "The parodist recognizes language as dialect or idiolect, as *characteristic* of some group or speaker. Taking speech as an index of its speaker or listener, he or she selects and draws attention to whatever most clearly uncovers their affectation or folly" (original emphasis).[18] Maher's humor focuses on this normative political dialect and subverts its control, its sense of rigid performance that is designed to lend it a sense of dignity.[19] But dignity, as the parody would have it, cannot exist in public discussions about oral sex, at least not when the president of the United States is at the center of those discussions.

Bakhtin argues that the parodist's voice has a higher "semantic authority" than the voice being parodied, to which Morson adds, "The audience of the conflict knows for sure with whom it is expected to agree."[20] But what gives the parodist's voice that semantic authority? The fact that he or she is the last to speak? The laughter produced through this particular form of ridicule? The belief that the parodist spoke the actual "truth" of the matter? I suggest that what gives the parodist semantic authority is his appeal to common sense. The use of the vernacular, the inverted codes, and so on help produce the humor. But what *appeals* to the viewer's sensibilities are the commonsense notions of how the world works that seem missing from this political end game. Common sense seems divorced from this series of legal processes that quickly arose but also rapidly spun out of control with no one apparently knowing how to stop them, despite the farcical level to which the events had risen. For instance, Special Prosecutor Kenneth Starr asked Lewinsky to give intimate details of her sexual relations with the president, such as the number of orgasms she achieved in any particular sexual encounter, whether the president achieved an orgasm in each encounter, her phone sex with him, the sexual accoutrements used (e.g., cigars), her book purchases, and her semen stained clothing. That such matters would become of "public importance" seemingly defied common sense, and therefore parody, jokes, and satire offered an important public language through which to question this affront to common sense. Irony, however, seems impotent because the public was offered two equally worthy sources of outrage—a selfish and careless president and his vengeful and obsessed political opponent, both of whom seem to be gross caricatures of the excesses that lie at the heart of the culture wars. Parody, jokes, and satire might be just the type of public language that was best suited for scathing political critique in this instance. Indeed, several journalists and social commentators reported the flood of jokes and "puerile humor" circulating on the Internet about the scandal.[21] The public, it seems, found great pleasure in using the scandal for folly, although we have no way of gauging the intent of such jokes as political critique. Maher's use of parody in this case, however, was just that.

The features of Maher's speech suggest how rhetorical formulations of common sense might give the parody its semantic authority. To see how that is so, we should examine what makes this parody commonsensical. First, we must map some ways in which it is possible to analyze common sense itself.

MAPPING COMMON SENSE

For Clifford Geertz, common sense is almost impossible to define, for to do so is to ignore the tremendous variance that comprises common sense across cultures. He simply says that common sense is "an interpretation of the immediacies of experience, a gloss on them; [it is] historically constructed . . . and subjected to historically defined standards of judgment." He argues that common sense is a cultural system, one that "rests on the same basis that any other such system rests: the conviction by those whose possession it is of its value and validity."[22]

Therefore, rather than using a definition as an investigative starting point, he contends that we should look for common sense more in the nuances of its presentation than in its content:

> It is precisely in its tonalities—the temper its observations convey, the turn of mind its conclusions reflect, that the differentiae of common sense are properly to be sought. . . . It is only in isolating what might be called its stylistic features, the marks of attitude that give it its peculiar stamp, that common sense . . . can be

trans-culturally characterized. Like the voice of piety, the voice of sanity sounds pretty much the same whatever it says; what simple wisdom has everywhere in common is the maddening air of simple wisdom with which it is uttered.[23]

Geertz, therefore, argues that common sense *can* be empirically uncovered, although not by cataloging its content, sketching its logical structure, or summing up its conclusions. Rather, such an analysis must account for its tone and temper by constructing "metaphorical predicates" that serve to "remind people of what they already know."[24] From these nuances or characteristics, he offers five such properties that he contends comprise common sense: *naturalness*—the "of course" quality that seems inherent and intrinsic to the situation; *practicalness*—the sagelike quality it bestows on something; *thinness*—its simpleness or literalness, or as Geertz notes, "Sobriety, not subtlety, realism, not imagination, are the keys to wisdom"; *immethodicalness*—its inconsistent, ad hoc, and disparate notions, often in the form of jokes, anecdotes, proverbs, epigrams, and the like; and *accessibleness*—its openness to all, the general property of all, and usually anti-expert and anti-intellectual.[25] Boaventura De Sousa Santos also employs such metaphorical categories for cataloging common sense by offering a similar list of qualities, substituting the terms *self-evident* for *naturalness, non-disciplinary* for *immethodical,* and *superficial* for *thinness.* He also adds two others that are particularly helpful: *rhetorical/metaphorical*—that common sense is used not to teach but to persuade or convince; and *pleasure utility*—fusing our use with enjoyment, the emotional with the intellectual and practical.[26]

Maher's parody obtains its semantic authority, I argue, through the appeal of its features *as* common sense. For instance, the *thinness* and simpleness embedded in the implied response—Isn't it clear that this case is about sex, not lying?; Why the need to spend millions of dollars and dominate public affairs with this legal wrangling when we all know that certain things are always true? Maher rhetorically argues this is not a case about destroying documents, murdered colleagues, land deals, laid-off workers, and the like. Rather, he suggests, anybody can clearly see the matter is about sex—that universal human behavior that everyone engages in except, according to Maher, the Special Persecutor, who can only engage in it vicariously or voyeuristically, whichever the case might be.

Having asserted the simple fact that the case is about sex, the situation is then naturalized, or offered as *naturalness.* Of course people lie about sex; Of course men in power have extramarital sex with young women; Of course Clinton has sex with women besides his wife (we elected him twice knowing that)—these are all inherent to the situation, his comments imply. Note that many of these sentences were not overtly stated. Michael Holquist, in his study of Bakhtin's concept of dialogism, argues that an utterance is a "border phenomenon," something on "the border between what is said and what is not said, since, as a social phenomenon *par excellence*, the utterance is shaped by speakers who assume that the values of their particular community are shared, and thus do not need to be spelled out in what they say."[27] By positing this case as simply about sex, many assumptions naturally follow, including sets of disparate or *immethodical* notions that both add humor and continue the focus on sex but have little direct bearing on the issues in the case: Starr is just doing this because he is a jealous nerd ("I'm sorry Ken Starr can't get laid"); The president is doing this because Mrs. Clinton is cold ("I'm sorry wives don't like giving oral sex"); It's okay that the president is doing this because he's overworked and under pressure ("I'm sorry I'm a flesh and blood human being in need of some affection and release in what some might consider a high-stress job").

These simple and natural facts made discernable and understandable are also made more *accessible* through Maher's significations of "work," "sex," "adultery," "lying," "peace and prosperity"—a language more easily understood than the elite formulations of "suborning perjury," "obstructing justice," "depositions," "impeachment proceedings," "special prosecutor," "DNA reports," and others that were used by Clinton's opponents and other institutional elites (such as journalists). Geertz's model of common sense would have it that publics can engage more easily in evaluation and judgment based on the accessible signs through which they are invited to make meaning in this situation. As Holquist reminds us, we "make sense of the world only by reducing the number of its meanings—which are potentially infinite—to a restricted set."[28] The paradigmatic signs used in Maher's vernacular discourse allow that sense making to be potentially more common.

Maher's speech also drips with a *style, tone,* and *attitude* that invite the viewer to adopt his semantic reformulations, features such as incredulous exasperation ("Are you people kidding me?" "Did this really happen?"), sarcasm ("Oh, I forgot, it's not about sex. Yeah, right, it's about lying"), anger ("grow up"), overstatement ("I go as a victim of treason"), and identification ("what guy hasn't lied about doing a fat chick?"). Holquist stresses the importance of intonation in utterances in assigning value and meaning. "Intonation," he argues,

is a material expression of the shaping role the other plays in the speech production of any individual self. The community of shared values gives different semantic weight to the physically articulated acoustical shifts in pitch or volume. We never convey objective information in our speech; we always pass judgment on whatever information is contained in what we say: "The *commonness of assumed basic value judgments* constitutes the canvas upon which living human speech embroiders the designs of intonation." (Emphasis added)[29]

In short, then, few (although some) of the constructions in Maher's monologue seem to represent any identifiable common sense *maxims* that have been traditionally formulated and circulated within American culture. They are, however, contemporary formulations that are selected, packaged, and presented—as the Geertzian model suggests—in ways that appeal to our common understandings of reality.[30]

Although the dialogic utterances that make up this commonsense reality are part of Maher's monologue, these utterances only make sense in relation to the social situation in which they exist. Bakhtin argues, "Any monologic utterance . . . is an inseverable element of verbal communication. Any utterance . . . makes response to something and is calculated to be responded to in turn. It is but one link in a continuous chain of speech performances."[31] Holquist adds, "An utterance is never in itself originary: an utterance is always an answer. It is always an answer to another utterance that precedes it, and is therefore always conditioned by, and in turn qualifies, the prior utterance to a greater or lesser degree."[32] Maher's monologue is part of a dialogue with the voices that literally preceded his parody only moments earlier on *Nightline*, the voices of primary political actors, analysts, and journalists who continued to frame the scandal and its meaning in their own terms of formal, legal, and political procedure mixed with talk of the details of oral sex. Maher is in dialogue with these and other voices that sought to establish "ways of speaking" these events, and the *Nightline* broadcast represents some of the voices from the political class.

Here are some excerpts from *Nightline*, cited randomly and not necessarily representing a sequential order as they appeared on the broadcast:

Michael Zeldin, former independent counsel (discussing the definition of sex approved in the Paula Jones case): Well, the definition was pretty specific there. It involved conduct by a person with respect to another person. It comes out of the criminal code. It's the sexual predatory conduct provisions of the criminal code. And so if he says this is a consensual relationship where something was done to me consensually rather than me to somebody else involuntarily, then he has the legal wiggle room to avoid a perjury trap.

Dan Quayle, former Vice President of the United States: Well, Ted, today is a sad day. It's a sad day for America. . . . Tonight [the president] admitted that he did, in fact, have a sexual relationship with Monica Lewinsky and by admitting that he also basically admits that he did, in fact, commit perjury. Perjury is lying. Perjury is a crime. I assume that this will now go to the Congress. Impeachment proceedings will probably begin in all probability on perjury, perhaps obstruction of justice and the suborning of perjury.

Congressman Bill McCollum (R, Florida), member of the House Judiciary Committee: What I'm prepared to say is that if, indeed, at the end of the day, after all is said and done, there is, indeed, sufficient evidence to clearly say the president lied under oath in a court proceeding, then I think that he should be impeached. I think it's a matter that's very highly, much in the constitutional issue of what is the rule of law and do we let a president stand above that rule of law? I think that's a very significant thing that cannot be dismissed even if there is nothing else here. And I think that's the question.

Ted Koppel, Nightline *Anchor:* There was also not much specificity, and I don't mean specificity in terms of the actual acts, but even a concession that there had been sexual contact between the two of them.

Sam Donaldson, ABC News Senior White House Correspondent: That's right. Inappropriate conduct, he said, but he did not specify what type of inappropriate contact. It's almost like in 1992, remember on his *60 Minutes* interview when he said to the country, "I think the country gets it." It was like, "wink, wink, you know what I mean." But sex is the problem and the description of it. . . . Apparently, from what we we're told, he did not answer many questions within the testimony when he was pressed by the prosecutors, questions that asked him to detail the type of sexual contact. And he cited privacy rights and he got upset.[33]

Some of these comments reflect the less accessible elite language and formulations that Maher's commonsense discourse exists in opposition to. Some of these comments exemplify why Maher could be so frustrated with political actors who think it is their right to know the intimate details of Clinton's sex life. And other comments reflect the insider tendency to define the scandal in terms of its threat to democracy. That is, Republican opponents of the president argued that Clinton committed perjury, and if the rule of law is to stand for anything, the highest of high must be treated the same as the lowest of low if our system of justice is to prevail.[34] Embedded in that claim is the assumption that law is impartial and fair, and that law must be uniform and equally applied to all. From the celebrated media cases of O. J. Simpson, to the Menendez brothers, to Lacresha Murray, Americans have witnessed a judicial system that could conceivably lead many observers to conclude that "justice" has little to do with telling the truth in a court of law, and much to do with other factors. These cases suggest that lying is simply part of the judicial process, and both sides of the aisle seem to practice it when it makes a difference between winning and losing. When the president of the United States does the same thing, especially when his lying is about sex with an intern, many Americans wanted to know what's the big deal. For instance, polls conducted by ABC News after the president's address and reported during the *Nightline* broadcast cited the following results to the questions, "Has the president said enough?" (59 percent yes, 39 percent no); "Do you believe the president has obstructed justice?" (52 percent yes, 41 percent no); "Should Kenneth Starr end his investigation of the president?" (69 percent yes, 29 percent no); "Should the president resign?" (28 percent yes, 68 percent no).[35] For some Americans, the civics textbook mantra—"the rule of law, not by man"—is simply an ideal that doesn't mesh with reality, and admitting as such doesn't undermine law or democracy.

As Maher pointed out when discussing the scandal (using the O. J. Simpson verdict as case in point), the fact that O. J. Simpson is legally innocent doesn't mean that law determines what is *right* and *just* or *true*. For true justice to exist, the law would not be such a malleable concept easily influenced by economic, social, and political forces. By joking about O. J., Maher attacks the notion that law and justice have some necessary relationship to each other. Mary Douglas argues, "The joke . . . affords the opportunity for realizing that an accepted pattern has no necessity. Its excitement lies in the suggestion that any particular ordering of experience may be arbitrary and subjective."[36] Republicans made the Clinton case out to be a textbook example of why, in a democracy, the law should apply to everyone. Jokes, however, provide the means to question this formulation because the public knows through common sense that such "ordering of experience" is not correct. Furthermore, the use of jokes to question such patterns of ordering also offers an opportunity to question the ideological basis of such notions through a commonsense critique. As Michael Billig reminds us, "The contrary elements [of common sense] can arise from different sources. They could be represented by the contradiction between possessing a theoretical ideology and at the same time living within a society whose everyday life seems to negate the ideology."[37]

To return then to the discussions of parody and Maher's monologue, Maher introduces a discourse of common sense through a parody of the day's surreal proceedings, inviting the audience to adopt a different perspective than that offered in the formal political theater of the president's speech, the *Nightline* broadcast, and any number of other representations and explorations of the events. The parody is in conversation with those who would seek to take the events as serious breaches of law and a threat to democracy, redirecting attention to what Maher considers the ludicrous aspects of the case—that the best the president's enemies could come up with is his lying about sex, and that their only hope is to drive him from office by making him discuss and admit it in public. The normative political dialect is subverted by a parody that ridicules the rigid performance intended to lend dignity to a public event. The intonations of common sense, however, suggest that the events are downright humorous.

The seriousness of the occasion—the chief law enforcement officer lying, his impending political troubles, the maneuvering of political opponents—were accompanied by great civic rituals, rituals for the prosecution of the matter through formal political procedures: civil and criminal proceedings in courts of law, the constitutional acts of impeachment, a Senate trial, and so on. The ritualistic aspects of the case, however, only increased the potential for a public reaction centered on humor. Anthropological theories of joking rituals show why.

THE COMMON SENSE OF NON-SENSE

Mary Douglas's research and writings on jokes offer a useful theoretical basis to assess the ways in which the joking structure of Maher's monologue reorganizes and challenges the elite formulations he is questioning, while also offering ways of assessing how jokes challenge non-sense with common sense. Douglas argues that a joke is a means of subverting control, of disorganizing and disordering formalized systems of thought. "It attacks sense and hierarchies," she argues.[38] "Whatever the joke, however remote its subject, the telling of it is potentially subversive. Since its form consists of a victorious tilting of uncontrol against control, it is an image of the leveling of hierarchy, the triumph of intimacy over formality, of unofficial values over official ones."[39] The elite sense of what the scandal means, how the case should be prosecuted, and what ritual performances surround that execution are all questioned by Maher's parody—in particular, the seriousness and formality of Clinton's address to the nation.

Presidential addresses to the public are important rituals in the American system of governance. The ceremonial practice of addressing the nation in times of celebration and despair, triumph and tragedy has become quite common.[40] It is a ritual performance of leadership and guidance, a ceremonial role the president is expected to perform as the one elected official who represents all of the people. Clinton's remarks on August 17, 1998, were surrounded by this context and general public expectations of presidential rhetorical behavior. The president sought to quell public fears (and shaky exchange markets) that all was in order, that the presidency was not under threat, and that despite his personal failings and the failings of his persecutors, the republic would survive. Even the elite voices that followed the president's address on *Nightline* were participating in the ritual performance of "democracy in action."

Douglas explains how jokes, however, destabilize these formulations. "Great rituals," she argues,

> create unity in experience. They assert hierarchy and order. In doing so, they affirm the value of the symbolic patterning of the universe. Each level of patterning is validated and enriched by association with the rest. But jokes have the opposite effect. They connect widely differing fields, but the connection destroys hierarchy and order. They do not affirm the dominant values, but denigrate and devalue. Essentially a joke is an anti-rite.[41]

Although the overall thrust of Maher's parody is an attack on Clinton's enemies, it would be hard to argue that the president emerges unscathed. In the parody, the ritual is inverted, for all of the political elites involved in the matter look farcical; the rulers have no clothes (pun intended). The president looks like a fool, but so do his pious and hypocritical opponents. The joke calls into question the political performances on all ends. Furthermore, the jokes reduce elite power positions to the level of the people. The parody allows the viewer the pleasure of claiming that politicians are really no different from everyone else, and that power relations around sex and lying are the same regardless of the social strata in which they occur. The scandal—and its parody—is not just humanizing of politicians, but also offers identification for viewers.

The jokes around the Clinton scandal are a product of the populist impulse of the decade. As populism rejects the arrogance of power and elite privilege, jokes can be used to invert or challenge traditional hierarchies by exploiting the exposed philanderers (not just Clinton, but his similarly guilty Republican opponents who were uncovered in the process, such as Representatives Henry Hyde, Bob Livingston, and Bob Barr) and reminding the people that elites are no better or worse than the electorate who put them in office.[42] The public is offered common identification through their laughter, a common understanding of politicians and politics at a moment in which they are actually easy to understand. As Douglas argues, "Laughter and jokes, since they attack classification and hierarchy, are obviously apt symbols for expressing community in this sense of unhierarchised, undifferentiated social relations. . . . [A joke] represents a temporary suspension of the social structure, or rather it makes a little disturbance in which the particular structuring of society becomes less relevant than another. But the strength of its attack is entirely restricted by the consensus on which it depends for recognition."[43] The Clinton scandal represented a populist moment in which publics were allowed to invert hierarchies that separate elites from "The People."

If the joke is based on commonly held assumptions and beliefs, or as we have discussed above, adopts the tonalities of common sense that invoke the "commonness of assumed basic value structures" (e.g., distrust of unchecked power, a sense of proportionality, the patriarchal belief that men should be afforded great leeway in their sexual indiscretions),[44] that consensus, at least among those who felt Clinton was being treated unfairly, will be all the stronger. When discussing the joker figure in society, Douglas reiterates the joker's role in expressing common sense. The joker, she contends,

> appears to be a privileged person who can say certain things in a certain way which confers immunity. . . . He has a firm hold on his own position in the structure and the disruptive comments which he makes upon it are in a sense the comments of the social group upon itself. He merely expresses consensus. Safe within the permitted range of attack, he lightens for everyone the oppressiveness of social reality, demonstrates its arbitrariness by making light of formality in general, and expresses the creative possibilities of the situation. From this we can see the appropriateness of the joker as ritual purifier.[45]

The joker in traditional society, from which Douglas's analysis is drawn, is more firmly connected to a community, and hence the disruptive comments he makes reflect the general feelings and attitudes of the group itself. The joker in postmodern, mass-mediated society is less connected to a specific community. Nevertheless, the celebrity status as "entertainer" that grants him entry into millions of homes provides an invitation to the self-selected "cliques and cults" of viewers who privilege a certain political and cultural knowingness and who identify with his political commentary. Maher's parody of presidential persecution may not have expressed a consensus in a nation of 270 million people, but it certainly offered "creative possibilities" to the "oppressive reality" of ritual political processes that up to 70 percent of the American public disagreed with and found arbitrary.

CONCLUSIONS

Elite sense—of what the president "did wrong" and the reasons why he must be punished—is questioned. Jokers like Maher (and the thousands, if not millions, of Internet and water-cooler satirists) offer nonsense instead because elite sense seemingly makes no sense. The non-sense overturns the reasons, justifications, and rituals of political performance to suggest that elite sense also lacks common sense. As Chris Powell and George Paton put it, "The bisociation of sense and nonsense suggested in the old but still toothy saw that 'truth is stranger than fiction' is a fertile area for humour in contrasting a more staid, normatively controlled social reality with an alternative reality, however absurd or surreal, so long as the humorous enunciation can be recognized as containing a germ of truth as to its feasibility or possibility."[46]

The semantic authority of Maher's parody is attained through its structured common sense, and it is this appeal that makes parody a much more powerful tool than the irony of journalism that Ettema and Glasser evoke. Journalistic irony (itself perhaps another form of "elite" sense making) does not induce public outrage over Clinton. Instead, humor, joking, parody, and satire are tools that allow for a subversion of the social order and provide the means through which publics can express their disillusionment with the social hierarchies and farcical elite arrogance that seemingly drove this series of events.

7

The Competing Senses of Political Insiders and Outsiders

I have common sense. I got one week of high school. I didn't go that week. Remember that. But I'm on this show. Here's a man with no education. I'm talking to brilliant people here because I have common sense. And that's what this country don't have. We're in a nap. We're nappy. We gotta wake up and smell the roses, smell the coffee.

—Pat Cooper, comedian and guest on *Politically Incorrect*

I must say I think that letting the process work makes a lot of sense because it brings—then people [in government] can lead public opinion rather than just follow it through the process.

—Cokie Roberts, co-host, *This Week with Sam Donaldson and Cokie Roberts*

For over a year, President Bill Clinton's affair with White House intern Monica Lewinsky and his alleged lying about the affair in a court deposition dominated public discourse about politics, including discussions on *Politically Incorrect*. Even when other social and political topics were discussed on the program, the Clinton scandal would often find its way into the conversation. The scandal was a widely popular topic because it not only involved America's highest elected official but also encompassed so many themes common to human behavior and cultural belief systems—sex, lying, adultery, persecution, sin, redemption, human nature. Most citizens could, in some form or fashion, understand the core issues involved in this case, as opposed to the highly complex arms-for-hostages or savings and loan scandals of the Reagan years. Moreover, this scandal provided tremendous opportunities for citizens to offer their own opinions, humor, and personal experiences. As a political

scandal, it also dominated discussions of politics on other television programs, including pundit talk shows. A political scandal almost always equates
to political vulnerability, and professional monitors of political power could
hardly talk of anything else.[1]

I argue up to this point that laity-based television shows like *Politically Incorrect* and pundit talk shows are fundamentally different in the types of political discourse that comprise their presentations. Indeed, many scholars and
political observers contend that political elites and the general populace speak
different languages when discussing politics.[2] This chapter seeks to understand
both how and why these differences exist and occur. Both political
pundits/elites and the lay participants on *P.I.* offer commentary on politics, both
have the job of assessing and evaluating the issues of the day, and both must
offer some form of presentational stylistics to attract television viewers. But that
is largely where the similarities end. Our interest here is the *conversations*, the
political discussions that both these types of shows offer the viewing public,
and what accounts for the differences in how those discussions are formulated.

Moreover, this book is interested in assessing how publics encounter politics in the everyday, and how and in what ways new political television offers cultural engagements with politics. We need to determine if programs
like *P.I.* contribute something new or different to the mediated public realm,
and what that means for public discourse about politics. Do these shows'
construction and presentation as "entertainment" render the discussions
nonsensical for serious public matters, as some critics maintain? Or does the
show's construction based on an eclectic mix of politically nonexpert guests
encourage the application of more universal sense-making strategies?

This chapter continues the examination of the commonsense thinking and
discourse in new political talk of political outsiders by directly comparing the
"sense" made or used on *P.I.* with the "sense" made or used on a pundit talk
show. The focus here is on what these different conversations and conclusions tell us about "what made sense" to its participants and why. The issue
discussed on both shows was the same—the Clinton scandal. This examination of competing discourses allows an entry point to probe factors that
might account for the disjunction between elite and public opinion on the
scandal. It also allows us to see how nonexperts and the professional political class engage politics in such dissimilar ways and then assess what this
means for public engagement with politics via television.

The analysis here centers on four weeks of programming on *P.I.*—January
26 through February 3, 1998, the first two weeks of revelations of the president's affair and his subsequent denial of any wrongdoing, and August 10
through August 21, 1998, the two weeks surrounding the president's admis-
sion of the affair to the American people and his testimony before a grand
jury. These dates were high water marks in the scandal, especially in regard
to public interest in the matter. The first was the "gossip" period, when ru-

mors and revelations were swirling concerning what the president did or might have done. The second date covers the period in which the president finally admitted and apologized for his transgressions.

The pundit show examined is *This Week with Sam Donaldson and Cokie Roberts*, also on ABC, which aired during the same time frame.[3] This show was selected for several reasons. First, it offers one of the more diverse mixtures of guests among the pundit talk shows. Many shows in the genre are dominated solely by journalists, or include journalists interviewing policy makers. Two senior broadcast journalists host *This Week*, and the roundtable discussion includes a former top White House official and advisor to President Clinton (George Stephanopoulos), an editor of a conservative journal of political opinion (Bill Kristol), and a conservative syndicated columnist (George Will). All three guests are active in Republican and Democratic policy circles, although none is an office holder. Their presence on the show is also designed to represent both left and right ideological perspectives. *This Week* was also selected because it appears on the same network as *Politically Incorrect*. Along with *Nightline* (included in the discussions in chapter 6), these three shows represent three major forms of political programming on ABC's schedule. Here we compare two of them directly.

THIS WEEK WITH SAM DONALDSON AND COKIE ROBERTS

One of the distinguishing features of the discussions on *This Week* was the high level of agreement among the participants. For an issue so discordant in American society and so contentious between political parties, there was relatively little disagreement over what the scandal "meant" at any given time on the program. Instead, these five participants arrived at their conclusions with relative ease. Their fundamental concern was for the political system, or the "constitutional order," as they referred to it. The primary issue that drove that concern was the supposed threat to the system that resulted from Clinton's lying. The singular explanation offered for this threat was the weak moral character of Bill Clinton, or "this man" as George Will often referred to him.[4] And finally, the discussants based their conclusion on an abiding faith (despite continued evidence to the contrary) that the American people would stop supporting Clinton once they realized the "truth" that these pundits knew would be made public through the institutional processes at work in the efforts of Kenneth Starr and the U.S. Congress.

From the time the scandal broke until the president's confession some seven months later, the primary issue these pundits were interested in was "did Clinton lie?" If he did, they contended, his presidency was through.

January 25:
George Stephanopoulos: Is he telling the truth, the whole truth and nothing but the truth? If he is, he can survive. If he isn't, he can't.

Sam Donaldson: If he's not telling the truth, I think his presidency is numbered in days. This isn't going to drag out. We're not going to be here three months from now talking about this. Mr. Clinton, if he's not telling the truth and the evidence shows that, will resign, perhaps this week.

August 16:
George Stephanopoulos: It all depends on what he does tomorrow. I think if he tells the truth and comes forward to the American people, he can at least go on with his presidency.

George Will: The presidency is over.

There was relatively little interest in *what* the president lied about or *why* he lied, questions that were of utmost importance on *P.I.* Instead, lying itself was simply unacceptable. The act of lying was so serious that its occurrence alone meant the president would have to leave office; hence, the unanimous predictions for his early departure. Lying, their arguments suggested, is harmful in at least three primary ways. First, it damages the president's ability to lead as a politician and as a moral leader.

January 25:
George Will: This man's condition is known. His moral authority is gone. He will resign when he acquires the moral sense to understand.

August 23:
Cokie Roberts: There is the question of can he govern if he stays in office? Can he go up and twist an arm and get a bill?

George Stephanopoulos: He can govern, but he can't advance his agenda.

George Will: The presidency is constitutionally a weak office. There is very little he can do on his own, other than by moving the country by rhetoric that acquires its power from the hold his personality and character has on the country. This week *The New Republic* begins its editorial saying, "It's official. Bill Clinton is a lout."

Second, lying is such a gross violation of political principles that it damages the president's relationship with his own political party:

August 16:
Bill Kristol: The Democratic Party needs . . . the president to say he was wrong and to apologize for it. That gets them off the hook and the party can say it was wrong. They can't appear to be covering up for the president.

August 23:
Cokie Roberts: You're seeing Democratic political consultants, for instance, saying, you know, "This guy lost the House for us in 1994. He lost the House for us in 1996. . . . Now he's about to lose it for us again in 1998."

The third and most important reason they consider the president's lying unacceptable is the threat it presents to the political system:

February 1:
George Will: This is a great uncontrolled experiment now under way about having vulgarians in the most conspicuous offices in the republic. And it can't be good.

August 23:
Bill Kristol: To let him stay now, I think, is fundamentally corrupting.

George Will: The metastasizing corruption spread by this man is apparent now, and the corruption of the very idea of what it means to be a representative.

Bill Kristol: The president is at the center of the constitutional order. Credibility in him matters.

The explanation for why Clinton lied is simple—he has no moral character. He is a "vulgarian," a "lout." As George Will argued, "He can't tell the truth. . . . I mean, that's the reasonable assumption on the evidence informed by the context in which it occurs, which is six years of evidence of his deceit."

The pundits continued to exhibit a fundamental faith in the American public, however. With "lying" as the centerpiece of this case, the pundits maintained a hope that eventually the public would realize the wrongs that had been committed and rise up to punish the president. Ultimately, the pundits' conception of "the people" was quite paternalistic, although not condescending. For instance, George Will seemed to suggest that the public would recognize the right thing to do (what the political class already knew) once the Starr report was released. The public, he argued, "will not be able to change their mind. . . . Once that report [by Kenneth Starr] is written and published, Congress will be dragged along in the wake of the public."[5] They saw a good and virtuous public, although one that was a bit naïve and unsophisticated. As Bill Kristol stated, "I think it is that the American people are nice people. They're too nice, in fact, too trusting" (February 1). It is a public fashioned in their own image, with little connection to what people were actually saying about the scandal.

August 23:
George Will: But beneath the argument there's a visceral process. And it has to do with the peculiar intimacy of the modern presidency. Because of television,

the president is in our living rooms night after night after night. And once the dress comes in and once some of the details come in from the Ken Starr report, people—there's going to come a critical mass, the yuck factor—where people say, "I don't want him in my living room anymore."

This unrealistic opinion of a supposedly virtuous public and its beliefs on the matter are just one part of their overall conception of the democratic system. The pundits on *This Week* continued to exhibit faith in the ability of the system to combat the wrongs committed, to survive this crisis and restore order through processes established and codified in the constitution.

August 23:
Bill Kristol: This is why democracy in elections are [sic] a good thing. . . . Right now, people can go on TV shows and say, "I'm not here to discuss that." . . . But the advantage of an election campaign, the advantage of a real debate, is one candidate will turn to the other and say, "If the president lied under oath, what do you think you should do about it? You as a member of the House of Representatives?" And I agree with George, it's the election campaign that makes this real, in a sense.

George Will: [This] is why I favor impeachment rather than resignation because I want to clear up what impeachment means in the constitution.

In summary, then, the pundits on *This Week* reduced the scandal to one fundamental question—did the president lie? If he did—which they all assumed was true because of Clinton's supposed pattern of deceit—then it would be necessary for him to depart the office, either willingly or unwillingly. The foundation of legitimacy in American democracy, they suggested, was based on the president's telling the truth, and should the president violate that cornerstone principle, then the system would remove him. It was also assumed that the public shared the same understanding of how the system works, and once the public realized the truth, they would respond in a fitting manner.

What produced these formulations, I argue, is that these pundits, as part of America's governing class, used "political sense" for assessing political matters. By political sense, I mean a learned understanding of how politics works, what actions and behaviors are admissible, correct, justifiable, and workable; an acquired sense of what matters and what doesn't. Political sense is like other intellectualized systems such as legal sense, scientific sense, artistic sense—a philosophy or an intellectual order. "Philosophy," Antonio Gramsci argues, is "official conceptions of the world" that are "elaborated, systematic and politically organized and centralized."[6] Practitioners of politics are trained (through schooling, professional experiences, upbringing, the media) to think in certain ways about how the system works.[7]

To be sure, as John Dewey argues, political sense, as philosophy or science, does not exist outside of common sense: "Neither common sense nor science is regarded as an entity—as something set apart, complete and self-enclosed." Rather, without common sense science cannot exist and "philosophy is idly speculative apart from [the rudiments of common sense] because it is then deprived of footing to stand on and a field of significant application."[8] Nevertheless, the interrelationships between elements of elite and lay thinking need not obscure the broader processes of sense making that lead to such dissimilar conclusions between pundits and citizens. Instead, political sense is different from common sense in that it is a conscious creation of an abstracted mode of thinking. As Dewey notes,

> Science is the example, par excellence, of the liberative effect of abstraction. . . . The liberative outcome of the abstraction that is supremely manifested in scientific activity is the transformation of the affairs of common sense concern which has come about through the vast return wave of the methods and conclusions of scientific concern into the uses and enjoyments (and sufferings) of everyday affairs, together with an accompanying transformation of judgment and of the emotional affections, preferences, and aversions of everyday human beings.[9]

What I am arguing is that political sense used by the pundits of the "political class" (to use George Will's term) is the product of just such a transformation, an alteration of the "emotional affections, preferences, and aversions of everyday human beings" into an abstraction with its own set of rules and understandings about what is valid, right, just, and legitimate.

According to political sense, politics in a representative democracy is centered around the social contract between the polity and the trust they bestow on their elected officials to conduct the affairs of state in an open and honest fashion, and operated in the people's best interest. Political legitimacy in such a system is based on public trust. A politician caught in a lie has naturally betrayed that trust. The pundits argued that the president is at the center of the constitutional order, and to not censure his violation of that order threatens the whole system and everyone in it. The pundits recognized that the political system is fragile. Its strength, their comments suggest, is that the constitutional order is designed to purge such individuals who betray that trust.

Those who employ political sense maintain a systematic logic—a structured understanding of the workings of a complex political system that guarantees the functioning of democracy. Within that system, however, the public is only one of several factors. Executive leadership, legislative agendas, and political parties are also crucial to the system's functioning, and hence the pundits found these issues just as relevant (if not more so) as topics of discussion. But the public was also key. The political sense employed by these pundits led to a paternalistic view of the public—a public that is good and decent, but one that would need to overcome its naïveté to understand the seriousness of Clinton's violations. The pundits placed faith not in the people whom the systemic structures are ultimately designed to protect, but in the system itself. The public's role in the scandal was simply to acquiesce in what the system needed to do—to purge the breaker of trust. This type of systematic logic was so strong that the pundits' political sense was generally incapable of recognizing the overwhelming evidence to the contrary. That is, an overwhelming majority of the public was not interested in the system purging itself.[10] Indeed, the public was an abstraction for the pundits, whereas the political "players" in the scandal (whom they all knew) and the arenas in which these players operated (with which they were all thoroughly familiar) were much more real than a capricious, passive, and unthinking public—a public that is only required to react to the events produced by the political class when called upon.

What these pundits would not entertain, however, is not only that citizens might not be the mythical public they had constructed, but that citizens might employ a different means of thinking about politics altogether. The fact that many citizens considered Clinton's lying about sex a private matter, not a public concern, was the product of commonsense thinking that allowed for different versions of truth from those offered by the political class. Nor would the pundits stop to consider that new television forums might provide a site where a different "sense" of political events could now be entertained. The laity on *P.I.* knew quite well that the president was lying. For them, however, the issue was not whether he lied but whether lying is permissible when it is about sex and when it is the president who is engaged in such lying. The thinking that would lead from these central concerns is quite important in understanding why the public didn't respond in ways pundits had hoped.

POLITICALLY INCORRECT WITH BILL MAHER

Although the discussions on *This Week* were generally void of meaningful disagreement, the discussions on *P.I.* were much more contested and fractious. And despite a wide variety of guests, the arguments tended to coalesce around several issues. The concern driving the discussion was not the political system, but rather how Clinton as an individual and as a leader should be judged. The central issue in the scandal was Clinton's sexual affair and his lying about it (not any procedural or juridical concerns such as suborning perjury, obstructing justice, etc.). Because he lied about sex, the arguments split over how to assess Clinton—as a human being (which made the actions normal, comprehensible, fathomable, and ultimately benign) or as a moral leader (which made the actions unacceptable, unfathomable, and therefore a threat). Those assessments were based on whether the lying was a public or a private matter, as the following exchange demonstrates.

August 13:
Carmen Pate (activist): If he would just admit it. If he would admit, "I was wrong."

Bill Maher: Why should he? It's his private life. Why should he have to admit anything to you?

Pate: It's not just his private life.

Maher: You're not his wife. Why should he have to come clean to you?

Pate: Because he represents the American people. He represents me.

Maher: Exactly. They cheat.

James Coburn (actor): Lie.

Maher: They lie. They steal office supplies. They try to get money off their income tax, and that's what I'm saying. He's just like them.

Another defense of Clinton was based on conceptions of human nature. Although Clinton may be guilty of lying, some panelists suggested, he couldn't help it because the need for sex—and lots of it—is part of the nature of men. Clinton did this, they argued, because he is a man, and it is a simple fact that men, in their efforts to fulfill these human needs, have extramarital sex and lie about it. Furthermore, that behavior is understandable, if not justified, because men need sex more than women. Behavior and agency are explained in essentialist terms, as seen in the second comment of the following exchange.

August 18:
Star Parker (author): We are a land of law. And if man starts to do whatever he wants to, then so is everybody else. And when you do it from the highest office so are the lowest.

Donzaleigh Abernathy (actress): [But] they have been doing it already. They have been doing it since the beginning of time. . . . It's the nature of men. They need to cast their seed everywhere they can.

Panelists who didn't embrace essentialist gender arguments might resort to claims that *all* humans are fallible, and therefore deserve mercy.

August 17:
Michael Moore (director): We are human beings. Have you ever made a mistake? Have you ever made a mistake?

August 19:
Jo-Ellan Dimitrius (jury consultant): You know why politicians are so concerned about this issue, though, is because there is a sentiment of, "There but for the grace of God go I."

Other panelists advanced the argument that Clinton is just a regular guy, an average American who is just like everyone else. Instead of exalting Clinton as a distant leader, these panelists embraced the notion that their leader was just like them. It was not his higher moral stature that garnered respect (or the lack thereof in both instances), but rather his position as both a political leader *and* a regular guy that inspired them. Citizens fashioned the president in their own image (as already seen in the comments by Maher cited above).

January 29:
Coolio (rapper): What it really is, is that he's human, and that's why people like Clinton because he's showing that, "I'm human. O.K., I had an affair, whether I admit it or not, or whether I did it or not, I'm human."

Dennis Prager (talk radio host): Exactly. A guy called my show and said, "Dennis, Clinton is the sort of guy I can see drinking beers with and chasing women with."

But arguments also ensued over Clinton's position as leader and role model, and the relationship of lying to leadership.

January 29:
Bill Maher: Over and over again, the polls say [the people] think he had an affair, and they don't care. So what they're saying is, let him live, we don't need him as a role model. We'll look to ourselves for our own moral guidance.

Brad Keena (political analyst): But it's important that we don't normalize this kind of behavior and that's what we're allowing to happen. . . . I think it is time to have a president, to elect a president who is a role model, someone who has good moral values.

Some panelists extended the conception of Clinton as leader a step further, invoking the metaphor of the country as a family. In the metaphor, Clinton is the "father" of the country, and by implication, the people are his "children," together comprising a "family," with the White House (the site of the indiscretions) as the family's "house."

January 26:
Eartha Kitt (singer/actress): President is head of the family. He sets an example for the rest of us. If he can't live by moral standards, then what does he expect of us?

August 13:

Jeffrey Tambor (actor): Any household can look within their own selves and their families and say, "There have been transgressions in my family." There are transgressions here. And the smart thing to do is separate the presidency from the man.

These arguments, in sum, form a central dialectic, a tension between the desires to separate Clinton-the-man from Clinton-the-leader. When viewed as a *leader*, a split occurred between those who argued that:

A. *Leaders and the people have different rules.* These discussants invoked history (all presidents have done this), explained power (men in power have affairs the world over), and made his job performance more important than his off-the-job activities (he can do whatever he wants if he's doing a good job).
B. *Leaders are not exempt from the same rules as the people.* Presidents get no special treatment when it comes to moral behavior.

When viewed as a *human*, a split occurred between those who argued that

C. *Clinton should represent the people by being better than they are as a moral person.* He should be a model for how the people should be.
D. *Clinton is no different from the people he represents.* He has the same flaws and he does the same stupid things that all humans do.

It seems, then, that panelists wanted it both ways—Clinton is like the average person and unlike the average person; the president deserves special rules yet must operate by the same rules as average citizens. Despite this contradictory positioning, both liberal and conservative guests tended to adopt these dual stances. The more liberal voices tended to use both arguments A and D (different rules as a leader, but Clinton the man is no different from the rest of us), while conservatives tended to use both arguments B and C (leaders have the same rules as the people, yet as a man he has different rules; he should be better than we are). From the perspective of political culture in the 1990s, we might argue that these positions are grounded in the larger popularity of populism (for instance, the suspicion of political elites disconnected from the people; a desire to have politicians like the people) and the culture wars (elites who have no morals; elites as hypocritical). These positions also represent the contradictory, disjointed, and multifarious dimensions of commonsense thinking that Gramsci, Clifford Geertz, and other theorists of common sense have described.[11]

MAKING SENSE OF COMPETING SENSES

Each of these programs' structures largely determined the type of discourse that it would produce. Pundit talk shows feature individuals whose primary purpose is to establish for other insiders (and political junkies who subscribe to this way of thinking or who simply enjoy monitoring power) what the events of the week "really mean." That is, they *produce* an agreed-upon reality that other insiders are expected to accept (at some level). The show, therefore, is not designed to produce wide-ranging explanations or diverse viewpoints. Rather, the whole point of the show is to narrow contentious issues and events and their "meanings" so that viewers can hear the précis and then move on to new matters that will arise in the week ahead. The discursive framework for *P.I.*, however, is designed for entertainment and information. An eclectic array of public persons appear on the program, and as a televisual cocktail party, this mixture is intended to guarantee debate, if not acrimony and laughter. *P.I.* is not interested in presenting its viewers with a single conception of what "makes sense" at any given moment. Indeed, its discussions are centrifugal, not centripetal (like the pundit shows). And by including guests who have little expertise in politics, the show is intentionally structured to sound not like political insiders, but more like the viewing public.

Interestingly enough, the discussions on both shows included, at times, similar arguments. Compare, for instance, the following statements made on both programs.

Heavy D: He's the father of our country. He's our dysfunctional father.

George Stephanopoulos: In many ways, it's like this whole episode has turned the whole country into a dysfunctional family.

Victoria Jackson: Because he lies about everything else, of course he's lying about that.

George Will: He can't tell the truth . . . that's the reasonable assumption on the evidence informed by the context in which it occurs, which is six years of evidence of his deceit.

Michael Moore: And they put him in office knowing exactly who he was and what he's done.

Cokie Roberts: But is that [lying] something new? Everybody knew that when they elected him.

Similarities in the discussions across the two shows were not pervasive, but they did exist occasionally. Yet it is not surprising to see similarities in various phrases, questions, and arguments that appeared on both *P.I.* and *This Week*. As in the point made by Dewey above, pundits must use their common sense about how the world works, while citizens on *P.I.* are often attuned to the general debates occurring in Washington and in the media. Citizens learn to appropriate the rudimentary terms through which political elites wage war with each other—terms like *suborning perjury, obstruction of justice, quid pro quo, depositions,* and so on. And pundits and citizens alike appropriate terms from other intellectual realms—terms like *dysfunction*—to explain the scandal. But as Hwa Yol Jung notes, "The ordinary language of political man precedes the objectified language of political science, and the second must be consistent with the first."[12]

The overriding differences in content, in focus, in overall concerns, and in the conclusions between the shows, however, were dissimilar. Whereas the "meaning" of the scandal for the pundits on *This Week* generally boiled down to how Clinton's lying presented a threat to the larger political system, the meaning of the scandal for the nonexperts on *P.I.* was whether Clinton's lying presented a threat to certain values. Guests on *P.I.* often employed arguments that included claims to universality, claims based on personal or group experience, which defined the situation in universalistic terms: "*Everyone* does this," "*All* politicians lie," "*Never* trust a liar," "*All* families have problems," "*All* men are this way." These claims to universality render the common sense inherent in these truisms reliable, even reassuring in that this is the way of the world. Clinton is not exceptional, they argue, nor is this case exceptional. Although the scandal had Washington in gridlock, the public can understand what is going on because it rings true with their understanding of the world. Its universality is its key to being understood.

One of the most prominent themes in citizen arguments over the scandal was conflicting notions of whether this was a public or a private matter. For those who argued the latter, the liberal notions of freedom and individuality drove their arguments. For those who argued the former, republican notions of responsibility and community came to bear. Rarely were these concepts enunciated as theoretical postulates, but rather as beliefs about how the world works. As Michael Billig and his colleagues argue, "Within the ideology of liberalism is a dialectic, which contains negative counter-themes and which gives rise to debates. These debates are not confined to the level of intellectual analysis; both themes and counter-themes have arisen from, and passed into, everyday consciousness. And, of course, this everyday consciousness provides the material for further intellectual debate."[13] American liberalism battles republicanism here, yet these ideological formulations appear simply as common sense:[14] "This is none of your business"; "This is between him and his wife"; "If his wife is O.K. with it, what concern is this of yours?"; "He did this in our house, the people's house"; "What type of example does this set for people/the children?"; "Lying is lying, so how can we trust a liar?"

This is the *natural, thin, immethodical, practical*, and *accessible* language of common sense outlined by Geertz and explored in the last chapter. Through this type of language and thinking, citizens are formulating answers to questions such as "Is this natural? Is this the way the world works? Is this the way human beings really are?" "Do I understand this; is this something I can judge?" "What aspects of my experience come to bear on this situation?" "Is this right?" These aren't political questions or terms at all. Panelists did not argue from the basis of political sense—the chief law enforcement officer lying, the implications for systems of justice, the precedent this sets for future presidents, the mandate of the special prosecutor, and so on. They use accessible terms that not only make sense but also make the scandal interesting and popular to discuss. They fuse use with enjoyment. In other words, the terms and conditions of the Clinton scandal (e.g., sex, lying, adultery, cigars, dresses, semen, fellatio) favor the application of common sense (certainly in ways that the savings and loan scandal did not). People can *relate* to this kind of politics, for it has resonance with their own lives. As one guest on *P.I.* intimated, "You know, I've been following this [scandal] 'cause I haven't seen [the soap opera] *All My Children* in a long time."

That remark is telling in that it exemplifies how politics is increasingly attended to in ways quite similar to entertainment and consumer culture, and therefore, the sense used in attending to those realms will also be used in making sense of politics. With the tendency for more and more politicians to both act like and be treated like celebrities, the public then finds no reason to engage politics differently from how they make sense of and use entertainment celebrities. David Marshall argues that "the celebrity offers a discursive focus for the discussion of realms that are considered outside the bounds of public debate in the most public fashion. The celebrity system is a way in which the sphere of the irrational, emotional, personal, and affective is contained and negotiated in contemporary culture."[15] He goes on to contend that celebrities are "intense sites for determining the meaning and significance of the private sphere and its implications for the public sphere. . . . The private sphere is constructed to be revelatory, the ultimate site of truth and meaning for any representation in the public sphere. . . . Celebrities . . . are sites for the dispersal of power and meaning into the personal and therefore universal."[16] By making politics personal and universal, the invitation is made to publics that all politics be evaluated on these terms. Political sense about how politics properly functions appears as nonsense, and publics revert to the means of thinking used in the other realms of their everyday existence. Defenders of Clinton appealed to the commonsense "truth" of the private realm, including essentialist claims about a man's needs or human biology, or personal identification with Clinton because of his human frailties. For some guests, Clinton-as-celebrity was easier to judge and easier to make sense of psychologically than Clinton-as-leader and politician. Clinton's actions as a celebrity seemed all too familiar when compared with other celebrities. The foibles of Bill Clinton's and actor Hugh Grant's sexual misconduct come to be seen in similar ways when such criteria are used for judgment.

But as Joshua Gamson points out, the celebrity sign is composed of oppositional characteristics that allow for different readings, depending on the situation. "Contemporary celebrity," he notes, "is composed of a string of antinomies: public roles opposing private selves, artificial opposing natural, image opposing reality, ideal opposing typical, special opposing ordinary, hierarchy opposing equality."[17] As the analysis above suggests, these are *exactly* the means through which *P.I.* panelists attempted to read Clinton as a political celebrity—Clinton as special or ordinary, better than the people or equal to the people, an ideal leader or a typical American. Pundit discourse based on political sense, a perspective that didn't position Clinton as a celebrity but as a politician required to play the game of politics by certain rules, was much more unified in how to make sense of the scandal.

CONCLUSIONS

The epigraphs that began this chapter come from participants on *This Week* and *Politically Incorrect* during this period of investigation. Both individuals embrace a particular form of sense as the means for putting the country back on a proper course. One openly acknowledges his particular brand of sense while the other seems oblivious to the fact that hers is a brand at all. The analysis of these competing senses suggests several conclusions. The means through which talk show guests think through the political matters of the day will greatly affect the discursive realities they create. The political sense of *This Week* tended to limit debate, efficiently organizing the scandal around a particular set of meanings beyond which other explanations made no sense. This particular ordering of political reality framed Clinton as a systemic threat, and the integrity and continuity of the system necessitated his exit from the system. Alternative means of making sense of the scandal were rarely entertained.[18]

The common sense that dominated discussions of *P.I.*, on the other hand, provided the means for a far-reaching exploration of what the presidential scandal meant for the nation. The assorted nature of common sense necessarily means that space exists for conservative and progressive notions, Stone Age and intellectual thinking. As this analysis suggests, common sense may be conservative, advancing patriarchal notions of male leadership or entertaining essentialist formulations that excuse male behavior. Conversely, common sense may be progressive, challenging hypocritical strictures of public morality cloaked behind legal terms and procedures. Whereas debate using political sense can amount to little more than the proper arrangement of dishes on the table, debate using common sense may result in arguments over whether the proper issue is the dishes, the table, the chairs, or the table-cloth. That is not to say that common sense is a means for liberational thinking. Common sense will not bring about a reordering of society, and it is certainly too haphazard to advance a unified or cogent substitute for that which it critiques. It does, however, provide a means for public reflection on issues in ways less commonly found in the traditional manifestations of political talk on television. Furthermore, its presence on a program like *P.I.* exemplifies the important shifts that are occurring in how publics are invited to make sense of politics through a cultural instead of a political lens.

The Clinton scandal also became an opportunity for citizens to explore a range of interpretations about the changing relationships between leaders and the public in contemporary America. Commonsense thinking led panelists to explore what Clinton as (fallen) archetypal hero means for America: Is this scandal just about him, an amoral and selfish baby boomer, or does this include the public in some way? Is Clinton representative of broader cultural factors, and in what ways do citizens identify with him? It also led citizens to investigate the nature of leadership and political privilege, and the normative expectations that should exist given contemporary realities. This new political television program, and the commonsense thinking it allowed for, offered a more wide-ranging exploration of the scandal than that offered by pundit television. By facilitating such an exploration, other citizen concerns become manifest in the discussions—concerns not derived solely from the immediate situation. For instance, these questions are constitutive of a populist political culture where citizens routinely ask politicians the price of a gallon of milk to check their "'of-the-people'" credentials. These questions arise from a political system that has seen the decline of political party affiliation, the popularity of independent candidates, and the increased role of media as the means through which we understand our leaders and their relationship to the polity. And these questions emanate from an entertainment culture in which politicians have increasingly become celebrities in their own right, trading in the currency of intimacy, gossip, image, and myth; a culture in which the lines of image and reality are hard to pin down, and in which privacy is a fleeting concept.

Geertz advocates investigations into common sense as a cultural system because those investigations should lead to "new ways of looking at some old problems, most especially those concerning how culture is jointed and put together, and to a movement . . . away from functionalist accounts of the devices on which societies rest toward interpretive ones of the kinds of lives societies support."[19] The argument I am making is that new political television offers viewers a means of discussing politics in a common vernacular. As such, the language of common sense points to means of enunciation and understanding through which societies think and argue about politics. Although such programming may come up short for advocates of a rational-critical public sphere—a functionalist account of a device on which societies *should* rest for many scholars—I argue that laity-centered talk shows are constitutive, representative, and contributive to the way publics commonly interact with, make meaning of, and deal with politics in their everyday lives. Common sense constitutes our cultural system, and our civic ideals should recognize its currency, its foundational presence in people's relationships with intellectualized constructions such as representative democracy. In a competitive media marketplace that exists within a political culture disdainful of politics, the language of common sense will continue to be an attractive means of addressing and incorporating audiences within television programming of politics.

It is ironic, we should note, that conservatives who led the move to impeachment had also been leading proponents in their rhetoric of a return to "common sense" government. Yet, when "the people" applied their common sense to the scandal, it actually worked against the political sense that many conservatives used in their efforts to remove Clinton from office. Indeed, the political sense of politicians, journalists, and other institutional elites recognized that to remove a sitting president, certain rules would have to be followed, certain evidence obtained, and certain arguments made to the public for why those actions were justifiable. Common sense, however, suggested otherwise.

IV

AUDIENCES FOR
NEW POLITICAL TELEVISION

8

Audience Engagement with *Politically Incorrect*

All in all, your show is an addictive pain in the ass. . . . I wish I had more self-control.

—Elwood, viewer correspondent to
Politically Incorrect with Bill Maher

Up to this juncture, I have argued various points about new political television (NPTV) that should be measured against audience understanding and engagement with the programming. First, the producers of NPTV have attempted both to offer programming that cuts through the fakery of public life and to act upon the somewhat populist desire to offer a voice that is different from the political establishment. Does the viewing audience find such properties in NPTV? Second, citizens are said to be increasingly disillusioned with traditional political institutions, including news and the reporters and pundits who've dominated political talk on television. Is this also the case for viewers of NPTV? Third, other studies suggest that citizens tend to see no difference between fiction and nonfiction, serious and entertainment programming when using these resources to make sense of the political world. Are viewers of NPTV similarly uninterested in drawing distinctions between "legitimate" and "illegitimate" sources of information? Fourth, we have seen how nonexperts examine different issues and concerns and formulate political reality in ways that are different from those of pundits. Does this disturb viewers? Do they, like critics of NPTV, have a problem with nonexpert celebrities discussing the "serious" business of politics? If not (as one would assume, since they choose to watch the program), then what do they think about such a nontraditional approach to political talk on television? Finally, I argue that one of the most prevalent forms of citizen engagement with politics is the textual activity they entertain (or create themselves) through various forms of media. The question to ask of viewers of NPTV is in what ways do they *engage* the program—both behaviorally and cognitively?

I have set out, then, to examine audience reception of NPTV through the program *Politically Incorrect*. As noted previously, this program offered several distinctive avenues for studying audiences, including the unique feature of audience auditions to be a "Citizen Panelist" on the program in several major U.S. cities. Another aspect of audience activity that is more pronounced for *P.I.* than for other shows is an active on-line discussion forum that has operated since 1997 (when *P.I.* moved from cable to network television) and continues to this day. Finally, my access to the show's producers also allowed me to examine viewer mail to the program. The specific methodological details of each of these investigations are discussed below and in the appendix. I therefore analyzed viewers who themselves had chosen to engage the program in some way: by writing a letter to the program, auditioning to be a participant on the show, being a studio audience member, or talking on-line with other viewers about the show. I was interested in learning what type of relationship they had with the program. That is, how did they engage it and why? What did the programming do for them, or why did they watch? How did they conceive of the programming in ways like or unlike other political talk programming?

Because these viewers are self-selected and therefore not representative in a statistical way, this means, of course, that my reading of these viewers is not necessarily that of the "typical" viewer. Yet, there is nothing to suggest that the feelings these viewers expressed are necessarily "atypical" of the majority of viewers either. The forms and motivations for engagement in each of the viewer activities I studied are so varied—attending a taping while on vacation, wanting to be on a television show, discussing politics while on the Internet, expressing one's pleasure or displeasure with Maher's beliefs and comments in a letter—that I think these viewers are not of a singular type (say, Über citizens, obsessive "fans," or other "abnormal" characteristics), and therefore come closer to approximating what the wide array of viewers might sometimes look like.

VIEWER MAIL

On average, *Politically Incorrect* received about seven pieces of correspondence a day (plus an additional thirty e-mails), according to Lizzy Scherer, who handled mail for the program in 2000.[1] The producers are hesitant to call this "fan mail," referring to it instead as "show response." Their reasoning is more than simple semantics: the show's staff recognizes that viewers are not simply writing to express their love for the show, request autographs, or propose to the host in marriage—more typical (and bizarre) motivations and behaviors for audiences that contact other entertainment shows. Instead, as Scherer contends, they think they are citizens in action. In reviewing correspondence to the show from February 1997 to March 2000, I too am struck by the burning desire of citizens, transformed from simply being viewers, to engage in political *conversation* with Maher. That is, it didn't matter if viewers agreed or vehemently disagreed with Maher or the comments by guests on the show—either way, they wanted to talk politics, sometimes at great length and sometimes with much vituperation. In fact, a vast majority of the mail I reviewed contained a politically discursive focus.

For instance, a man from Rocky Point, New York, notes, "I'm writing in response to your show on October 30, 1997 about the population explosion. I agree with you 100%. I'd like to put my thirty two cents in" (the cost of a postage stamp at that time). For a page and a half, this gentleman discusses government policies that supposedly exacerbate the population problem (e.g., tax exemptions) but also discusses other issues that appeared on several of *P.I.*'s episodes—oil reserves and mandatory voting, invoking his agreement with the celebrities who advocated these issues, Ben Stein and Rod Steiger, respectively. In other instances, correspondents would attempt to answer the question that Maher had posed on the show for the panelists to discuss. The viewer had the answer, and therefore wrote to share it. "On a recent program," one viewer wrote, "you discussed whether a school in Oregon should teach Black History . . . [because] the school is virtually all white, so why bother?" He answers, "Why not?" and then sets out to explain the merits that "the truth is worth knowing" no matter where one attends school. This writer also enclosed an article for Maher to read, another common rhetorical tactic in viewer efforts to either persuade Maher or simply to share the information that supports their point.

Again, perhaps the defining feature of this correspondence is the desire to engage in conversation about political issues. Here are a few examples.

> "Thank you for expressing some of my views. . . . We concur on women, population explosion, personal responsibility, and reprehensible Republicans."
> "Here are a few comments on subjects discussed on PI in recent days. The subjects are the free classical music CD's and the protesters at abortion clinics."
> "I am very excited finally to have the opportunity to contribute something to the lively discussions which have kept me fascinated and entertained these past few years."

David Thelen's analysis of letters to members of Congress regarding the Iran-Contra scandal (reviewed in chapter 2) suggested that letter writers were often motivated by a perceived threat to their fundamental values. That is much less the case here. The one belief or value that viewers felt compelled to write about was freedom of speech, not because it was being challenged, but because the show exemplified it so well (as is discussed below). The other value was religion, which many viewers believe Maher often denigrates. Overall, the dominant reason most viewers made the effort to write a letter to the show was to continue the conversation that Maher and his guests had begun.

Part of that conversation was the need to criticize Maher and/or his guests. "I was sort of hoping you would be better informed," intoned one guest, while another authoritatively stated, "You are a perfect study into totall [sic] ignorance and liberal stupidity." Other writers were offended more by the guests, such as one who notes, "What bugs me about your show is that some of your guests can't get a word in edgewise without some uncontrolled blabbermouth (i.e., Leslie Abramson, Sheryl Lee Ralph, etc.) shooting their mouths off and rudely interrupting other guests!" In both instances, the writers were generally intent on connecting the issues espoused with the personal characteristics of the person espousing them. As one viewer noted, "I used to think you were intelligent and witty, and I enjoyed finally seeing a show where people could talk freely, with intelligence, thoughtfulness and humor, and not have to 'tiptoe' around issues that are often shyed [sic] away from. However, lately your attitude towards women . . . makes you appear . . . like an obnoxious, sour man." The politics and the personal, the person and the idea are not so easily separated—at least not in the form of political conversation this show creates or by the people who enjoy/dislike watching it.

If one of the dominant themes in the letters was the desire to engage in political conversation, a close second appeared when writers were interested in offering their opinions about how the program should be run. That is to say, viewers were well aware that the political conversation is *also* a television program. Since viewers feel just as knowledgeable (if not more so) about what makes good television as about what makes for good laws, they freely made suggestions about how the program should be different. According to the show's producers (and I concur from my own review of the letters), the two most requested changes in the show's format were for it to be an hour long (instead of thirty minutes) and for the show to include an average citizen (which came to be known as the "Citizen Panelist" when the show finally did institute this feature for a brief period). Audiences often felt that the conversation ended just when it caught some momentum. They also expressed that although they enjoyed watching celebrities discuss politics, the show needed "someone from the 'real world,'" as one writer put it, someone who "might be able to give more insight into a particular problem or situation." Many of these writers, as one might imagine, also volunteered themselves for that role.[2] Again, why watch and listen when you really desire to contribute (or become a "celebrity" yourself)?

A second set of suggestions popular with writers was requests for specific guests to appear on the show, as well as for particular issues to be discussed.

For instance, one writer offered this issue: "Here's a question that I hope you ask someday: Why do individual politicians need large sums of money to run a campaign?" Another proposed, "One issue I would like to see discussed is this: In male-female relationships, notice that it is politically incorrect to show on TV any male ever winning a game, contest, or competition with a female." One writer from Canada assembled a list of thirty-six different panels she would like to see on the show, complete with names linked to particular subject matters. To discuss the issue of "The Monarchy, the Paparazzi, and the 'Tabloidization' of America (re. Diana's death)," she proposes "Arianna Huffington, Karen Finley, Jerry Springer, and Ann ? (political Irish singer with Chumbawamba)." To discuss foreign aid she nominates Colin Quinn, Kathy Lee Gifford, Toni Morrison, and Peter Berg. I'm not sure what the intellectual powerhouses Colin Quinn and Kathy Lee Gifford, in particular, bring to the table in discussing foreign aid, although this viewer obviously does. But that, of course, is the point: viewer desire in helping produce this television show is not necessarily based on what specific guests have to offer intellectually to a subject as much as on the viewer's identification with and pleasure in seeing these particular celebrities or public persons engage the issues of the day. These comments suggest that it is the particular *assemblage*, and control of that assemblage, that is important to viewers as they participate in popular culture. This phenomenon was perhaps represented best by Nick Hornby in his book (and the film based upon it) *High Fidelity*, as the characters found great personal significance and gratification in the meticulous construction and specific order of music play lists, whether anyone else was listening or not.

What these unsolicited contributions and recommendations amount to, I argue, is the recognition by viewers that television can and should *represent* them in some way—either their bodily representation through the surrogate citizen panelist (or guests known for a particular point of view), vocally through the issues they wish to have aired publicly, or mentally (i.e., their fantasy) through the "dream team" they would like assembled for discursive battle. For them, television is a participatory realm, one in which that participation can be facilitated by contacting the show. To see one's self, one's desires, and one's concerns shared and experienced publicly is what makes popular culture such a powerful attachment in modern society. For a program to articulate these ritualistic ways of attending to television and popular culture with the political realm offers a whole new avenue for viewer pleasure. Viewer activity around *P.I.*, then, demonstrates an articulation between lifestyle pleasures and concern for civic life.

The third common theme in viewer letters is their expressions of pleasure and enjoyment with the program based on its mix of entertainment and intelligent conversation. Contrary to the belief by critics that entertainment and information belong in separate realms, many viewers wrote to express just the opposite: their sheer joy at finding both intelligent and entertaining programming. "There's just nothing like *Politically Incorrect* for its intelligent, fascinating, and entertaining combination of news, humour, and opinion," wrote one viewer, while another contends that the show "offers humor, thought and criticism and absolute pure enjoyment with the many 'crazy' current events of our time." One viewer was even more specific in locating why she likes the program: "Your show makes me think and laugh and sometimes get a little riled up and I really enjoy it."

Fourth, but closely linked to this sense of enjoyment and pleasure, is perhaps a more democratic yearning that led viewers to praise the show for what it does for American democracy. That is to say, many viewers wrote to express their belief that the show was a distinctive and compelling addition to television discourse because it offered a forum for conversation, for diverse and competing viewpoints and opinions. "Thanks to you and your guests' discussion of important issues from diverse political views," wrote one woman from Oregon. The forum itself was key for many letter writers. "Your show . . . does present a forum like virtually no other," notes one viewer, while several others said "thank you for making this program available," "thanks for giving the little people something REAL to watch," and thanks for "giving the viewing public the most refreshing and thoroughly enjoyable program to ever hit the air waves." For them, television was finally offering something that was politically meaningful because of the type of forum it was creating. As one viewer noted, "I had damned-near stopped watching television at all . . . but the resulting lonely cynicism was getting to be a bit much."

It is in these letters where we find the strong belief in "freedom of speech" and the importance of deliberation percolating to the surface. One writer expressed her love of the show for its willingness "to tackle issues no one seems to want to talk about," something she found "refreshing in these times when 'free speech' is more expensive than ever." She applauded the show for its efforts to "*expand* dialogue and get rid of the P.C. bullshit—speech has never been more limited than it is currently," and very smartly noted, "what *P.I.* does is showcase the *limits* of speech while it simultaneously attempts to expand those boundaries" (original emphases). The more common formulation involved references, directly or indirectly, to the First Amendment (however mythological and inaccurate that clichéd "right" has become). "I, too, defend the freedom to say what we want. I hate flag burners, but defend the right to burn flags," wrote one viewer. Another writer critiques Maher in saying, "I was somewhat offended when you called me illiterate.[3] But since I support everyone's First Amendment rights, as you do, I will always defend your right to say whatever you wish."

Another strain of letters waxed philosophical about the waning of proper discourse in America. "Americans seem to have truly lost the ability to think for themselves, examine the facts and form a variety of opinions that might contradict the latest buzz word of the day," argued one writer. Another noted, "I think the ability to debate issues is a dying art, and it's good to see people debating intelligently (for the most part)." This writer and others also pointed to the fact that the show creates political conversation in their homes—sometimes between husband and wife, sometimes between parent and child. The writer noted, "I encourage my 14-year-old daughter to watch (the show) . . . so that she can learn debating skills and develop her own ideas about issues. We talk about the various topics, and the guests responses, during commercials and I think she's learning a great deal." Another letter signed by husband and wife (although written by the husband) notes,

> Although I don't always agree with you, the topics never fail to bring about great conversation around the house. I believe that conversation (real talk mind you) is what is missing in many homes. . . . Your show won't save the world, but it has expanded at least a couple of minds.

Finally, this forum for free speech, conversation, and diverse opinions is also praised for offering something that these writers find absent elsewhere on television—realness, frankness, honesty, and common sense. *Politically Incorrect*, one writer argues, is "the only show not afraid to say things as they are," while another praises Maher for his "efforts to voice your unqualified opinions on issues" and the "courage to speak what you feel." The following quote from one viewer is instructive in the ways the writer juxtaposes *P.I.* and Maher with other programming on television that she finds timid, fake, and manipulative, and as a result, both deceitful and monotonous.

> What I find most riveting about your show is your frankness about your own opinions concerning issues that no one else on television attempts to broach. It seems to me that you have no hidden agenda in voicing your views, and I guess that's why I find your show . . . non-tiresome. You come across as a real person, someone I might work with or socialize with, an unusual thing when it comes to the media of television. Your integrity is refreshing and should be an example to all other types of shows.

And with a program that sports an anti–political correctness moniker, it was common for viewers to praise the show and Maher for being "commonsensical." As one representative letter put it, "For the most part I usually agree with your views although not because I think your [sic] smart . . . but because they involve good and common sense."

For an entertainment show, in summary, a defining feature of these letters is the desire to talk about politics. While critics argue that the language and logic of television has led voters (and political candidates) away from issues and toward *imagery* in political campaigns, what stands out about these letters is how the opposite is true. Writers want to talk politics, making very specific,

reasoned, and impassioned statements about a variety of political issues, policies, and programs. In fact, Bill Maher characterizes his audience as quite smart
and desirous of discursive engagement. "I'm just amazed at the volume of intelligent mail I get, people who really care and want to add to the debate. . . .
There's a large segment of smart people yearning for something challenging."[4]
With that said, the letter writers also recognize the program for what it is: a television show that provides both edification and enjoyment. Therefore, these
viewers think like television producers, volunteering their ideas for how to
make the presentation more meaningful, interesting, informative, or pleasurable. Part of that pleasure is the feeling of being represented, of participating
in some way, and in being both entertained and informed at the same time.
The writers also acknowledged that *P.I.* was something different, a unique forum that allowed for different voices to be heard—voices that could be honest
and frank in saying what (for them) was right and true. Hence, viewers wrote
to express their appreciation for such a show—and, of course, to continue arguing politics.

AUDIENCE INTERVIEWS

Over the course of nine months in 1999–2000, I interviewed approximately
sixty-five people in four major U.S. cities. In three of those cities—Houston,
Baltimore, and Atlanta—these individuals had shown up early on a Saturday
morning at their local ABC affiliate to audition for a guest spot as "Citizen Panelist" on *Politically Incorrect*. In the fourth case, I interviewed people outside
the studios of CBS Television City in Los Angeles as they waited in line to
serve as the studio audience for two tapings of *P.I.* Some interviews lasted less
than five minutes, while some lasted as long as twenty-five minutes. Some
people had seen the show only a couple of times, while others were regular
viewers of the program, some even from its days on Comedy Central. Although the majority of the people I interviewed were fans of the show, by my
count, at least twenty were neither fans nor non-fans—they simply didn't care
one way or another. These included local actors who had shown up at the auditions hoping to win a spot on television, spouses and friends of those who
were auditioning, and tourists who simply thought that watching a taping of
P.I. was more interesting than watching a taping of *The Price Is Right*. Although in some cases my "interview" turned into a conversation, the questions I used to guide each interaction are included in the appendix.

In general, I sought to explore these viewers' opinions on three central
points. I first wanted to know why they watched *P.I.* and what they liked and
disliked about the program. Second, I queried them about their consumption
of various forms of mediated political talk (e.g., talk radio, pundit TV, television news, letters to the editor, the Internet), and in particular, how *P.I.* com-

pares to pundit political talk (although in their responses they usually grouped television news into this same category). Because one of *P.I.*'s distinguishing features is its eclectic mix of nonexperts talking politics, I also asked them what they thought about potentially uninformed celebrities discussing politics. Finally, I asked them if they thought *P.I.* was good for American democracy, and, if so, how or why.

The responses I received for why they watched the program and what they enjoyed about it were similar to the reasons offered in the viewer mail. That is, their responses tended to coalesce around the distinctive and unusual qualities that the show offered. As with the letter writers, these viewers also appreciated the mix of entertainment and information they felt the show delivered. "I don't think that [the show] illuminates any big issues," one person noted, "but I think it is kind of interesting. I think you have to have that balance between entertainment and information." Another stated, "It's very humorous. And I think with that type of genre, instead of, 'This is *Nightline*' [said in a droning monotone voice], it's more entertaining and it excites people more." These viewers recognized the entertainment imperatives of the program but contended that this doesn't really matter. One person noted that a person should "take the show with a grain of salt. It's obvious that it's for entertainment . . . other times, [Maher] raises good points." Several respondents took the glass half-full/half-empty approach by looking at it from a different perspective. That is, they appreciated the fact that the show didn't stick to just "serious political issues" but would also bring in other topics that, as one person put it, "are so stupid or inane [yet] are funny." In other words, these viewers didn't mind the seriousness but appreciated the change of pace through the varied topics or the humor to "lighten it up." But again, most respondents emphasized the smartness of the discussions, refusing to focus on just the humor and entertainment aspects. As one person argued, "It's intelligent people discussing intelligent topics."

Also similar to viewer mail, many interviewees appreciated the distinctive qualities that Maher brought to the program as host, finding him humorous, opinionated, unpredictable, yet fair and balanced. Several viewers found Maher to be quite bold and iconoclastic for a television personality. For instance, one person noted, "I found him telling a citizen panelist to shut up. She didn't know what she was talking about. And he had no fear of repercussions later like, "Oh God, my public's gonna hate me now because I told that citizen panelist to shut up." Similarly, another viewer argued, "The key about Maher is, the show is so successful and his personality is such a key ingredient, that he doesn't have to care about being liked; he can be respected. And most TV people want to be liked; respect is an adjunct." There is an appreciation, then, for Maher's "damn the torpedoes" approach, but also for his desire to hold honest conversations. One viewer smirkingly noted, "He's a bastard, but he has to be a bastard given what he does."

Many interviewees, as with letter writers, appreciated the show for the significant role that argumentation plays within the program, and how that then
structures their relationship to the show. Numerous viewers I talked to said
they generally enjoy watching people argue and hearing other people's
opinions. One interviewee maintained that the show "encourages" a particularly agonistic environment. Furthermore, she noted, "People will say
things that may sound completely off the wall and bizarre, but when they
stand up and fight for it, that's what makes it worthwhile and one of the
things you really enjoy seeing on the show: someone who's willing to take a
stand and work it and fight it." This same viewer also maintains that the show
won't allow the viewer to remain neutral when watching it, but instead it
"kind of forces people to take a side, one way or the other."

This description accurately portrays the program's effect on some viewers
due to the fact that they tend to become involved in joining the conversation
in one way or another. That is, several people reported that the program
"spark[ed] lively debates" between themselves and their spouses, including
providing rhetorical ammunition in long-running arguments. As one woman
from Tennessee revealed, "See, my husband is a real conservative and I'm
fairly liberal. We both watch it and it's like, 'Hey, did ya hear that? Did ya hear
that? Hey, I told you so!'" Others noted how the program drew them into the
debate. "I project myself on[to the program] hoping that somebody would
ask the question that I would want to ask," noted one male respondent. Another person stated, "I just love the issues, even if somebody is completely
off the wall, because I sit there and think, 'What would I say or what would
I think about that issue?'" And leading the viewer to consider the issues the
program presented was a common attraction for many of my interviewees.
One viewer put it succinctly when she said, "Overall, it does stir the mind
and causes you to pause and think about what the issues are."[5]

A natural question that arises here is, what makes *P.I.* distinctive? Can't one
derive the same type of argumentative "pleasure" from the pundit talk
shows? About half of the interviewees said they watched the traditional pundit talk shows some of the time. Typically, they felt ambivalence about them,
tending to emphasize the role the shows play in imparting information, but
not expressing any fondness for them. The other half, however, communicated strong disdain for shows such as *Crossfire*, *Meet the Press*, and *The
McLaughlin Group* (all named specifically as examples). Some viewers
stated their disconnect with insider talk very bluntly, as one woman did
when she remarked, "The thing that Washington forgets is that things that are
serious inside the Beltway, the rest of the country doesn't give a rat's ass
about." Other viewers found the talk on pundit shows too "scripted." "I think
the people that go on the news shows," one woman noted, "so much of what
they say is packaged, and so much of it is formatted that there is no spon-
taneity, there's no reality, and they're all worried about their careers." For

her, the nonexperts on *P.I.* had less to lose, and hence their discussions were more real *because* they were spontaneous.[6] And one male respondent put his feelings about the differences between *P.I.* and the pundit shows into explicitly populist terms:

> We've got into this whole thing in our country where political expertise is warped into some sense of elitism. . . . We need more people in the mainstream process of running this country. And we've got this elitism going on . . . where, it's like only lawyers, and only these people have views. Or either the media elite, they're talking down to people, where you know we all have the same fundamental right in the country and in society. . . . We all have one vote and we all have one voice, and I think Bill [Maher] at least gives a little bit of that power to the people.

Other viewers framed their enjoyment of *P.I.* by emphasizing the distance they felt from the world that pundit shows create, a world that seems foreign to these viewers' real life concerns. Hence, the interviewees asserted that both the issues and the type of language used on *P.I.* were more accessible and "real" for average citizens. One viewer argued that *P.I.* "deals with real issues that are on people's minds, the questions that are out there," while another contended that the show "touches on more, I guess you'd say, the topics that your 'regular' people have more concerns about." Other respondents focused on the accessibility of *P.I.* versus the distance they felt from insider political talk. For instance, "The issues [on *P.I.*] are simple as they are presented without a lot of the doublespeak. The variety of the panel is guaranteed to draw in a diverse market versus watching the shows where the stiff political pundits are there. [That] turns me off a lot of times." Another viewer argued that *P.I.* is "more like real life discourse. Like, you know, five people in a bar sitting around talking about something," while another compared the talk to "the same tenor of conversation around the water cooler." One person was perhaps more blunt when he argued that the guests on *P.I.* were "not afraid to say the dumb things that everybody's already thinking."

Some viewers also find the program more indeterminate than the pundit shows. One man contended that on the Sunday morning talk shows, "They're either interviewing a Republican or a Democrat and they're saying the other one is wrong no matter what." And a female viewer asserted, "The whole world isn't black and white, and that is one thing I like about [*P.I.*]. It's the biggest gray area on television, and nobody's preaching to you how you should feel." Finally, others liked *Politically Incorrect* because it was what the label advertised—a special forum in which taboo speech could be enunciated. A woman argued, "On this show you can actually say what you feel. And now days, there are very limited venues in which you can do that. . . . That's why I like it, because I do feel suppressed. You have to be so careful [these days]." A fellow viewer also contended that "political correctness has gone way too far, and [Maher] just doesn't play by those rules. . . . It's a common sense approach is what I like about it."

After they expressed their enjoyment for *P.I.* and their general dislike for pundit talk shows, I asked these viewers what they thought about nonexperts talking about politics in such a public forum. Did it bother them (as it does many critics) that celebrities who appear on the show may be generally uninformed about the issues they are discussing? To my surprise, the interviewees universally embraced the role that celebrities played on the show. Indeed, their responses were quite perceptive yet also surprisingly aware of the tradeoffs associated with the show's format. These viewers were very honest about the role that fascination with celebrity plays in many people's lives. They also recognized the fact that celebrities (including celebrity politicians) are *the* primary figures in public life that people care about. As one man simply put it, "Well, people listen to celebrities." There was also, of course, the enjoyment many people expressed in seeing how celebrities they "knew" from other pop culture venues felt about political issues. Somewhat recognizing his own confusion between fiction and reality, one viewer noted, "So many times you see somebody play a character and you think that's how [the actor] think[s], and then you get to see what the actual person thinks." Other viewers expressed their interest in witnessing whether the celebrity was actually smarter or dumber than they had previously imagined ("that person's such a bimbo, that person's such a dork, or very intelligent," one person noted).

But again, these viewers were very forthcoming in stating the place that celebrities occupy in their lives. "I like to see what people that I watch and care about, even in a small regard, what they have to say about things," one woman intoned. Another viewer expressed her dislike of the citizen panelists that appeared on the show, stating, "I just always want to choke them." Although the citizen panelist feature was one of the most heavily requested features that viewers communicated to the program's producers, very few of the viewers I interviewed actually liked them when they were given the chance to appear. Perhaps these viewers felt that they could have done a better job. In the meantime, however, celebrities offered the voices they were most interested in hearing. This same woman admitted,

> You want to hear the famous person talk. . . . Honestly, I'd rather know what the [celebrity] has to say about it than someone I can visualize as my next door neighbor. That's sad, but that's why we have celebrities on the show. That's just our culture.

Other viewers agreed with the respondent who noted, "People like to see *their* stars or people they're familiar with, with a degree of fame, in a unique dimension" (emphasis added). One interviewee waxed philosophical about how celebrity was being used here and its value, not just for the program, but also for society:

> We attach so much value to entertainers—celebrities, musicians, whatever—that it is an interesting dynamic to have these entertainers. You're using their celebrity to draw viewers, but then you're putting them in a position where they're not usually seen. You're asking these people to act like human beings. In that regard, it's a very compelling show. And it's a very smart use of celebrity that isn't being used [elsewhere]. . . . We're asking them to talk about issues of the day; [it's] rather compelling because there is no other forum where you're going to see that.

Given the other responses this man made in the interview, he is advocating a role and place for celebrities in bringing politics to people who are generally disconnected from political life and who are somewhat uninformed (more on this later). He also made a point worth considering when he asserted that celebrities were not "politicized" public persons, and therefore their opinions could be evaluated more fairly without the preconceptions and baggage that come with the ideological alignments and partisan commitments of traditional (and familiar) public rhetors.

When these viewers were asked if we should be concerned that these celebrities may not be very informed on the issues they were discussing, numerous people responded with remarks such as, "Most people are not particularly informed; it's representative," and, "I think a lot of us are kind of ignorant in the political arena. They're no worse than anybody else, as far as I'm concerned." Another respondent stated the point more eloquently when he said,

> To a certain extent, *Politically Incorrect* is more where you see political discourse on a raw level, whereas if you watch, like, *Meet the Press*, it's been refined. But if you take the person who is . . . a singer or an actor, they're not reading position papers. They're essentially forming their opinions not much differently than a person sitting at home watching the program. I'm not certain one is more valid than the other.

As with this person, the populist leanings are also evident when a woman dismissed the notion of expertise entirely in favor of other, more important criteria: "It's great to have someone that is not a professional politician to speak from their heart or to speak on the issues, whether they are misguided or not."

This identification with celebrity as a "representative" figure for the viewing audience should not come as a surprise, according to David Marshall. He contends that "the celebrity is both a proxy for someone else and an actor in the public sphere. . . . From this proxy, the celebrity's agency is the humanization of institutions, the simplification of complex meaning structures, and principal site of a public voice of power and influence."[7] As traditional institutions (e.g., political parties and the news media) are increasingly seen as less legitimate representatives of public concerns, the celebrity as representative sign has stepped in to fill the public void. The "simplistic" political analyses that celebrities might offer that so frustrates critics yet pleases some audiences is the natural outcome of the celebrity's role as public proxy, for as the viewer above argued, the celebrity's knowledge of politics derives from the same sources as the general public's. Celebrity lack of knowledge, therefore, represents the same lack possessed by the viewing public, and hence, suggests that this talk is just as valid as pundit talk. In that regard, celebrities are paradoxically *more* representative (in a certain respect) than the expert players in politics, including politicians.

Marshall argues further that "celebrity is the site of intense work on the meaning of both individuality and collective identity in contemporary culture. It is the capacity of these public figures to embody the collective in the individual, which identifies their cultural signs as powerful."[8] Again, as one respondent noted (as quoted above), because celebrities do not maintain the partisan or ideological baggage that other political representatives do, their ability to be new and enticing voices in the realm of politics (as unexpected representatives of multiple collectivities) is enhanced. As the viewing public attempts to make sense or make meaning of political life, a television program that offers such representative public personalities with whom audiences maintain an affective relationship (from other cultural sources) is embraced for the *feelings* it ignites, more so than any reasoned logic these celebrities might offer. As Marshall argues, "What is privileged in the construction of public personalities is the realm of affect. Affect moves the political debate from the realm of reason to the realm of feeling and sentiment."[9] In short, then, audiences have embraced a program that simply intensifies broader processes that are at work within public life as citizen-viewers maintain intense commitments to popular culture while politics is increasingly kept at arm's length.

The final major question I asked the viewers of *P.I.*, given their overall support for the show, is whether they believed the program offered something good for American democracy. With the exception of two college students interviewed in Los Angeles, every respondent gave some explanation for why they believed the show contributes positively to political discourse and even to the education of viewers who are less attuned to politics.[10] One point to note here is that when queried, very few people referred to themselves in this response. A question about democracy led them to speak about why the show was good for citizens other than themselves, perhaps displaying somewhat of a third-person effect in their thinking (or perhaps representing the "philosophical" nature of the question itself).[11] Or perhaps, as people who enjoy political discussion and debate, they realize from direct experience that many people in their lives—friends, family, and colleagues—are not of the same ilk and do not enjoy the same relationship with politics. Nevertheless, their responses display insight in understanding (beyond pure individualistic pleasure) the potentiality of entertainment television in political life.

One common response is the argument that the American public is generally uninformed about politics and political issues, yet does not necessarily want to be that way. A program like *P.I.*, then, could make politics more accessible and therefore serve an educational role at some level. Here are two representative responses in this regard:

> It is going to get some of the people that would never watch something like *Crossfire* to watch and maybe understand a little bit more about the current issues and what's going on. So often they always talk about the apathy with the elections and that sort of thing. You know, most people just don't know. You got some people that even if they do try to watch something like *Crossfire* and all that, [pundits] are talking on a higher level, assuming that everybody knows all the background, but [viewers] don't get it. They don't understand it, so they don't get involved in it. So I think [*P.I.*] definitely adds to the education of the public.
>
> People can be intimidated by the political process. They, for whatever reasons, feel as though issues are beyond their own personal grasp, or beyond their own level of contributing. I think that [*P.I.*] reduces some of the barriers to entry for people. . . . People want to be able to talk about things.

Anecdotally, one woman who identified herself as a dental assistant perhaps attests to the accuracy of these statements. She noted that she formerly didn't vote because she didn't think it mattered. Although she recently registered to vote to please her boss, she contends that now "*P.I.* has actually gotten me into looking at more political things because I can deal with the way they discuss it a lot better than the hardcore politicians."

Other viewers took a "something-is-better-than-nothing" approach by embracing the show's accessibility to the wider public. "Maher has done a good job in trying to inject politics into pop culture," argued one viewer, "and make it somewhat entertaining for people who don't have a clue about the political process, which is the majority of Americans in my opinion." Others echoed this statement, noting things such as "just at least to hear the dialogue [is] better than not having any clue," or "just the idea of getting issues on the table, whether it's the budget, whether it's Kosovo . . . or affirmative action" is a good thing because somebody is "gonna go, 'You know, I didn't even think about that.'"

Beyond accessibility and the potential for clandestine education about politics, a final group of viewers made the case for pluralism and the simple importance of the airing and exchange of opinions and ideas. One person argued, "*P.I.* is a good vehicle to discuss the controversial topics without being the definitive answer. You're not solving anything, but at least you get to discuss it." Another viewer noted,

> Perhaps [*P.I.*] might be one of the purest forms of media, of being able to express yourself on a particular topic. And even if someone doesn't agree, you still can try your best to get your point across. Regardless of whether you are trying to convince someone, just to be able to say, "Well this is how I feel about it. Regardless of what you think, this is what I feel."

Finally, a woman simply said, "Anything that will stimulate thought is good. Anytime you can exchange ideas is great." The point here that audiences understand, yet critics of these types of shows seemingly don't, is that what is discursively produced on television is not a *product* to be chosen (i.e., the most intelligent thought or rationally correct idea). Instead, what they desire is simply the *process* of being able to speak and hear others speak, of bringing about public thinking in a language they understand and that (as noted above) is heartfelt and sincere, despite the possibility that such thinking might be misguided. The audience implicitly asserts that it is within *them* that truth and meaning will be made, not selected from choices developed by "experts." The facilitation of thinking public thoughts is the benefit of televised political discourse for these viewers. The irony, it seems to me, is that critics of this form of television are the ones advocating a citizen-consumer model, whereas the viewers who attend to the programming are interested in a more thoughtful and deliberative process for understanding politics.

In summary, then, the viewers of *P.I.* that I interviewed generally had no problem with the mixture of entertainment and information that the show presented. Instead, they recognized the enjoyment of such a coupling, while suggesting that perhaps these features would also bring less politically engaged and astute citizens into the fold. The show is seen as being accessible because it includes people with whom the viewing public is familiar, because it discusses issues that people are concerned about, and because it does it in a way that is not intimidating. On the other hand, many viewers expressed their dislike of traditional political talk on television, seeing it as scripted, predictable, and unaffecting. Furthermore, because such talk is somewhat inaccessible for many viewers, it tends to leave people feeling inadequate and uninformed. The irony, then, is that rather than leading people to be informed about politics, pundit shows repulse some citizens by reminding them of all that they do not (though perhaps should) know. Finally, the public also wonders why they should care about pundit talk (and by association, the issues covered there) because they don't really know who is doing the talking and why. As one woman exclaimed, "Pundits! You know, you always have pundits, pundits, pundits all the time. You just want to smack 'em around and tell 'em to get a job or something instead of just being a pundit." As she makes abundantly clear, those who typically discuss politics on television are seen as not sharing much in common with the average viewer. "Why listen to you?" this woman seemingly asks. Given what she and others have stated above, the response to pundits seems to be, "We don't know who you are, what you do for a living, what you are talking about, or why you are on television, and furthermore, we really don't care."

Who or what many of these viewers do "know" or care about are celebrities. The celebrity guests seen on *P.I.* are familiar because of the affective relationship that viewers maintain with these characters who comprise popular culture. The political opinions celebrities state are seen as more real, more heartfelt, and pronounced in a language that is more easily understood than pundit talk. These celebrities, for the most part, are not politicized persons. Therefore, audiences don't feel they must endure the entrenched positions or the predictable and scripted lines that typically accompany televised political talk. Celebrity political talk emanates from the same sources as the audience, and it is stated in the same raw and unrefined ways as one would find in a bar or at work (and as a result, enhances its validity). Therefore, the audience appreciates the means and manner in which the program and its celebrity guests have articulated the public with the private. Marshall argues that because the celebrity "text" retains such affective power, it can move easily between the public and private spheres. He notes,

> Fundamentally, celebrities represent the disintegration of the distinction between the private and the public. This disintegration, as represented by celebrities, has taken on a particular form. The private sphere is constructed to be revelatory, the ultimate site of truth and meaning for any representation in the public sphere.[12]

As with the discussion that occurred on *P.I.* about President Clinton (examined in chapter 7), the private sphere becomes the site for establishing truth and meaning as both celebrity discussants and the viewing audience attempt to make the public sphere more closely resemble the private.[13] Critics have increasingly argued that it is television or politicians that are responsible for this blending or merging of the public and private as politics and pop culture, celebrity and politician are supposedly becoming one and the same. The data offered here suggest that perhaps it is a public that is disillusioned or disaffected from previous models of political representation and discourse that is driving this change as a means of achieving something more real and relevant to their lives.

ON-LINE DISCUSSION GROUPS

Since the early days of the Internet, a discussion forum known as Usenet News has been available for those who have been knowledgeable about how and where to access it.[14] Usenet is not really a "news" site, but a place where discussions and the sharing of information occur on tens of thousands of subjects. Specific group names designate the topic of discussion within particular forums/groups (such as soc.culture.asian for Asian culture, or rec.aviation.hanggliding for recreational sports), and all manner of discursive activity occurs there. It is also an asynchronous form of communication, meaning that once a message is posted, other users have the opportunity to respond by posting a reply message at any time in the days, months, and even years ahead. As such, conversations can be carried on for some time, allowing multiple respondents to also join in the discussion should they desire. Although Usenet was made more widely available through the website Deja.com, it is perhaps most easily accessed these days through the Internet at Google.com (although there are myriad means for connecting to Usenet groups, such as through commercial and educational Internet service providers). Anyone with Internet access, in theory, can participate in these discussion groups.

Of all political talk shows on television, the discussion forum dedicated to *Politically Incorrect*—alt.tv.pol-incorrect (henceforth referred to as ATPI)—has been the most frequented on Usenet, with over 98,000 postings since the group's inception in February 1997 through February 2004. Indeed, none of the pundit television shows (*Meet the Press, Crossfire*, etc.) have Usenet discussion sites related to them (for the public is not really invited into those discussions), and the number of postings in sites dedicated to new political television programs such as *Dennis Miller Live* and *The Daily Show with Jon Stewart* pale in comparison.[15] Perhaps because of *P.I.*'s format, it is seen as an inviting and inclusive forum for anyone to discuss politics and the program.[16] And that, of course, is what occurs there, among other things.

I studied the postings made to alt.tv.pol-incorrect for the month of February for every year between 1997 and 2003 (the entire run of the show on ABC), as well as for August 1998 (when President Clinton admitted his affair with Monica Lewinsky and testified before a grand jury) and September 2001 (when Maher's comments on the 9/11 terrorist attacks created a popular uproar against him) (see the appendix for methodology). Because of the nature and focus of my analysis, I decided not to become personally involved in the discussions and not to interview the people who participated in them. Rather, I have treated the discussions and the people who posted them—the message content and "purpose," as well as the posters' intentionality and relationship to the site—as a text to be read by anyone who might happen upon them. Whereas I directed the conversation in the personal interviews discussed above, here I am merely a witness to the discursive activities that others have created, offering yet another vantage point from which to assess audience activity around the text that is Bill Maher and *Politically Incorrect*.

Usenet discussion groups are strange yet interesting places, with norms, ritual behaviors, patterns of interaction, and a culture all their own. A useful analogy in understanding these forums is to a neighborhood bar (although for ATPI, one with a higher IQ). Like a bar, the discussion group is frequented by regulars, those who drop by occasionally, and those who just happen to wander by and decide to "have a drink (e.g., make a posting) and check out the joint." As such, the regulars are the most frequent posters, and therefore come to know each other quite well. They develop levels of trust, fondness, and support for each others' ideas, as well as general disdain for some of the more annoying regulars. They set the tone for how discussion will generally occur, become de facto experts on the program, perhaps create longer discussion threads by responding more frequently to each other, and take the liberty to be either generous or rude to those just passing by (although rudeness is generally not the dominant motif here). Also like a bar, the talk is a combination of seriousness and irreverence, reflection and playfulness, bluntness and cleverness. Although the myriad activities that go on in a bar also can occur here (i.e., petty fights, drunken banter, cattiness, etc.), it is the focus on the show, Maher as host, and politics in general that remain central to the larger flow of discursive activity and overall purpose people have for coming to this forum.[17]

In some ways, discussions on ATPI are similar to those that occur in other on-line forums where television programming is discussed. For instance, Nancy Baym's study of on-line soap opera discussions reports four primary fan practices that occur there: *informing* others of what occurred in missed episodes; *speculating* about where the show's content will or should go; *criticizing* the show, its narratives, its actors, or other postings; and *reworking* the show's text in various ways.[18] All of these activities occur in ATPI as well. For example, discussants in ATPI share information about a specific program that others may have missed. Under the posting title "What happened on the 5 year celebration Show?" (2/23/02), for instance, a person asked, "What did Ann Coulter say. [sic] What were the three topics? Thanks for the info," followed by numerous replies that harshly criticize Coulter, discuss the guests that appeared that evening, review things viewers thought were funny and comments that they found either right or wrong. The conversation then segued to a discussion of Dennis Miller's recent episode, and the production facilities of both *P.I.* and *Dennis Miller Live* in Los Angeles (where both shows were taped). This discussion thread typifies the way in which a comment on one subject can carom through numerous issues or subjects that people want to discuss. Sharing information, then, is also interlaced with the tendency to share one's feelings or opinions about the program.

ATPIers also speculate about Maher or guests on the show, debating, for instance, whether John McCain is a racist for anti-Vietnamese remarks (2/22/00) or whether the comedian Carrot Top is Jewish (3/11/98). The act of criticizing—Maher, the program, and the guests that appear—is one of the most frequent activities that occur in the forum. Indeed, Maher and his guests, from my observations, are more frequently criticized than celebrated.[19] In fact, it is probably a mistake to call these participants "fans" of the show (just as with many of the letter writers above), but rather, "regular viewers." For instance, one poster proclaims about Maher, "He comes off as a [sic] arrogant know it all. If you don't agree with him your [sic] 'crazy' or way off base" (2/9/01). Other posts attack various guests, from their perceived weight gain (Ben Affleck), to their need for a face lift (Ann Richards), to their grating and vacuous comments (Victoria Jackson). Perhaps the number one pariah for these viewers is Ann Coulter, the skinny blonde conservative "pundette" that Maher and *P.I.* essentially put on the political map. One discussion thread that began on February 2, 1998, with the comment, "Does anyone ever take a look at Ann Coulter and just want to offer her a plate of food?" lasted for five years through ninety different postings, ending with a conversation begun on February 22, 2003, that asked, "Did anyone else notice that when the anorexic Nazi had her hair tucked behind her ear she looked shockingly similar to a Vulcan?" Of course, this highlights another important feature of on-line discussion in general—the ability for a conversation to never really end (for better or worse).

Finally, as is similar with on-line viewer discussions in other television-dedicated forums, the participants in ATPI rework the program in various ways. As with letter writers, one popular form of reworking is the (re)construction of favorite past panelist lineups or assemblages the audience should see. One poster requests participants to "Vote for the funniest *P.I.* panel ever!" (2/6/98), while another, under the heading "Lets [sic] get some smart people on *P.I.*," asks, "Hey, folks, what's your *P.I.* panel of choice? My choice: Dennis Miller (of course), Patrick Buchanan (It can't be too one-sided), The guy who plays Munch on *Homicide* (Christ I can't remember his NAME!!!), Jerry Falwell (comic relief)" (2/1/99). Other reworkings might include clarifying Maher's statements or his particular thinking on issues, requesting changes in set design, inserting pop culture references, or integrating outside information to "fill out" the text in some way. This reworking is central to the pleasure that the show provides, thereby allowing viewers to participate in the construction of what the show then means to these viewers. For instance, under the heading, "The week according to me," one poster begins by stating, "Here's my take on the past week," and then offers a list of five points—the first two being criticisms of specific guests, then the "best line of the week," "best new word of the week," and "best shouting match of the week" (2/1/98). The discussion that ensues brings forth other viewers' pleasures and dislikes related to these items—most notably, their favorite or least favorite guest celebrities.

As seen in these actions, the program as a political talk show does not stand apart from the wider array of popular culture and its meanings to television viewers. Indeed, the program's format (i.e., its inclusion of all sorts of public persons, including mass media stars, authors, musicians, politicians, etc.) is designed to link all of these popular people and their opinions to the issues of the day. The reason, of course, that the program is heavily criticized by political elites and cultural arbiters is that it has supposedly constructed this unholy union between sacrosanct politics and profane popular culture. What is important to note, however, is that such a linkage already exists in the minds of viewers—whether *P.I.* has facilitated it, created it, or not. Conceiving of politics as a distinct field of thought or realm of activity that stands apart from the rest of public culture is simply ludicrous. Such attempts at segregation (in the pursuit of "rational thought") do exist on the pundit shows, but not in the minds of viewers. The same viewers who hold smart, rational, informed, and thoughtful discussions of political issues in ATPI are the same viewers who carry in their heads a whole array of politically irrelevant but culturally attuned information. A discussion thread on presidential candidates, for instance, will stand next to another on where one can download full episodes of *Seinfeld* on the Internet. Or better yet, a discussion of presidential candidates will include references to music and parental advisory lyrics that candidates' wives have inserted into popular culture (2/23/00). As seen in many of the examples given above (and by the research by Michael Delli Carpini and Bruce Williams reviewed in chapter 2),[20] governors and senators stand in the viewer's mind next to public personalities such as inane comedians (Carrot Top), religious and secular pundits (Falwell and Buchanan), and characters found on fantasy television shows (*Star Trek*), police dramas (*Homicide*), or obnoxious advertisements (Miss Cleo). These are all essentially players on the same public stage.

Of course, some viewers might pat themselves on the back for being both politically knowledgeable and culturally savvy, and as John Thornton Caldwell argues, post-network television prides itself on flattering the viewer in just this way.[21] But one discussant in ATPI took another poster to task for displaying his arrogance in this regard, and in the process, displayed her own version of intellectual-cultural agility that seems foundational for those attracted to new political television:

I suspect if Dennis Miller read (your) assessment of his comedy he'd say,

Hang on, li'l buddy, it ain't Swiftian genius because I throw the Professor and Maryann, Bilbo Baggins, Urkel and Boomers drinking bong water martinis together in a sentence—its pop culture, dude, not Oscar fucking Wilde, 'kay? I'm a working hack, and the day I get so fucking full of myself that my act requires a perfect, nay, even decent SAT score, HBO pulls the plug and I'm back to prop comedy, begging Carrot Top for the right to be his opening bitch at Catch a fucking Rising Star—so, to end this rant, I turn to my old pal, Billy Maher and say . . . GET OVER YOURSELF.

She ends her attack by noting, "You don't need a bloody Ivy League educa-tion or the width and breadth of an Einstein . . . to 'get' Dennis Miller. All you need is a sense of humour that isn't served by the Tim Allens of the world, and a passing knowledge of television/drug/intro to English Lit 101 culture." Perhaps the key point here is her claim that certain audiences *aren't being served* by certain television presentations. The same could be argued for tele-visual presentations of politics that attempt to segregate politics from the het-erogeneous world that many people live in—one heavily influenced by pop-ular culture. This is a lack, I argue, that *P.I.* and new political television (including Dennis Miller) attempt to address.

Perhaps the most important component of ATPI yet to be discussed is the way in which an entertainment television program has been the base from which quite extensive and substantive discussions of politics regularly occur. Like the letter writers and my interview subjects, participants in ATPI really want to talk about political issues, and as one might imagine, these discus-sions occur on numerous topics: welfare, gun control, immigration, environ-mental regulations, taxation, animal rights, free speech, education, race, vio-lence, health care, law enforcement, and so on. The discussants bring with them their own personal characteristics and experiences from different parts of the nation (and Canada). For instance, one reader complained that Maher unfairly characterizes her age-group (Gen Y) as unwilling to work in grunt or entry-level jobs. A discussion then ensues in which people offer their per-spectives based on personal experiences with twenty-somethings in the workplace (3/26/02). Similarly, a show that included Arsenio Hall discussing his family's time on public aid blossoms into a conversation about Food Stamp cards, with posters contributing information about the success or fail-ure of these electronic cards in their home states of Texas, Illinois, and Min-nesota (2/21/98).

P.I., then, becomes the jumping-off point for political discussion. Someone will comment on a recent show, and a political discussion that can be very specific or wide-ranging will typically occur. For instance, on a program that dealt with the case of a ten-year old girl suing another child for sexual ha-rassment, Maher was particularly belligerent toward his guest Gloria Allred, a lawyer who supported the girl's litigation. The original post complained that Maher wouldn't let her speak, but the discussion that followed quickly turned to the issue of sexual harassment policies, laws, and norms of be-havior and control. When Maher acted similarly toward guest David Duke on another episode, a Duke supporter appeared in ATPI with numerous links to websites supporting Duke's arguments. Again, although the actual program may not have been the best forum for the wide exchange of ideas in certain instances, ATPI allowed viewers to hold a much more extensive, dispassion-ate, and reasoned argument than that hosted on the program. In a different vein, a comment by Maher that society should "stop punishing the smokers"

(2/17/98) becomes the beginning of a conversation where posters, in a single thread, discuss taxation policies, freon, smog, the framers of the constitution, Thomas Paine, various books to read, libertarianism, and other issues.

One might wonder, however, whether these viewers should go to another forum to talk politics—say, for instance, alt.talk.politics. What is significant, however, is that they don't (or if they do, they still come to ATPI). They link their pleasure in watching a television program that features wide-ranging discussions of politics to then activate their interests in participating in their own wide-ranging discussions of politics. They desire to share information (news articles, hyperlinks, experiences) and engage in knowledge formation. As one user wrote to the group, "Thanks [for the postings], I often lol [laugh out loud] and the level of discussion has stopped me in my tracks more than once." And they do so in a rather civilized manner (for I find participants in this forum are less likely to engage in ad hominem attacks and are much less ideologically polarized than the participants in some political discussion forums, such as alt.fan.rush-limbaugh).[22] And as with the other two sets of *P.I.* audiences discussed above, the participants here desire to assert their *own* views, however profound or trivial. In short, the show activates a certain set of desires for political engagement that *P.I.* often initiates and that ATPI hosts. Television may seemingly be a one-way communication technology, but the Internet certainly is not. And again in reference to Caldwell's point about post-network television, ATPI can perhaps be seen as an example of the successful new relationship that television producers have attempted to create among networks, programming, and audiences.[23]

Another point worth noting is that the discussions in ATPI represent behavioral activity around television that isn't necessarily derived from a love for the show. As noted above, there is no shortage of commentary and discussion on Maher as host and political commentator, on the various guests that appear, or on the production of the show. Yet by my reading, the discussants don't necessarily like Maher that much, nor do they necessarily find him or the guests to be especially smart or insightful. Some other pleasure is derived from this experience of watching and talking about the program, guests, or issues. Watching the show alone—especially a show *based* on discussion—is not as much fun as watching and discussing it with others. And that is the point—watching television and discussing it on the Internet are two activities that the regular participants of ATPI ritually engage in, media-based activities that in some way comprise the patterns and rituals of their lives (as they do for many citizens). Add to this their interests in political discussion and/or humor and satire, and both of these media have facilitated engagement with politics in some way.

Without talking directly to these participants, one must be careful in assigning particular intentions to their actions. But based on the behaviors exhibited in ATPI, it seems that the multiple practices they engage in serve their needs or complete their viewing experience in some way. These seemingly include the desire for argumentation, hopes for information gathering, expression of various feelings, tapping into other pleasures and interests, participating in human relations, and being a political person (that is, being connected to the nation and its needs, knowing where it is headed and what it has done, feeling when it has been right or wrong in its policies, etc.). Again, many of these "needs" could be served through numerous other discussion forums or subjects—religion, music, or *Buffy the Vampire Slayer*. Instead, they are addressed through an entertainment television show dedicated to political discussion.

In summary, then, *P.I.* provides a starting point for a whole range of discursive practices by viewers in the ATPI forum, the most important of which are the numerous and varied political discussions that are spawned as a result of conversations that began on the show. With that said, the show also serves as a linking mechanism between politics and other viewer interests, and between various domestic media practices and activities in which viewers regularly participate. Those who post messages argue political issues but also discuss hair style or weight gain of panelists, second-guess the show's producers, applaud the wit of guests, address Maher directly, debate the validity of arguments, introduce evidence from other media sources as rebuttal, attack each other personally, speculate on panelists' sex lives or denounce them as moronic, and so on. Viewers tend to engage the program as both politics *and* television. That is, they read *P.I.* on its own terms—part real, part constructed, part important, part frivolous, part serious, part playful, part engaged, part distant, part ironic, part outraged, part sanctimonious, and part satisfied.

Furthermore, on-line viewer activity parallels the assumptions of new political television: that politics is not something that is attended to separately, cordoned off from the rest of one's identity, activities, or existence in the world. Politics is one of many facets of a person's life, and it too includes drama and humor, seriousness and entertainment, importance and triviality. Both *P.I.* and the on-line audience activity surrounding the show reflect that understanding. In short, the evidence here suggests that new political television is important as a spark for drawing viewers toward greater discursive participation in politics—one that includes their lives as citizens *and* as cultural beings.

CONCLUSIONS

Looking across these three areas of investigation into how audiences relate to *Politically Incorrect*, three primary conclusions stand out. First is the overriding desire of viewers to engage in political conversations that they feel comfortable participating in. They use *P.I.* as a means to talk about political issues with their family and friends, with Maher directly, and with strangers and virtual acquaintances they find on-line. In this process, they also talk about, criticize, and celebrate the component parts of popular culture that *P.I.* also offers—Maher as comedian host and the celebrities and public persons that appear there. The show, then, is an *instigator* of a broad range of discussion on various political, social, and cultural topics. But again, the show only begins the discussion—it is the overriding desire of the audience to take the discussions a step further through their discursive participation in politics in the private realm that shows how *P.I.* (and NPTV) contributes to our civic culture.

Second, *P.I.* is a *connector*, articulating these viewers' lives as consumers of media to public life. It connects their concerns for the nation and the issues it faces with their interests, desires, pleasures, and behaviors as private individuals. Here the show offers celebrities with whom audiences identify and, at some level, care for—the people who inhabit the cultural landscape that viewers ritually engage. Furthermore, the show offers different issues (and different ways of thinking about them) than what regularly appears on the political agenda set by political elites and the news media. It therefore connects the more immediate concerns of viewers with public life by expressing them in a nationally televised forum. It bridges their interests in being informed with their desires to be entertained, while simultaneously connecting their routines and behaviors of watching television (and in some instances, surfing the Internet) to public life. The program, therefore, doesn't stand apart as something separate (as pundit shows might lead viewers to believe about politics) but is integrated within their panoramic view of life in its totality. In short, *P.I.* links their identities as both citizens and consumers, making the connections between the public and private spheres more seamless and perhaps more meaningful.

Finally, the show serves as an alternative to traditional forms of political talk on television, namely pundit television and the news. *P.I.* is seen by its viewers as offering talk that is more real, honest, and accessible than what emanates from political elites. It is therefore often more interesting and pleasurable to these viewers. Through Maher and the celebrities who offer this type of talk, the program is seen as more *representative* of the issues, concerns, language, and thinking that audiences possess and that they desire to see portrayed on television. And many viewers freely volunteered their suggestions (to the producers or to fellow viewers) for how the program could represent them even more through specific issues or guests, including the average citizen as guest or through all-star celebrity lineups.

In sum, I argue that viewers engage their citizenship through *P.I.* in various ways—behaviorally, by becoming active discussants of politics, and cognitively, as they constantly weigh the points in which they agree and disagree with the show and the issues it presents based upon their beliefs, ideology, knowledge, and experiences. Furthermore, they are socially engaged, as they share information and listen to the viewpoints of others through their ritual behaviors, and culturally engaged, as they link their interests, pleasures, desires, and identities as consumers of popular culture with their general concern for a shared democratic life.

9

Conclusion: Entertaining Politics in American Civic Culture

Teachout likes to "thesaurusize" words on the computer. . . . She is hard at work looking for a word to replace "citizen." "It would be a word to describe someone for whom politics is part of their personal life and social life."

—News article describing Zephyr Teachout, director of Internet organizing for the Howard Dean for President Campaign[1]

They're tapping into people's love for the Internet and people's love for being online. [Dean's] added a whole new dimension to that lifestyle, the political dimension.

—Corey Sommers, Howard Dean for President Campaign volunteer[2]

In the late summer and fall of 2003, the news media awoke to a puzzling political surprise—a former governor from a small northeastern state had vaulted to the front of the pack of prospective Democratic presidential candidates through a combination of honest and aggressive political talk and a savvy recognition that the Internet is a medium of communication that plays an important role in people's lives and their interactions with others. Utilizing weblogs, message boards, and the grassroots organizing site, Meetup.com, the Dean campaign invited Internet users to take an active and participatory role in defining, constructing, and organizing the campaign from the bottom up (or at least seemingly so). Much of that civic activity was discursive. That is, the primary activity for these "Deaniacs" (as these Dean "maniacs" came to be called) was the exchange of ideas, observations, and information via the computer keyboard. They participated in constructing the running narrative on the campaign's official weblog, and hence the *narrative* that was Howard Dean for President.

What the Dean campaign either knew or learned (indeed, what America learned) is that people were hungry for meaningful engagement with politics, and the Internet provided an accessible avenue for such participation. People who regularly logged on to the weblog welcomed the opportunity not just to be spoken *to* but also spoken *with*. And they realized they could do so while enmeshed in the myriad of other activities that consumed their daily lives (such as work, family, entertainment, etc.). The pleasures of intellectual engagement with the world in which they live had become manifest in the pleasure of entertaining politics in new and engaging ways. Many Deaniacs were even willing to move away from the keyboard to meet up with others in their local communities who also felt a resurgence of political activism deriving from their on-line activities. Cynics and traditionalists will undoubtedly ridicule these feelings as false or temporal, or perhaps even naïve or lazy (that is, Deaniacs as "armchair activists").[3] Yet Dean's ability to raise over $40 million in campaign contributions and (for a time) become the presumptive party nominee and front-runner largely as a result says something about people's desire or willingness to be civically engaged in both traditional and nontraditional ways. The Dean example also shows that people are not interested in segregating politics from other activities in their lives that they enjoy and with which they routinely participate. This is not "lifestyle politics" (a term for me that has always seemed a pejorative means of dismissing political activity that doesn't derive from class, religious, ethnic roots or traditions), but instead signals nascent steps toward a political engagement that is part and parcel of one's life as lived—a new form of integration of the public and private spheres obtained through communication technologies.

Similarly, I contend, the forms of new political television discussed throughout this book are part of this same general tendency away from segregating politics into a separate realm that publics must enter when engaging it. New political television challenges the artificial boundaries that have existed between politics and popular culture, between that which is considered "serious" and that which is "entertainment." In the process, audiences are invited to link their interests, habits, and pleasures to political life and to be engaged (discursively, cognitively, etc.) on their own terms. New political television offers the option for thinking differently about politics through narratives that are not bounded by the thinking, logic, or control of political insiders. Comedians with a different license to speak have reinvigorated political humor as a vehicle for serious critiques of power and as a different way of making sense of the events and issues of the day. Humor (with its semantic authority rooted in commonsense thinking) provides a vernacular that all audiences speak and a vehicle for attracting broader audiences to politics. It links the pleasures of laughter with the displeasure and outrage over abuses of public trust. Moreover, the celebrity comedian serves as a public proxy, a televisual representative who vocalizes issues, ideas, and values in accessible and inviting language. And the comedian-host has constructed a hybrid viewing experience that simultaneously redefines and critiques existing genres of televisual talk, again articulating the viewing audiences' likes and dislikes in newly creative ways.

As I note above, the changes in new political television (NPTV) should be viewed not only for what they have added to television but also for what they contribute to public life in the process. That is to say, the ultimate measure for what these changes portend should be centered on answers to these questions: how is NPTV involved in the processes of citizenship, how does it shape our political culture, and how does it affect how Americans see themselves as citizens? A useful means for arriving at answers to these questions can be reached by examining NPTV as it relates to our "civic culture."

NEW POLITICAL TELEVISION AND CIVIC CULTURE

Over the course of several articles, Peter Dahlgren has developed a theory of "civic culture," a concept he defines as "cultural attributes prevalent among citizens that can in various ways facilitate democratic life."[4] Through this theory, Dahlgren is interested in highlighting the linkages that exist between culture and politics. Indeed, he argues that "civic culture is anchored in the practices and symbolic milieu of everyday life," including our uses and relationships with mass media.[5] He conceives of civic culture as "a resource, a storehouse of assets that individuals and groups draw upon and make use of in their activities as citizens."[6] In labeling this theory, he contends that the word "politics" connotes *doing*, whereas "civics" suggests the "pre-condition" to doing.[7] As such, he argues that scholars should analyze the ways in which our *cultural* practices (such as media usage and its central role in the processes of meaning making) participate in shaping these civic pre-conditions. He offers civic culture as an analytic construct, a way to help "organize analyses of how the media, via their modes of representation as well as the newer forms of interactivity that they offer, are contributing to the decline of traditional political life and the emergence of newer forms of involvement."[8]

This helpful heuristic, then, serves as a guide for discussing and analyzing the ways in which new political television is involved in contemporary processes of citizenship. The six "pre-conditions" that comprise civic culture, Dahlgren advances, include discussion, practices, values, knowledge, affinity, and identities. Each is discussed in turn.

Discussion

As with many democratic theorists, Dahlgren contends that discussions among citizens are the "cornerstone" of democratic practice. As we have seen, new political television contributes to this democratic practice not only through the new types of political discussion it presents, but also in its role as an instigator of discursive activity outside of the act of watching television. First, new political television offers various modes of discourse about politics that appeal to a wide variety of interests, tastes, comfort levels, and preferred modes of political discourse—from serious, humorous, theatrical (performative), and argumentative to deliberative, emotional, and nonchalant. As we saw in our comparison of political talk by pundits and laity, pundits operate by certain tacit rules that tend to circumscribe democratic debate, limiting the discussions to issues derived from specific ways of thinking. Laity-centered discussions, however, are much more open and wide-ranging, incorporating numerous perspectives and approaches across the social and political spectrum as well as the public and private spheres. Such expansiveness derives from these discussions, emanating from a values-driven approach to political thinking. Furthermore, the audiences for *Politically Incorrect* believe that the program offered the ability for a diversity of people to speak and to be heard about issues in a deliberative manner. Many felt disconnected from pundit talk, and instead, contended that they themselves were responsible for establishing the *meaning* of politics through the processes of political discussion. They too found discussion central to their own democratic practices, and hence they appreciated a program that facilitated such public thinking.

Audiences also believed that *P.I.* allowed for discussions of issues that they care about in a language that is accessible and not intimidating, yet also conducted by certain *people* that they care about. They found the discussions heartfelt and sincere, and they appreciated the commonsensical thinking that Bill Maher and others provided. Finally, we saw how the program instigated further conversation and discussion outside of the direct viewing experience. Viewers were mobilized to talk with family (and occasionally friends and co-workers), and even strangers on-line. That impulse registered even when talk could not produce a true conversation, such as their desire to engage in conversation with Maher through the letters they wrote him or by talking back to the television set. In short, the forms of new political television analyzed in this book encourage the discussion of politics in ways that have proven meaningful and engaging to various audiences.

Practices

"Democracy must be embodied in concrete recurring practices," Dahlgren contends, that also have a routine and "taken for granted" quality.[9] As we have seen, critics regularly criticize the role that television plays in the daily routines of citizens—a medium that supposedly distracts from their civic duties and trivializes the political process by making it an amusing spectacle. Yet I argue that this is a shallow view of the role and place of television both in democratic politics and in the lives of citizen-viewers. For many citizens, politics is increasingly understood *as* a discursive practice (a textual activity), and as such, we must recognize the ways in which new political television not only instigates discursive activity (discussed above), but also provides accessible interpretive procedures for making sense of the political world through that process. Television is a ritualized *practice*, and politics is one of many topics that audiences interact with on a daily basis. New political television has its own ritual appeal, repeatedly hailing the viewer with attention to pressing current events, and its changing casts of familiar yet politically novel characters. Its cross-generic construction (part pundit, part late-night talk; part celebrity, part policy wonk; part sketch-comedy, part roundtable) also invites the audience's attention to something distinctive on television. New political television's strength is in its ability to connect our affective relationship to popular culture—our "mattering maps"—with politics, offering a much stronger articulation between public and private life than previous political talk television has been able to achieve beyond one's "duty" to be an "informed citizen." Indeed, NPTV is linked to other cultural practices (such as our attention to other media and media usage), inviting our cognitive connections between and across these concerns. Political practice is then part and parcel of our cultural practices and is therefore more thoroughly embedded in our daily lives.

Values

Dahlgren is correct to point out that the components of civic culture have little meaning if disconnected from shared values upon which democracy rests. He notes that these values can be substantive (such as liberty, justice, equality, and solidarity) or procedural (such as tolerance, openness, reciprocity, and accountability/responsibility). The question for us is whether (and how) new political television participates in maintaining and/or reinforcing common values such as these. As seen in the analyses of programming content, the political discussions held there are largely products of a value-centered (as opposed to an instrumental) approach to politics. Issues are taken up, conversations held, parodies performed, and rants delivered largely on this basis. Two of the dominant values that permeate the programs are the belief in truthfulness and honesty (and the lack thereof) in public life—whether the issues discussed were a presidential sex scandal or the international scandal of a unilateral military invasion. Laity-based talk about President Clinton was not procedurally based, but rather, derived from the values that his indiscretions threatened. Panelists on *P.I.* were divided between those arguing for responsibility, truthfulness, and justice on one side, and those demanding tolerance, reciprocity, and equality on the other. Similarly, discussions and parodies of governmental action in response to the 9/11 terrorist attacks again derived from the belief that both government and the news media jointly participated in constructing dazzling falsehoods. NPTV provides a forum then where these values can be explicated and mulled over publicly.

The usage of commonsense thinking by the hosts and guests on NPTV is an appeal to the values that are held in common. The modernist response of the comedian-host is to remind viewers of the need to return to these values. That NPTV traffics in such appeals is not surprising. David Thelen's study of television viewers who watched the Iran-Contra hearings showed how they were mobilized to take direct political (discursive) action because their central values were threatened by what they witnessed in the congressional hearings and news reports. Similarly, Michael Billig contends that through social conversation, we process central value-laden or ideological dilemmas embedded in our language.[10] In short, television audiences may not always understand the minutiae of insider political discussions (e.g., arms-for-hostages in covert operations schemes, or suborning perjury and obstructing justice in a grand jury testimony), but they usually get the bigger picture of dishonesty, loyalty, accountability, and the like, and feel comfortable discussing politics on those terms. New political television, then, provides a forum where those discussions and that level of analysis, based on values held in common, are not only welcomed but encouraged.

Knowledge

For democracy to remain viable, people have to be informed about the world in which they live. To be informed, people must have reliable information that accurately represents the social-political world. As we have seen, the concern over new political television programs is that they have supposedly become a central source of information for a minority of young citizens. Because the stated mission of these shows is entertainment, they are considered to be "naturally" unreliable. Yet as we have discussed, the other stated mission of these programs is their desire to puncture holes in the lies, fabrications, and distortions that are circulated in the public sphere, lies repeated "until they become true," as both Maher and Jon Stewart contend. A three-minute report on Fox News and CNN, I argue, is just as capable of painting an incomplete picture of "reality" as is a five-minute rant by Dennis Miller. Reliable information in this era of hyperreality is hard to establish, and new political television programs (through both humor and serious discussions) are just as involved in trying to establish knowledge from what is true and accurate as any other televisual construction of reality.

An important subset of knowledge, Dahlgren argues, is competencies and the ways in which people make sense of and understand their world. Much of the discussion so far has focused on the ways in which new political television allows for politics to be discussed, entertained, and made sense of through the commonsense thinking of its narratives, group discussions, and parodies. As the examination of audiences also attests, viewers find such thinking accessible because of the linguistic and cultural proximity of the discussions and guests who articulate them. *P.I.*'s audiences displayed their competencies in numerous political and cultural areas, and indeed, it was their pleasure in integrating and publicly displaying such competencies that added value to their viewing experience. Knowledge, therefore, is established not by segregating politics from other things that matter in people's lives, but rather, by finding linkages between them—between politics and culture and between mediated reality and lived experiences. Sonia Livingstone and Peter Lunt and Paolo Carpignano et al. found similar results in their analyses of audience discussion programs. Audiences often rejected or challenged the knowledge claims made by "experts," and instead asserted their own knowledge claims based on lived experience.[11] And as both Doris Graber and Lawrence Grossberg contend, that which we "know" as citizens is intimately linked to that which we *care* about.[12] For politics to be made meaningful, then, it must have some relationship to that which we value. New political television, I argue, provides avenues for such alternative ways of knowing about politics as those offered by political pundits.

Knowledge is also built on the diversity of viewpoints and issues that new political television offers for consideration. Rappers from South Central L.A. and basketball players from Alabama sit next to blueblood policy advocates and Christian conservatives discussing everything from mandatory prison sentences and food stamps to school vouchers and the war in Kosovo. The discussions produced in such encounters may not always fulfill every viewer's desire for "enlightened" political discourse, but one cannot deny that democratic pluralism is alive and well in such instances. Furthermore, the wise fools of new political television offer critiques of power rarely entertained in traditional political talk forums. In short, although the inside-the-beltway thinking found on pundit talk shows still dominates political talk on television (and indeed, has even proliferated thanks to cable news channels), new political television creates an alternative public space (to paraphrase one audience member) "for those not served by" the Tim Russerts, Tucker Carlsons, and Colin Powells of the world.

Affinity

Democratic life, Dahlgren contends, must be sustained by a civic culture
that supports some minimal sense of commonality despite all of the differences that exist in heterogeneous societies. Two aspects of new political television, I argue, help construct and maintain such affinity. The first is the humor that is central to each program's meaning. In a decade in which
ideological polarizations have intensified and in which political rhetoric has
grown increasingly coarse and harsh, the use of humor as a means of molli-
fying such tendencies is vitally important. As Charles Schutz argues, "Comic
rationality is nondogmatic, [and] in its negative response to political excess it
serves to restore equilibrium to politics." Furthermore, he argues, "The successful reception of the [political] humor depends on its audience's agreement on the standard. Then comic rationality reminds of common values; it
does not declare revolutionary standard of politics."[13] In an era replete with
cultural struggles—such as a morally questionable president engaging in
sexual liaisons in the White House followed by another president operating
by the dictates of Christian fundamentalism—the presence and usage of humor in political discussions can help restrain, in such ideologically driven
battles, the tendency for "adversaries" to be seen as "enemies," as Murray
Edelman warns us.[14] The most notable example of this in new political
television is Jon Stewart's contention that his ability to criticize the Bush administration's war on Iraq without being branded a "traitor" is largely the
product of his critiques' humorous packaging (and the audiences' expectations of such).

The second area of commonality central to new political television is that
viewers are able to witness their ideas, voices, and/or concerns being represented in the public arena. This may at first seem counterintuitive due to the
presence of celebrity hosts and guests. Yet I contend that when viewers feel
that public life does not include them in these ways, it becomes quite easy
to shunt aside one's necessary relationship to the community and the "common good." If a citizen believes that his or her thoughts and ideas matter,
however, that citizen is more likely to invest in the common endeavors of
public life. In his study of audiences of the televised Iran-Contra hearings,
Thelen found that viewers became quite active and animated when they
found public voices that in some way represented their thoughts and feelings in the debates. As he notes, "By defending their values at the hearings,
their champion encouraged citizens to feel connected once again to each
other and to government. . . . The thrill of hearing their thoughts come
through the voice of a defender . . . was the thrill of renewed confidence in
the community."[15] Similarly, in the examination of audiences for *Politically
Incorrect*, we see how some viewers found no affinity with political talk
show pundits, the issues the pundits discussed, or the ways in which they

discussed them. Viewers instead expressed their belief that Maher or other celebrities who appeared on the program were more representative because they were also nonexperts who tended to think in politically similar ways and enunciate their thoughts and feelings in a similar language, and hence were just as valid arbiters of political reality as the so-called experts. The paradox, of course, is that celebrities are seen as being "closer" to the people than journalists, largely because journalist/pundits have erected barriers to discursive participation through their particular epistemology, language, and claims to expertise.

Identities

As Dahlgren notes, democracy needs for people to see themselves, in some way, as "citizens" (despite the fact that the word itself seemingly retains little value in today's society, as the epigraph suggests). With the crisis of legitimacy that western governments are experiencing, the need for civic culture to support such personal identification with democratic practices seems ever more pressing. Dahlgren is not, however, emphasizing overt nationalism or even an enhanced patriotism. Rather, of the many forms of identity that individuals maintain in late modern society (for instance, an individual's identity as a student, gay man, African American, and jazz musician, all held and balanced simultaneously), one aspect of that composite self should include that of "citizen." The programming I describe recognizes that politics is simply one of many things that viewers identify with and carry around as part of "who" they are. By exploiting the linkage between culture and politics, it invites viewers to resist segregating their citizenship to a place that receives little attention or recognition. And who knows— perhaps even Maher's desire to make politics "cool" will prove successful as a result.

ENTERTAINING POLITICS

The arguments I present are likely to fall on deaf ears if the reader still holds onto the mistaken idea that television's primary role in politics is to educate voters. Television rarely serves that function well. Instead, its strengths are in the circulation of conversations—its role as a political and cultural forum where ideas, issues, events, people, values, and beliefs are entertained in a myriad of ways. Television is a primary means for ritual attendance to our common culture. The broader and more eclectic the conversations found there, the more meaningful its viewers will find it to be. Certainly neither comedians nor pundits have a monopoly on the circulation of inane, naïve, or misguided thinking, or for that matter, the ability to be brilliant, insightful, and prescient on all political matters. But both participate in offering different avenues for political discussion for television viewers, and both provide different types of narratives about politics which viewers can draw upon in making sense of politics. New political television, however, takes such pluralism one step further by integrating culture and politics in ways that can enrich and enliven the processes of a discursively active citizenship. The audiences for new political television themselves have shown that it is in the *process* of public thinking about politics that one's identity as a citizen is largely defined through television.

As the above discussion attests, new political television provides a public space where preconditions of citizenship can be cultivated, displayed, affirmed, and maintained. As such, the entertaining politics offered by new political television is not just a product of popular culture, but also a contributor to the ever-shifting shape and form of our political culture. And in an age when public commitment to a shared democratic future is continually questioned, an enhanced and more vibrant political culture is no small matter.

Appendix: Methodology for Audience Research

VIEWER MAIL

The staff of *Politically Incorrect* granted me access to all letters sent to the program since its move to ABC. Hence, I examined letters dating from February 1997 through March 2000 (the month I visited their studios). I scanned through almost all of the letters, selecting and photocopying ones that I felt were representative of the various types of viewer response the show received. I photocopied approximately ninety-five pieces of mail for in-depth analysis.

INTERVIEWS

Interviews with viewers were conducted on these dates at these locations: KTRK, Houston (6/18/99); WMAR, Baltimore (10/15/99); WSB, Atlanta (11/20/99); and CBS Television City (studios for *Politically Incorrect*), Los Angeles (3/21–22/00). In Houston, Baltimore, and Atlanta, the interview subjects were auditioning to be a "citizen panelist" on *P.I.* In Los Angeles, interviewees were queued outside *P.I.*'s studio to watch a taping of the program.

Interview subjects were asked some or all of the following questions:

1. Do you watch the program? If so, how often?
2. [If program is on too late in the evening] Do you tape the program to watch the following day?
3. Do you enjoy the program? Why?
4. Who in your family watches this show besides yourself?

5. Does the show lead to political discussions or arguments with others who watch in your family?
6. Do you discuss the show with friends or co-workers?
7. Is this an entertaining show? How so?
8. Is this an informative show? How so?
9. What do you think about the guests that appear on the program?
10. Do you watch based on who is appearing that evening?
11. Are there particular guests who frequently appear that you really like/dislike? Why?
12. Does it bother you that few of the guests are political "experts"? What do you think about celebrities discussing politics?
13. What is your opinion of Bill Maher as a host?
14. Do you talk back to the television set during the program?
15. Do you ever get mad or frustrated enough with the show to turn it off? Why?
16. Do you think this program is good or bad for American democracy?
17. Do you listen to talk radio?
18. Do you read a daily newspaper? Do you read letters to the editor?
19. Do you watch pundit/Sunday morning talk shows? Why? How do they compare with *P.I.*?
20. Do you participate in political discussion sites or groups on the Internet?
21. How would you characterize your current attitudes toward politics (in general)?
22. Do you identify with a single political party? Which one?

ONLINE DISCUSSIONS

Postings to the Usenet News site dedicated to *P.I.*, alt.tv.pol-incorrect, were examined for the following months. Listed are the number of postings that occurred during that period, as well as the major event (if any) that corresponded with that period:

February 1–March 1, 1997: Newsgroup is formed; Program moves to ABC network.
20 postings.

February 1–March 1, 1998: News of the Clinton-Lewinsky affair surfaces in the media.
329 postings.

August 1–September 1, 1998: Clinton admits affair and testifies before a grand jury.
337 postings.

February 1–March 1, 1999: [No major events of note]
2,870 postings.

February 1–March 1, 2000: Presidential primaries.
1,510 postings.

February 1–March 1, 2001: Bush inauguration two week's earlier; contested election results.
2,900 postings.

September 11–October 11, 2001: Terrorist attacks; Maher makes "controversial" comments.
7,840 postings.

February 1–March 30, 2002: Announcement made of show's imminent cancellation.
3,900 postings.

February 1–March 1, 2003: *Real Time with Bill Maher* premiers on HBO.
1,030 postings.

Between February 1, 1997, and February 1, 2004, the newsgroup has received approximately 98,000 postings. ABC began hosting a similar discussion forum on its website dedicated to *P.I.* in 2000, but no data was collected from that forum (which has since been removed).

Bill Maher began hosting a discussion forum (boards.billmaher.com) on his personal website, BillMaher.com, on May 23, 2000. As of January 5, 2004, the site had received approximately 259,319 postings—substantially more than the Usenet site. I can only surmise that the greater number of postings is related to broader knowledge of and easier access to the World Wide Web than to Usenet. Because Maher's discussion boards also allow for better data gathering, we can also note that the larger numbers are partially attributable to the enormous number of postings by single individuals. Approximately 2,532 users are registered to use this moderated site, yet only 52 people account for approximately 68 percent of the postings (with 30 percent of the postings made by just 8 people). In other words, there is a small number of people who are very heavy users of the site. Unfortunately, no similar data are available for the Usenet site. My general observations, however, suggest that although there are frequent users who post more than others in Usenet (the "regulars"), there is nowhere near this level of domination of discussion by such few individuals.

Notes

CHAPTER 1

1. Interestingly enough, Rush Limbaugh was not among those who attacked Maher. Instead, he actually defended Maher by saying, "This was, in my mind, one of the few things Bill Maher has ever said that's correct. In a way, he was right." Of course, since Maher's comments also amounted to a critique of President Clinton's policies, Limbaugh is less interested here in defending Maher than he is in welcoming another critique of Limbaugh's prime enemy—Bill Clinton. Joe Kovacs, "Rush Limbaugh: Bill Maher 'Was Right,'" *WorldNetDaily.com,* 2001, www.worldnetdaily.com/news/article.asp?ARTICLE_ID=25267 (3 February 2004).

2. Early in the show's run, one reporter wrote, "Bill Maher's *Politically Incorrect* is no more about politics than MTV's *The Real World* is about the real world. And watching *Politically Incorrect* for a discussion of newsworthy events of the day makes no more sense than watching *The Real World* for life lessons." Edith Sorenson, "The Politics of Cool," *Houston Press,* 14 November 1996, theater section. At the end of the show's run, one journalist argued that *P.I.* "belittled and degraded public life for the sake of cheap laughs—and couldn't even get them. . . . If this is what passed for non-professional political debate, why bother with it at all?" Josh Ozersky, "The 'Correct' Thing to Do: Kill the Show," *Newsday,* 27 March 2002.

3. David Wild, "Checking in with Bill Maher," *Rolling Stone,* 25 April 1999, 57.

4. We do know, however, that Clinton returned the favor during Maher's own "scandal." That is, Clinton is reported to have telephoned Maher after Maher's remarks about 9/11 and the ensuing controversy.

5. For a detailed discussion of the impact of competition on the television industry from cable and satellite programmers, see John Thornton Caldwell, *Televisuality: Style, Crisis, and Authority in American Television* (New Brunswick, N.J.: Rutgers University Press, 1995).

6. When queried why he wouldn't talk to reporters during the campaign, candidate Bill Clinton responded, "You know why I can stiff you on the press conferences? Because Larry King liberated me by giving me to the American people directly." (Quoted in Caldwell, *Televisuality*, 256.) King's 1993 book on the election, *On the Line: The New Road to the White House*, lists candidate appearances not only for his program, but also for others within the genre during the 1992 election. See Larry King, with Mark Stencel, *On the Line: The New Road to the White House* (New York: Harcourt Brace and Company). For criticisms of this phenomenon, see Leslie Phillips, "BCP-TV: Bush, Clinton, Perot," *USA Today*, 5 June 1992, 7A; Ed Siegel, "Playing the Softball Alternative," *Boston Globe*, 7 October 1992, 17.

7. The programs, respectively, are *24, Alias, The Agency, The X-Files, The West Wing, First Monday, The Court, Spin City, JAG, AFP: American Fighter Pilot*, and *The American Embassy*. Institutional branches of government, it seems, have finally become a programming subgenre similar to police, lawyers, and hospital dramas.

8. James Poniewozik, "The New Capitol Gang," *Time Magazine*, 1 April 2002, 64.

9. www.americancandidate.com. In Britain, plans were also announced for a similar type of program from the producers of *Pop Idol* and *Big Brother*. Gaby Hinsliff, "Power Idol? Now Politicians Audition for Votes," *The Observer*, 4 January 2004, http://observer.guardian.co.uk/pring/0,3858,4828824-102279,00.html.

10. Governor Howard Dean, Ambassador Carol Mosley Braun, General Wesley Clark, Senator John Edwards, Representative Dennis Kucinich, Senator Bob Graham, Senator Joseph Lieberman, and Reverend Al Sharpton all appeared on one or both of these shows in 2003–2004. In other words, all of the 2004 Democratic presidential candidates appeared except for John Kerry.

11. Jill Abramson, "Hyperreality TV: Political Fact Meets HBO Fiction," *New York Times*, 24 August 2003, AL1, 8.

12. Jennings is quoted as saying, "Stewart is an essential character in the national political landscape. There's nothing mean about him. And in a society where there's so much mean talk, someone who punctures the balloons with grace and elegance and humor is just a blessing." Bruce Fretts, "In Jon We Trust," *Entertainment Weekly*, 31 October 2003, 34.

13. Sheryl Gay Stolberg, "Whoop, Oops and the State of the Political Slip," *New York Times*, 25 January 2004, 4:3.

14. Mark Jurkowitz, "Manhunt Gets Prime-Time Priority on Crime Program," *Boston Globe*, 13 October 2001, A11.

15. Katherine Q. Seelye, "TV Drama, Pentagon-style: A Fictional Terror Tribunal," *New York Times*, 31 March 2002, 1:12.

16. Those countries were Brazil, India, Russia, Italy, Egypt, the United Kingdom, and the United States. Barbara Slavin, "Sex, Politics, but No Rock 'N' Roll: Powell Talks Openly with World Youth," *USA Today*, 15 February 2001, 10B.

17. The producers claim "the series will educate, inform, and inspire the average citizens around the world about America's front-line defense/offense against those who have declared war on the U.S. and our democratic allies." Jeffrey Jolson-Colburn, "Bush Backs New Terrorism TV Series," *E! Online News* www.eonline.com/News/ Items/0,1,13584,00.html (26 February 2004).

18. Neil Postman treats the phenomena as relatively new and the direct product of television. He uses the Lincoln-Douglas debates to argue that citizens had attention

spans that allowed them to attentively listen to the minutiae of politics for hours and days on end (as compared to today's culture shaped by television). Neil Postman, *Amusing Ourselves to Death: Public Discourse in the Age of Show Business* (New York: Penguin Books, 1984), 44–49. Michael Schudson, though, correctly points to the civic culture of mid-nineteenth–century America that treated such debates as entertainment. Michael Schudson, *The Good Citizen: A History of American Civic Life* (New York: The Free Press, 1998), 136–37. See also Charles Schutz, *Political Humor: From Aristophanes to Sam Ervin* (Rutherford, N.J.: Fairleigh Dickinson University Press, 1977), who argues that politics is drama, and hence is part of show business.

19. John Street, *Politics and Popular Culture* (Philadelphia: Temple University Press, 1997.

20. Or when they do, it is survey data such as number of viewing hours, number of television screens per household, channel surfing habits, viewing habits, and so on. In short, they don't speak with viewers to see what the medium actually *means* to them.

21. Susan Pharr and Robert Putnam, eds., *Disaffected Democracies: What's Troubling the Trilateral Countries?* (Princeton, N.J.: Princeton University Press, 2000); Pippa Norris, *The Virtuous Circle: Political Communications in Post-industrial Societies* (Cambridge, U.K.: Cambridge University Press, 2000); Patricia Moy and Michael Pfau, *With Malice toward All? The Media and Public Confidence in Democratic Institutions* (Westport, Conn.: Praeger Press, 2000); Michael Delli Carpini and Scott Keeter, *What Americans Know about Politics and Why It Matters* (New Haven, Conn.: Yale University Press, 1996).

22. Peter Dahlgren, "Media, Citizenship, and Civic Culture," in *Mass Media and Society*, ed. James Curran and Michael Gurevitch (London: Arnold, 2000), 310–28; John Gibbons and Bo Reimer, *The Politics of Postmodernity* (London: Sage, 1999).

23. As discussed at length below, *P.I.* was a twist within the genre of talk television. It differed from the traditional political talk show by offering a comedian as host/star of the show, by offering a comedic monologue of political jokes, and by featuring guests who are not "experts" or insiders to talk about politics. It altered the late-night variety/interview show by focusing on serious *political* issues—something the other shows largely avoid—in a discursively conflictual but also entertaining manner. And it altered the daytime talk show formats by dealing with social issues in specifically political ways, in offering guests the opportunity to talk to each other without having to talk through the host or to invited "experts" but reducing the role of the studio audience to observers.

24. For instance, the Clinton-Lewinsky scandal may produce discussions on issues such as privacy, morality, leadership, individuality and freedom, law and justice, and gender relations. See, Michael Billig, Susan Condor, Derek Edwards, Mike Gane, David Middleton, and Alan Radley, *Ideological Dilemmas: A Social Psychology of Everyday Thinking* (London: Sage, 1988); Michael Billig and Jose M. Sabucedo, "The Rhetorical and Ideological Dimensions of Common Sense," in *The Status of Common Sense in Psychology*, ed. Jurg Siegfried (Norwood, N.J.: Ablex Publishing, 1994).

25. This Usenet News discussion forum, alt.tv.pol-incorrect, has registered approximately 98,000 messages posted since February 1, 1997. ABC ran a similar bulletin board through its website, but it was relatively short-lived (existing for less than two years). Nevertheless, ABC's decision to use the show as an opportunity to direct

viewers to its website is similar to efforts by other television networks described in chapter 3.

26. E. J. Dionne Jr., *Why Americans Hate Politics* (New York: Simon and Schuster, 1991); John Dillin, "American Voters Disgusted, Angry with Politicians," *The Christian Science Monitor,* 17 October 1990, 1.

27. Peter Dahlgren, "Reconfiguring Civic Culture in the New Media Milieu," in *Media and the Restyling of Politics,* ed. John Corner and Dick Pels (London: Sage, 2003), 154.

CHAPTER 2

1. Roderick P. Hart, *Seducing America: How Television Charms the Modern Voter* (New York: Oxford University Press, 1994); Matthew Robert Kerbel, *Remote and Controlled: Media Politics in a Cynical Age,* 2d ed. (Boulder, Colo.: Westview Press, 1999); Jeffrey Scheuer, *The Sound Bite Society: Television and the American Mind* (New York: Four Walls Eight Windows, 1999); Neil Postman, *Amusing Ourselves to Death: Public Discourse in the Age of Show Business* (New York: Penguin Books, 1984), 44–49; Neil Gabler, *Life: The Movie: How Entertainment Conquered Reality* (New York: Knopf, 1998).

2. Robert D. Putnam, "Tuning In, Tuning Out: The Strange Disappearance of Social Capital in America," *PS: Political Science & Politics* (December 1995): 677; Robert Putnam, *Bowling Alone: The Collapse and Revival of American Community* (New York: Simon and Schuster, 2000).

3. Putnam, *Bowling Alone,* 246.

4. His use of the analogy to a crime is even more stark in a 1995 journal article: "I have discovered only one prominent suspect against whom circumstantial evidence can be mounted. . . . This is not the occasion to lay out the full case for the prosecution, nor to review rebuttal evidence for the defense. However, I want to illustrate the sort of evidence that justifies indictment. The culprit is television" (Putnam, "Tuning In, Tuning Out," 677).

5. Pippa Norris, *The Virtuous Circle: Political Communications in Post-industrial Societies* (Cambridge, U.K.: Cambridge University Press, 2000). See also Pippa Norris, "The Impact of Television on Civic Malaise," in *Disaffected Democracies: What's Troubling the Trilateral Countries,* ed. Susan J. Pharr and Robert D. Putnam (Princeton, N.J.: Princeton University Press, 2000), 231–51. Here Norris contends that it matters what you watch and how much you watch.

6. Doris A. Graber, *Processing Politics: Learning from Television in the Internet Age* (Chicago: University of Chicago Press, 2001).

7. Michael Schudson, *The Good Citizen: A History of American Civic Life* (New York: The Free Press, 1998), 136–37.

8. Jay G. Blumler and Michael Gurevitch, "Rethinking the Study of Political Communication," in *Mass Media and Society,* 3d ed., ed. James Curran and Michael Gurevitch (New York: Oxford University Press, 2000), 166; Lawrence Grossberg, *We Gotta Get Out of This Place: Popular Conservatism and Postmodern Culture* (New York: Routledge, 1992), 15.

9. H. Bausinger, "Media, Technology and Daily Life," *Media, Culture and Society* 6 (1984): 343–51.

10. James W. Carey, *Communication as Culture: Essays on Media and Society* (Boston: Unwin Hyman, 1989).

11. Peter Dahlgren, "The Transformation of Democracy?" in *New Media and Politics,* ed. Barrie Axford and Richard Huggins (London: Sage, 2001), 85.

12. Dahlgren, "The Transformation of Democracy?" 85.

13. John Street, *Politics & Popular Culture* (Philadelphia: Temple University Press, 1997), 60.

14. Street, *Politics & Popular Culture,* 21.

15. Street, *Politics & Popular Culture,* 57–58.

16. Kevin Barnhurst, "Politics in the Fine Meshes: Young Citizens, Power and Media," *Media Culture & Society* 20 (1998): 212.

17. Schudson, *Good Citizen,* 197.

18. Schudson, *Good Citizen,* 9.

19. Schudson, *Good Citizen,* 310–11.

20. Bausinger, "Media, Technology, and Daily Life"; James Lull, ed., *World Families Watch Television* (Newbury Park, Calif.: Sage, 1988); Roger Silverstone and Eric Hirsch, eds., *Consuming Technologies: Media and Information in Domestic Spaces* (New York: Routledge, 1992); Roger Silverstone, *Television and Everyday Life* (New York: Routledge, 1994); Shaun Moores, *Satellite Television and Everyday Life: Articulating Technology* (London: University of Luton Press, 1996).

21. This summary is provided by Ian Ang, "The Nature of the Audience," in *Questioning the Media: A Critical Introduction,* ed. John Downing, Ali Mohammadi, and Annabelle Sreberny-Mohammadi (Thousand Oaks, Calif.: Sage, 1995), 217.

22. The term *lifestyle politics* has also been used but is often a part of the larger conception of postmodern political practice. See Peter Dahlgren, "Media, Citizenship and Civic Culture," in *Mass Media and Society,* ed. Curran and Gurevitch, 310–28; John Gibbons and Bo Reimer, *The Politics of Postmodernity* (London: Sage, 1999); Barrie Axford, "The Transformation of Politics or Anti-Politics," in *New Media and Politics,* ed. Axford and Huggins, 22–25.

23. Dahlgren, "Media, Citizenship," 312.

24. Dahlgren, "Media, Citizenship," 318.

25. Margaret Scammell, "Citizen Consumers: Towards a New Marketing of Politics?" in *Media and the Restyling of Politics,* ed. John Corner and Dick Pels (London: Sage, 2003), 117–36.

26. Dahlgren, "Media, Citizenship," 312.

27. Gibbons and Reimer, *Politics of Postmodernity,* 113.

28. Blumler and Gurevitch, "Rethinking," 163–64.

29. Blumler and Gurevitch, "Rethinking," 162.

30. Blumler and Gurevitch, "Rethinking," 167.

31. Barnhurst, "Fine Meshes," 201–218.

32. Barnhurst, "Fine Meshes," 216.

33. Barnhurst, "Fine Meshes," 216.

34. Barnhurst, "Fine Meshes," 216.

35. Barnhurst, "Fine Meshes," 209.

36. Michael X. Delli Carpini and Bruce A. Williams, "Constructing Public Opinion: The Uses of Fictional and Nonfictional Television in Conversations about the Environment," in *The Psychology of Political Communication,* ed. Ann N. Crigler (Ann Arbor: University of Michigan Press, 1996), 160.

37. Delli Carpini and Williams, "Constructing Public Opinion," 161–62.

38. Delli Carpini and Williams, "Constructing Public Opinion," 153.

39. Delli Carpini and Williams, "Constructing Public Opinion," 173.

40. Ron Lembo, *Thinking through Television* (Cambridge, U.K.: Cambridge University Press, 2000), 113.

41. Lembo, *Thinking through Television,* 111–12.

42. Lembo, *Thinking through Television,* 170.

43. Lembo, *Thinking through Television,* 190–91.

44. Lembo, *Thinking through Television,* 169.

45. Lembo, *Thinking through Television,* 234.

46. David Thelen, *Becoming Citizens in the Age of Television* (Chicago: University of Chicago Press, 1996).

47. Thelen, *Becoming Citizens,* 5.

48. Thelen reports that over one-quarter of all letters sent to Congressman Lee Hamilton were signed by both a husband and a wife. Thelen, *Becoming Citizens,* 102.

49. Thelen, *Becoming Citizens,* 47.

50. Thelen, *Becoming Citizens,* 105.

51. Thelen, *Becoming Citizens,* 23.

52. Thelen, *Becoming Citizens,* 67.

53. Thelen, *Becoming Citizens,* 75–77.

54. Thelen, *Becoming Citizens,* 9.

55. Sonia Livingstone and Peter Lunt, *Talk on Television: Audience Participation and Public Debate* (London: Routledge, 1994), 29.

56. Thelen, *Becoming Citizens,* 2.

57. The military metaphor is Thelen's as he describes how citizens moved from "the dismissive role of monitor to the activist role of citizen-soldier." Thelen, *Becoming Citizens,* 46.

58. Jerome Bruner, *Acts of Meaning* (Cambridge, Mass.: Harvard University Press, 1990), 34 (emphasis added).

59. Bruner, *Acts of Meaning,* 95.

60. Bruner uses the term "folk psychology," although he allows for the more common term "common sense." Bruner, *Acts of Meaning,* 34–35. See also Antonio Gramsci, *An Antonio Gramsci Reader,* ed. David Forgacs (New York: Schocken Books, 1988); Clifford Geertz, "Common Sense as a Cultural System," *Antioch Review* 33 (Spring): 5–26; Michael Billig and Jose M. Sabucedo, "The Rhetorical and Ideological Dimensions of Common Sense," in *The Status of Common Sense in Psychology,* ed. Jurg Siegfried (Norwood, N.J.: Ablex Publishing, 1994); Serge Moscovici, "The Phenomenon of Social Representations," in *Social Representations,* ed. R. M. Farr and Serge Moscovici (Cambridge, U.K.: Cambridge University Press, 1984); Jeffrey P. Jones, "Rethinking Hegemonic Common Sense in Media Studies," in *Creating Sense: Texts and Realities,* ed. D. Allison (Singapore: National University of Singapore, 1999), 61–82.

61. Horace Newcomb and Paul M. Hirsch, "Television as a Cultural Forum," in *Television: The Critical View,* 4th ed., ed. Horace Newcomb (New York: Oxford University Press, 1987).

62. Geertz, "Common Sense," 8.

63. Bruner, *Acts of Meaning*, 35.

64. Bruner, *Acts of Meaning*, 42. Geertz, too, argues that common sense cannot be found "by cataloguing its content, which is widely heterogeneous. . . . One cannot do so, either, by sketching out some logical structure it always takes, for there is none. And one cannot do so by summing up the substantive conclusions it always draws, for there are, too, none of those" (Geertz, "Common Sense," 25). Instead, he suggests we look to the "tone," "temper," and "style" of common sense if we wish to uncover it.

65. Bruner, *Acts of Meaning*, 35.

66. For instance, audiences who were shown both a news report and a docudrama about the effects of toxic pollution on children were equally moved and convinced enough to foreground concerns about children in their discussions, despite the potentially fictional aspects of the docudrama. Delli Carpini and Williams, "Constructing Public Opinion," 166.

67. Hegemony theory recognizes the spaces for contestation and opposition, of course. But again, the point here is not capitalist dominance but the ways that pluralist thinking occurs within the limitations of liberal capitalist societies.

68. Bruner, *Acts of Meaning*, 95.

69. John Ellis, "Television as Working Through," in *Television and Common Knowledge,* ed. Jostein Gripsrud (London: Routledge, 1999), 55.

70. Ellis, "Working Through," 55.

71. Newcomb and Hirsch, "Television as a Cultural Forum," 459.

72. Newcomb and Hirsch go on to say, in an important caveat, that television "is an effective pluralistic forum only insofar as American political pluralism is or can be." Newcomb and Hirsch, "Television as a Cultural Forum," 461.

73. Michael Billig, Susan Condor, Derek Edwards, Mike Gane, David Middleton, and Alan Radley, *Ideological Dilemmas: A Social Psychology of Everyday Thinking* (London: Sage, 1988); Michael Billig, *Ideology and Opinions: Studies in Rhetorical Psychology* (London: Sage, 1991); Billig and Sabucedo, "Rhetorical and Ideological Dimensions."

74. Billig, *Ideology and Opinions,* 71.

75. Ellis, "Working-Through," 57–58.

76. Livingstone and Lunt, *Talk on Television*; Paolo Carpignano, Robin Anderson, Stanley Aronowitz, and William DiFazio, "Chatter in the Age of Electronic Reproduction: Talk Television and the 'Public Mind,'" in *The Phantom Public Sphere*, ed. Bruce Robbins (Minneapolis: University of Minnesota Press, 1993).

77. Carpignano et al., "Chatter," 96.

78. Thelen, *Becoming Citizens*, 13–14. Thelen reports that "between 1934 and 1981 the number of communications to Congress rose from an estimated 6 to 9 million pieces in the first Roosevelt Congress to an estimated 92.5 million pieces in the first Reagan Congress. Congress received, on average, a communication from 5 percent of all Americans in 1934 and from 25 percent of Americans in 1981." Thelen, *Becoming Citizens*, 23. See also Roderick P. Hart, "Citizen Discourse and Political Participation: A Survey," in *Mediated Politics: Communication in the Future of Democracy,* ed. W. Lance Bennett and Robert M. Entman (Cambridge, U.K.: Cambridge University Press, 2001), 407–32.

79. Carpignano et al., "Chatter," 119. For me, this is a declaration that is quite similar to arguments made by Carey and Dewey. See Carey, *Communication as Culture*, and John Dewey, *The Public and Its Problems* (Athens, Ohio: Ohio University Press, 1954).

80. Street, *Politics & Popular Culture*, 9. See also Grossberg, *We Gotta Get Out of This Place*; Simon Frith, *Music for Pleasure* (Cambridge, Mass.: Polity Press, 1988), 123.

81. Bruner, *Acts of Meaning*, 52.

82. Dahlgren, "Media, Citizenship," 323.

NOTES TO CHAPTER 3

1. See Schudson's argument about periods of civic culture in American history, including the Informed Citizen model that grew out of the Progressive Era reforms of the early twentieth century and that, in many ways, we still operate under today. Michael Schudson, *The Good Citizen: A History of American Civic Life* (New York: The Free Press, 1998).

2. Eric Alterman, *Sound and Fury: The Making of the Punditocracy* (Ithaca, N.Y.: Cornell University Press, 1999); Alan Hirsch, *Talking Heads: Political Talk Shows and Their Star Pundits* (New York: St. Martin's Press, 1991). Alterman provides an interesting discussion of the history of punditry on television dating back to Walter Lippmann's writings in newspapers. See also Bernard Timberg, *Television Talk: A History of the TV Talk Show* (Austin: University of Texas Press, 2002).

3. Indeed, Nielsen ratings for the Sunday morning talk shows suggest that over ten million audience members still tune in to these programs. For instance, average audience ratings for the Sunday morning pundit talk shows for the 2001–2002 television season are: *Meet the Press* (4.5 million); *Face the Nation* (2.9 million); *This Week* (3.0 million) (A. C. Nielsen Company).

4. Included in this discussion is political talk programming that appeared with the first generation of cable programming; that is, on CNN during the 1980s. Although appearing on cable, this approach to political talk was very similar to that found on public television and the networks, with only slight modifications that led to an increase in spectacle performances. It was not until the 1990s when numerous new cable channels began appearing (what I call the second generation of cable programming) that pundit political talk would be both challenged by other forms of talk and expanded upon using similar generic features.

5. See Rick Ball, *Meet the Press: Fifty Years of History in the Making* (New York: McGraw-Hill, 1998).

6. Dan Nimmo and James E. Combs, *The Political Pundits* (New York: Praeger, 1992), 6.

7. Nimmo and Combs, *Political Pundits*, 8.

8. William F. Buckley Jr., *On The Firing Line* (New York: Random House, 1989).

9. Hirsch, *Talking Heads,* 13.

10. For reasons that have been hard to identify, liberals have never been successful as hosts of pundit programming. MSNBC tried to counterprogram against Fox's conservatism by making Phil Donahue their lead prime time host in 2002, but his show was cancelled just as America was preparing to invade Iraq (a war that Donahue opposed) in 2003. Allison Romano, "Liberal, and Proud of It," *Broadcasting & Cable* (15 July 2002): 12.

11. The ever-changing lineup has included shows such as *Hardball with Chris Matthews, Hannity and Colmes, The Drudge Report, Equal Time, Politics Today, The Beltway Boys, Special Report with Brit Hume, Imus in the Morning, Scarborough Country,* and the old talk show stalwarts, *Geraldo* and *Donahue,* which were reformatted for cable. See Alterman, *Sound and Fury,* for a more thorough accounting of these shows.

12. Hirsch, *Talking Heads*; Alterman, *Sound and Fury.*

13. Pat Buchanan was Richard Nixon's speechwriter and also worked in the Reagan administration; John McLaughlin was personal friends with Reagan, and his wife was appointed secretary of labor by Reagan; Chris Matthews worked for Jimmy Carter; George Will was close personal friends with Ronald and Nancy Reagan, and his wife worked in the Reagan White House and was also a manager in Bob Dole's 1996 presidential bid.

14. The case of television pundit and columnist Robert Novak's "outing" of an undercover CIA agent at the behest of "unnamed" Bush administration officials in 2003 is perhaps the most glaring recent example of this.

15. Alicia Mundy, "Showtime in the Capitol," *MediaWeek* 6 (15 January 1996): 20–22.

16. Hirsch, *Talking Heads,* 181.

17. Nimmo and Combs, *Political Pundits,* 43–44.

18. As Alan Hirsch warns, since success breeds imitation, most commentators "now travel the celebrity path" and probably will not heed the warning of celebrity pundit Jack Germond: "Celebrity impinging on your ability to do your job well is a genuinely serious concern and it requires people to be damned careful." Hirsch, *Talking Heads,* 182–83.

19. As Wayne Munson asks, "Is it 'talk' or 'show'? Conversation or spectacle? Both? Neither?" Wayne Munson, *All Talk: The Talkshow in Media Culture* (Philadelphia: Temple University Press, 1993), 15.

20. Although one might argue that Jimmy Carter, with his outsider positioning and homespun persona, began the current trend, it was Reagan who essentially ran against the job he wanted to occupy. He took anti-politics to a new level, one we are still living through today.

21. Or as Robert Dallek puts it, Reagan's "pronouncements on everything from abortion to welfare proved to be more symbolic than substantive" proving his "extraordinary mastery of public symbols that resonated so effectively with millions of Americans." His "public goals satisf(ied) psychological needs as much as material ends." Robert Dallek, *Ronald Reagan: The Politics of Symbolism* (Cambridge, Mass.: Harvard University Press, 1999), viii, xiv, xxiv.

22. See Allen D. Hertzke, *Echoes of Discontent: Jesse Jackson, Pat Robertson, and the Resurgence of Populism* (Washington, D.C.: Congressional Quarterly Press, 1993).

23. Michael Oreskes, "As Problems Fester, Voters Send Pink Slips," *New York Times,* 23 September 1990, 4:5; John Dillin, "American Voters Disgusted, Angry with Politicians," *The Christian Science Monitor,* 17 October 1990, 1.

24. For analyses of Perot as a "populist," see Dennis Westlind, *The Politics of Popular Identity* (Lund, Sweden: Lund University Press, 1996); Linda Schulte-Sasse, "Meet Ross Perot: The Lasting Legacy of Capraesque Populism," *Cultural Critique* (Fall 1993): 91–119.

25. See Larry King, with Mark Stencel, *On the Line: The New Road to the White House* (New York: Harcourt Brace and Company).

26. Maureen Dowd, "Populist Media Forums and the Campaign of '92," *New York Times*, 3 November 1992, A14.

27. Harvey Mansfield, "Newt, Take Note: Populism Poses Its Own Dangers," *Wall Street Journal*, 1 November 1994, A1. For a more general assessment of the 1990s as a "populist" political era, see Sean Wilentz, "Populism Redux," *Dissent* 42 (Spring 1995): 149–53; Paul Piccone and Gary Ulmen, "Populism and the New Politics," *Telos* 103 (Spring 1995): 3–8. For commentary on how the populist overtones of the decade don't live up to the "true" definition of "populism," see Molly Ivins, "Just What Is a Populist, Anyway?" *Austin-American Statesman*, 6 February 1996, A9; Michael Kazin, *The Populist Persuasion: An American History* (New York: Basic Books, 1995).

28. See E. J. Dionne Jr., *Why Americans Hate Politics* (New York: Simon and Schuster, 1991); Seymour Lipset and William Schneider, *The Confidence Gap*, 2d ed. (Baltimore: Johns Hopkins University Press, 1987); Susan Pharr and Robert Putnam, eds., *Disaffected Democracies: What's Troubling the Trilateral Countries?* (Princeton: Princeton University Press, 2000); Christopher Lasch, *The Revolt of the Elites and the Betrayal of Democracy* (New York: W. W. Norton and Company, 1995).

29. Albert Gore, *Common Sense Government: Works Better and Costs Less* (New York: Random House, 1995); Philip Howard, *The Death of Common Sense: How Law Is Suffocating America* (New York: Random House, 1994).

30. See "Bad Justice," editorial, *New York Times*, 21 February 1995, A18; Joe Klein, "The Birth of Common Sense: Bill Clinton Outflanks the Republicans on Regulatory Reform," *Newsweek* 125, 27 March 1995, 31.

31. David Marshall, *Celebrity and Power: Fame in Contemporary Culture* (Minneapolis: University of Minnesota Press, 1997).

32. In the 1992 presidential election, Thomas Patterson compared ten questions asked of candidates by citizens with ten questions asked by journalists in campaign debates and press conferences. One of the conclusions he arrives at is that the press conducts its business in a language that is foreign to the concerns of the citizenry. Thomas Patterson, *Out of Order* (New York: Random House, 1993), 55–56.

33. For instance, John Thornton Caldwell quotes a former adviser to the FCC and the White House and board member of the National Association of Broadcasters as saying, "'There will be a plethora of niche [cable] networks responsive to the needs of specific cultural groups within our multicultural society.' In addition to providing 'ownership opportunities' for minorities, 'these culturally specific niche networks will require management teams that are sensitive and responsive to the needs of their target audience.'" John Thornton Caldwell, *Televisuality: Style, Crisis, and Authority in American Television* (New Brunswick, N.J.: Rutgers University Press, 1995), 257.

34. A representative work of this utopianism is Howard Rheingold, *Virtual Community: Homesteading on the Electronic Frontier* (New York: Simon and Schuster, 1991). For a critical assessment of the false illusions presented by communication technologies, see Theodore Roszak, *The Cult of Information* (Berkeley: University of California Press, 1994). The polarizations of utopianism and distopianism became so pronounced by the end of the decade that a group of "middle-of-the-roaders" went so far as to advance what they call a "technorealism" movement, a manifesto grounded in "reality" that should ground us all. See Andrew Shapiro, "Technorealism: Get Real!" *The Nation* 266, 6 April 1998, 19–20.

35. Todd Gitlin, *The Twilight of Common Dreams: Why America Is Wracked by Culture Wars* (New York: Metropolitan Books, 1995).

36. The impeachment and trial of President Clinton were examples of the culture wars for *New York Times* columnist Frank Rich. He argues, "The cultural fault lines of the moment are those of 30 years ago, and potentially just as explosive. The right-wing rage once aimed at long-haired, draft-dodging, sexually wanton hippies (a caricature of the left even then) is now aimed at Bill Clinton, whose opportunistic, split-the-difference politics is actually closer to the old mainstream G.O.P. than to the 60's left but who nonetheless has become the right's piñata for all it hates about the Vietnam era's social and sexual revolutions." Frank Rich, "Let It Bleed," *New York Times,* 19 December 1998, A15.

37. For a representative example of scholarly works focusing on these types of talk shows, see Munson, *All Talk;* Jane M. Shattuc, *The Talking Cure: TV Talk Shows and Women* (New York: Routledge, 1997); Timberg, *Television Talk;* Andrew Tolson, "Televised Chat and the Synthetic Personality," in *Broadcast Talk,* ed. Paddy Scannell (London: Sage, 1991), among others.

38. See Sonia Livingstone and Peter Lunt, *Talk on Television: Audience Participation and Public Debate* (London: Routledge, 1994); Paolo Carpignano, Robin Anderson, Stanley Aronowitz, and William DiFazio, "Chatter in the Age of Electronic Reproduction: Talk Television and the 'Public Mind,'" in *The Phantom Public Sphere,* ed. Bruce Robbins (Minneapolis: University of Minnesota Press, 1993).

39. Doug McIntyre, a writer and guest on *Politically Incorrect,* once called these shows "human cockfighting." See Joshua Gamson, *Freaks Talk Back: Tabloid Talk Shows and Sexual Nonconformity* (Chicago: University of Chicago Press, 1998); Laura Grindstaff, *The Money Shot: Trash, Class, and the Making of TV Talk Shows* (Chicago: University of Chicago Press, 2002); Kevin Glynn, *Tabloid Culture: Trash Taste, Popular Power, and the Transformation of American Television* (Durham, N.C.: Duke University Press, 2000).

40. See Peter Laufer, *Inside Talk Radio: America's Voice or Just Hot Air* (New York: Carol Publishing Group, 1995), and Howard Kurtz, *Hot Air: All Talk, All the Time* (New York: Times Books, 1996), for accounts of talk radio's success and the personalities that drove it. For an analysis of talk radio's supposed influence on political behavior, see David C. Barker, *Rushed to Judgment: Talk Radio, Persuasion, and American Political Behavior* (New York: Columbia University Press, 2002).

41. Caldwell, *Televisuality,* 292.

42. Caldwell, *Televisuality,* 4.

43. Caldwell, *Televisuality,* 251.

44. Caldwell, *Televisuality,* 256.

45. Carpignano et al., "Chatter."

46. Carpignano et al., "Chatter," 116–17.

47. Livingstone and Lunt, *Talk on Television,* 102.

48. Livingstone and Lunt, *Talk on Television,* 178. They argue that this is occurring in British televised drama, documentary, and current affairs programming.

49. Tolson, "Televised Chat," 198.

50. Munson, *All Talk,* 6.

51. Munson, *All Talk,* 15.

52. Tolson, "Televised Chat," 198.

53. This section is based upon a more complete discussion found in Jeffrey P. Jones, "Vox Populi as Cable Programming Strategy," *Journal of Popular Film & Television* 31 (Spring 2003): 18–28.

54. John Dempsey, "Newest Cable Act Child: America's Talking," *Daily Variety,* 27 June 1994, 32.

55. Rich Brown, "America's Talking Cable Channel Takes Off," *Broadcasting & Cable* 124 (4 July 1994): 16.

56. Scott Williams, "America's Talking–The All-Talk Cable Network–Bows on July 4th," *Associated Press,* 1 July 1994.

57. Dennis Wharton, "Debuting Cable/Sat Net Tuned to the Right," *Daily Variety,* 29 November 1993, 4.

58. Linda Moss, "'C-SPAN with Attitude' Will Launch December 6," *Multichannel News* 14, 15 November 1993, 14.

59. Phil Kloer, "CNN Interactive Program Will Raise Back Talk to a New Level," *Atlanta Journal and Constitution,* 11 July 1994, A1.

60. Marc Rice, "People, Faxes, Computers Debate the Issues on New CNN Program," *The Associated Press,* 22 August 1994.

61. Bob Sokolsky, "'TalkBack Live' Touts Town Meeting Format," *The Press-Enterprise* (Riverside, Calif.), 5 August 1994, B5.

62. Rice, "People, Faxes."

63. CNN cancelled *TalkBack* as America geared up for war on Iraq in 2003. CNN noted the decision for change was based on a "heightened news environment." Yet as America debated the need to go to war when most of its allies did not support such a decision, CNN obviously was uninterested in hearing what viewers and audience members had to say about such a decision. The show averaged between 600,000–700,000 viewers (many over 55 years old). Caroline Wilbert, "CNN Pulls Plug on Afternoon 'TalkBack,'" *Atlanta Journal-Constitution,* 8 March 2003, 1E.

64. As discussed in chapter 7.

65. Dan Trigoboff, "3 Nets: News, Views, Confused," *Broadcasting & Cable,* 11 March 2002, 10.

66. That is to say, MSNBC moved from news to almost all talk programming in the summer of 2002. It eventually fired liberal talk host Phil Donahue and tried to imitate Fox News by hiring ultra-conservative hosts such as former Republican Congressman Joe Scarborough. Douglas Quenqua, "MSBNC Shifts Focus from Reporting to Commentary," *PR Week* (10 June 2002): 3.

67. For the typical weekday programming schedule in September 2002, for instance, CNN aired talk shows from 2:00 P.M. to 5:00 A.M. (EST), Fox aired talk from 4:00 P.M. to 6:00 A.M., and MSNBC aired news only from 9:00 A.M.–12:00 P.M. Tim Rutten, "Talk is Cheap, or at Least Cheaper Than Newscasts," *Los Angeles Times* (7 June 2002): D2.

68. Nimmo and Combs conclude that talk show punditry is persistent in American television because it offers the nation a form of "symbolic healing," providing viewers a therapeutic medicine of symbols and myths in confusing and complex times. Nimmo and Combs, *Political Pundits,* 167–69. The continued prominence of "expert" voices in cable talk programming perhaps reflects this theoretical observation.

69. *Politically Incorrect* began on Comedy Central in 1993, followed by *Dennis Miller Live* on HBO in 1994. *The Daily Show* did not appear until 1996, and Jon Stewart did not fill the "anchor" chair until 1999.

70. *Nightline* on ABC also airs at this time, but with it consistently running third in the ratings, I don't consider it a "dominant" type.

71. Although the first two were cancelled after nine years, both Maher and Miller have reappeared in 2003-2004 with new shows on cable in a similar vein—*Real Time with Bill Maher* (HBO) and *Dennis Miller* (CNBC).

72. Lawrence Christon, "Not For the Humor-Disabled: A Talk Show with No Holds Barred," *The Record,* 7 September 1993, D08.

73. Wayne Walley, "NCTA Surfer; Clashing Opinions Fuel 'Incorrect,'" *Electronic Media,* 8 May 1995, 39.

74. An exception to that claim might be *The Late Late Show* featuring Tom Snyder or *Later with Bob Costas,* but in both instances, those shows were interview programs simply conducted in an informal manner (not to mention the very late time slot in which they appeared).

75. Terry Kelleher, "Comedy Central's Cocktail Party," *Newsday,* 25 July 1993, 3.

76. Jack Tapper, "The Salon Interview: Bill Maher," *Salon.com,* 11 December 2002, http://archive.salon.com/people/interview/2002/12/11/maher/print.html.

77. Tapper, "The Salon Interview."

78. Mary Voelz Chandler, "Dennis Miller Gets the Last Laugh," *Rocky Mountain News,* 16 September 1994, 3D.

79. Ray Richmond, "Saturday Night Live: Dennis Miller Gears Up for HBO," *Los Angeles Times Weekend Magazine,* 26 March 1993, 20.

80. John McKay, "Miller Rants Come to Canadian TV," *The Ottawa Citizen,* 18 January 1999, C11.

81. Terry Morrow, "'The Daily Show' Mocks Presentation of TV News," *Pittsburgh Post-Gazette,* 12 June 2000, D5.

82. David Folkenflik, "Humorists Enter the War Zone," *Baltimore Sun,* 20 April 2003, 2F.

83. Bruce Fretts, "In Jon We Trust," *Entertainment Weekly,* 31 October 2003, 30–35.

84. Rodney Buxton, "The Late-Night Talk Show: Humor in Fringe Television," *The Southern Speech Communication Journal* 52 (Summer 1987): 377–89.

85. Buxton, "The Late-Night Talk Show."

86. Phil Rosenthal, "Worker Bee Dennis Miller Has Jokes, Not Answers," *Tampa Tribune, Florida Television,* 12 May 1996, 7.

87. Stewart explains that the inclusion of celebrities, as opposed to more high-powered political guests, is a product of the show's understaffing; that is, it's easier to do celebrity interviews. "Honestly, one of the reasons that it's there is we just can't write that much. We've tried to make the interview segment somewhat different from what you might see on other [late night shows]. But the truth is, it is what it is and we do the best we can with it. It's not part of the show that any of us necessarily go, 'I can't wait to get hold of that interview segment and make it happen.'" Aaron Wherry, "News and Laughs at 11," *National Post,* 5 October 2002.

88. See audience data in chapter 8.

89. *Real Time with Bill Maher,* HBO broadcast, 27 February 2004.

90. Josh Ozersky, "The 'Correct' Thing to Do: Kill the Show," *Newsday,* 27 March 2002.

91. Munson, *All Talk*, 111.

92. Scott Carter, interview by Jeffrey P. Jones, 5 February and 29 March 1999.

93. Indeed, perhaps political television is unique in that it invites certain viewers to watch the show because they explicitly dislike or disagree with certain persons or opinions found there but enjoy the political engagement or rhetorical challenge nonetheless.

94. Don Aucoin, "In the Midnight Hours; A New Generation of Hosts Livens Up the Late Shows," *Boston Globe*, 23 May 1999, N1.

95. Robert Laurence, "Room for Rant; From Stand-up to Sports, Dennis Miller's Trademark Diatribes Belie a Man Riding the Raves of Success," *San Diego Union-Tribune*, 12 August 2001, F1.

96. Bernard Weinraub, "The 2000 Campaign: The Comedians; Election's Barometer: Barbs of Late-Night TV," *New York Times*, 19 January 2000, A16.

97. Dennis Miller, *Ranting Again* (New York: Doubleday, 1998), 143.

98. Judy Woodruff, "Jon Stewart," *Inside Politics*, CNN, 3 May 2002; see also Jane Ganahl, "'Daily Show' Host Jon Stewart is TV's King of Irony," *San Francisco Chronicle*, 23 April 2002, D1, for another response.

99. According to Maher and *Politically Incorrect*'s producers, as well as my own observations of fan comments in viewer mail and on-line, one of the most frequent questions from the audience was why the show lasted only thirty minutes.

100. Stephen Armstrong, "I Can Scratch the Itch," *The Guardian* (London), 17 March 2003, 8.

101. Aucoin, *Midnight Hours*, N1.

CHAPTER 4

1. Larry King offers a chronological listing of 48 candidate appearances in these "alternative" forums during the 1992 campaign. See Larry King, *On the Line: The New Road to the White House* (New York: Harcourt Brace and Company, 1993).

2. Diane Rehm, "The 'Talk-Show Campaign' Isn't Showbiz: Angry Voters Really Want to Be Heard," *Washington Post*, 25 October 1992, C1; Jeff Greenfield, "TV Talk Shows are Right Spot for Candidates," *Chicago Sun-Times*, 14 June 1992, 41.

3. Ellen Debenport, "Candidates Try to Cut Media Filter," *St. Petersburg Times* (Florida), 11 June 1992, 1A.

4. See also Tom Patterson, *Out of Order* (New York: Random House, 1993).

5. Viacom, owner of Nickelodeon, was essentially attempting to extend its popular *Nick at Nite* format to twenty-four hours on a separate channel. Of course, *Nick at Nite* would compete with this new channel.

6. Dave Andersen, vice president of public affairs for Cox Cable Communications, agreed: "There just isn't a need for two comedy channels." Adam Buckman, "Cable Operators Favor Comedy Services Merger," *Electronic Media*, 16 April 1990, 2. Unless otherwise indicated, all quotes from Scott Carter come from telephone interviews with the author, conducted on 5 February and 29 March 1999.

7. This was an astounding development simply because the two companies were involved in a $2.4 billion antitrust lawsuit brought by Viacom. Nevertheless, both

companies were losing a tremendous amount of money, estimated at $40 million annually. The merged channel would launch with 15 million subscribers. See John Higgins, "Peace at Hand in Comedy Wars," *Multichannel News* 1, 24 December 1990, 1; Sharon Moshavi, "Merger Brings Comic Relief to Cable," *Broadcasting,* 24 December 1990, 26. In 2003, Viacom bought out AOL-Time Warner's 50 percent share for $1.25 billion. David A. Vise, "AOL Time Warner Sheds Comedy Central," *Washington Post,* 23 April 2003, E05.

8. Steven Herbert, "Comedy Central Hopes to Get First Laugh on State of the Union," *Los Angeles Times,* 28 January 1992, F1.

9. Herbert, "Comedy Central Hopes to Get First Laugh," F1.

10. Rick Du Brow, "TV Comedy Channel: Politics and Punch Lines," *Los Angeles Times,* 4 July 1992, F1.

11. For instance, the Democratic Party explicitly recognized the convention as little more than a media variety show in 1992 by designating one evening "Ladies Night at the Democratic National Convention," an intentional effort to "counterprogram" against CBS's broadcast of Major League Baseball's All-Star game. Kit Boss, "Unconventional Coverage Achieves Network Parody," *Seattle Times,* 15 July 1992, A1.

12. Scott Williams, "Not the News: Comedy Central Plans Convention Coverage," *Associated Press,* 27 April 1992.

13. In early 1992, Comedy Central reached 22 million homes; by early 1994, that number had increased to only 31 million homes (half as many subscribers as USA network and TBS).

14. Rich Brown, "Comedy Channel Unveils Laughing Matter," *Broadcasting & Cable* 123 (29 March 1993): 18.

15. For instance, MTV was bringing in a 0.4 rating before *Beavis & Butt-Head* but saw their ratings climb 25 percent with the hit animated series. Richard Katz, "Comedy Central: Good Reviews, Lackluster Ratings," *Multichannel News* 15 (25 July 1994): 19.

16. Maher was thirty-seven years of age when *P.I.* first went on the air in 1993.

17. Ownership was very important in allowing the show to end its contract with Comedy Central and move to broadcast television. The network has tried to prevent such departures more recently by owning the material it airs, such as *South Park.*

18. Mick LaSalle, "Political Satire Among the Ruins, Cable TV's 'Politically Incorrect,'" *San Francisco Chronicle,* 16 December 1993, D1.

19. Brian Lowry, "'P.I.': Where Celebrity Guests Fear to Tread?" *Los Angeles Times,* 31 March 2001, F1.

20. Jae-Ha Kim, "Speaking with . . . Bill Maher," *Chicago Sun-Times,* 15 November 2002, Weekend Plus, 3.

21. Douglas Rowe, "'Politically Incorrect': A Hybrid Talk Show Aiming for Laughs," *Associated Press,* 22 July 1993.

22. Wayne Walley, "ABC Eyeing 'Incorrect'; Post-'Nightline' Slot Discussed," *Electronic Media,* 2 October 1995, 3.

23. Ginia Bellafante, "Politically Incorrect," *Time* 150, 14 July 1997, 76.

24. Walley, "ABC Eyeing 'Incorrect,'" 3.

25. LaSalle, "Political Satire among the Ruins," D1.

26. Richard Zoglin, "Politically Incorrect," *Time* 143, 30 May 1994, 67.

27. Quoted in Scott Shuger, "Comic Relief: Real Issues, Barbed Wit and Celebrities Galore," *U.S. News & World Report* 122, 20 January 1997, 59–65.

28. Ana Marie Cox, "Lite Night with Bill Maher," *Mother Jones* 23 (January–February 1998): 67–68.

29. Andrew Stuttaford, "Politically Incorrect—Not," *National Review,* 10 March 1997, 56–57.

30. Walley, "ABC Eyeing 'Incorrect,'" 3.

31. Walley, "ABC Eyeing 'Incorrect,'" 3.

32. Stephen Battaglio, "'Incorrect' Move May Be to ABC," *Hollywood Reporter,* 26 September 1995.

33. Glenn Doggrell, "Bill Maher Keeps Them Guesting," *Los Angeles Times*, 22 December 1995, F1.

34. Aaron Barnhart, "Filling the 'Politically Incorrect' Gap," *New York Times*, 11 November 1996, D9.

35. Comedy Central's subscriber base equaled 22 million in 1992, 29 million in 1993, 31 million in 1994, 34 million in 1995, 42 million in 1996, 45 million in 1997, and 53 million in 1998.

36. See a 1998 discussion in *Multichannel News* on the impact of Comedy Central's hit show *South Park* for increasing network launches. "Do Hit Shows Drive Network Launches?" *Multichannel News,* 4 May 1998, 158. Carriage on cable is vitally important to profitability because cable networks make a substantial portion of their money on subscriber fees that range from 50 cents to $2 or more a year for each subscriber. See Barnhart, "Filling the 'Politically Incorrect' Gap."

37. Laura Blumenfeld, "Arianna Huffington, Getting the Last Laugh," *Washington Post*, 14 August 1996, C1.

38. Mike McDaniel, "'96 Republican National Convention: Political Barbs on Comedy Show Hitting the Mark," *Houston Chronicle,* 16 August 1996, 19.

39. Ray Richmond, "Changing of the Off-Guard on Tap at Comedy Central," *Daily Variety,* 4 November 1996, 27. *Politically Incorrect* was Comedy Central's first major step on the road to success. But it would be the animated series *South Park* that truly took the network to the big time, garnering an 8.2 household rating in 1998—the highest rated series in basic cable history to that point—while helping the network achieve an additional five million subscriber homes in just six months' time. Laurence Lerman, "Comedy Central Moves Uptown," *Daily Variety,* 12 October 1998, 27.

40. Whereas Maher (through Brillstein-Grey Productions) had retained control of the program when on Comedy Central, the move to ABC meant that he had to sell the show's rights to the network.

41. As New York *Newsday* reported, the network has experienced about a dozen failed attempts to fill the midnight time slot since *Nightline* first appeared in 1980. For a review of those flops, see "No More Captain Midnight? The Sinking of a 'Political' Ship," *Newsday*, 18 March 2002, B23.

42. Battaglio, "'Incorrect' Move."

43. Battaglio, "'Incorrect' Move."

44. Renee Graham, "'Incorrect' Maher Must Be Doing Something Right," *Boston Globe*, 9 October 1996, F1. According to Carter, the network had been looking "to get that time slot back from their affiliates and to expand their day." Many affiliates even delayed *Nightline* because entertainment programming was more profitable. By late 1995, after two years in which ABC had been working to improve clearance for *Nightline*, only 81 percent of the country could receive the program live. Battaglio, "'Incorrect' Move."

45. Graham, "'Incorrect' Maher," F1.

46. *P.I.* suffered from live clearance problems with affiliates, and hence was often pushed back in the schedule and didn't compete directly with other late-night talk shows. One trade press article reported that after 44 weeks on ABC, *P.I.* was averaging a 3.7 household rating (a 12 share) in the 20 markets where it airs opposite Leno and Letterman.

47. Kay McFadden, "In the Hot Seat: Bill Maher of '*Politically Incorrect*' Takes On a Host of Issues," *Seattle Times*, 15 March, 2002, H5.

48. Koppel has, however, done a lead-in for *Jimmy Kimmel Live*, the show that replaced *P.I.*

49. Unless noted otherwise, all Griffiths quotes are from a telephone interview with the author, January 8, 2004.

50. When the program began, it had 63 percent live clearance. Two and a half years later (May 1999), that number had risen to only 78 percent.

51. The problem was exacerbated by the fact that affiliates around the country were "embroiled in a long-standing financial-compensation battle centered on programming inventory and how much revenue affiliates receive from network programming." *P.I.*, then, was simply a pawn in this financial game between affiliates and the network. Dusty Sanders, "'Incorrect' a Victim of the Battle of the Buck," *Denver Rocky Mountain News*, 2 September 1999, 2D.

52. In the end, the producers went to approximately twenty-five to thirty cities, including Portland, San Francisco, Philadelphia, Boston, Baltimore, Dallas, Houston, Orlando, San Diego, Atlanta, Detroit, Tucson, New Haven, Seattle, and St. Louis, among others.

53. Telephone interview with the author, 24 July 2002. This was also reported in the *Los Angeles Times*: "Various sources close to the show say, '*Politically Incorrect*' lacks an advocate in upper management at the network, which would prefer a less abrasive personality following its stately news franchise, '*Nightline*.'" Paul Brownfield, "Troubled Timing Makes Maher Beyond '*Politically Incorrect*,'" *Los Angeles Times*, 26 September 2001, 6:1.

54. Yet another example is the amount of advertising inserted between *Nightline* and *P.I.* (again, a move than can be deadly without a lead-in). Jerry Nachman, former executive producer of *P.I.* in 2000, said, "There were discoveries I made . . . that I still shake my head over, like . . . when Ted [Koppel] says, 'I'll be right back with the final word' and then when [viewers] first see Maher. That's seven minutes [of commercials]. Not an exaggeration." The cumulative effect of all of this was that ratings for *Nightline* would come in around a 3.5; for *P.I.*, about a 2. "No More Captain Midnight?" B23.

55. Sheila Griffiths, interview by Jeffrey P. Jones, 24 July 2002.

56. Scott Carter, interview by Jeffrey P. Jones, 5 May 1999.

57. Sheila Griffiths, interview by Jeffrey P. Jones, 8 January 2004.

58. Lowry, "'P.I.': Where Celebrity Guests Fear to Tread?"

59. Bill Maher, interview by Jeffrey P. Jones, 2 February 2004.

60. "The last straw" is Maher's phrase to describe the effect of his 9/11 "cowardly remarks." Bill Maher, interview by Jeffrey P. Jones, 2 February 2004.

61. See Tony Peyser, "Political Incorrectness Strays into Boorishness," *Los Angeles Times*, 26 January 2001, B9; Richard Huff, "Catholics Call Maher Religiously Incorrect," *Daily News* (New York), 12 November 1999, 129.

62. Taken from transcript of the program found at www.abc.com.

63. Brownfield, "Troubled Timing," 1.

64. Again, as the *Los Angeles Times* reported, "Lee Antonio, spokeswoman for Sears, says the calls started coming in Tuesday—around 50, most of them from Houston and many unfamiliar with the particulars. 'People that called me didn't even know the show's name,' she said." Brownfield, "Troubled Timing," 1.

65. Susan Sontag wrote, "Where is the acknowledgement that this was not a 'cowardly' attack on 'civilization' or 'liberty' or 'humanity' or the 'free world' but an attack on the world's self-proclaimed superpower, undertaken as a consequence of specific American alliances and actions?" Brownfield, "Troubled Timing," 1.

66. Lisa de Moraes, "WJLA Pulls 'PI' a Second Time," *Washington Post*, 28 September 2001, C07.

67. The White House press office later removed the "watch what you say" segment from their transcript of the meeting.

68. Moraes, "WJLA Pulls," C07.

69. Kim, "Speaking with," 3.

70. Caryn James, "They're Celebrities, and You're Not," *New York Times*, 8 February 2004, 2: 28.

71. Bill Maher, interview by Jeffrey P. Jones, 2 February 2004.

72. Bill Maher, interview by Jeffrey P. Jones, 2 February 2004.

73. Bill Maher, interview by Jeffrey P. Jones, 2 February 2004.

74. Bill Maher, interview by Jeffrey P. Jones, 2 February 2004.

75. As Maher confides, "the press used to criticize *Politically Incorrect* for having one stupid guest on who said stupid things, and I would say, 'Yes, of course. We have five shows a week, four guests each show, [so] that's twenty guests a week. Not every one of them is going to be Bertrand Russell. But remember: we're on [the air] against Jay [Leno] and Dave [Letterman]. If you're going to start criticizing [us] about not enough intellectual content, you're right. Our show is not purely intellectual content. Theirs is none.'" Bill Maher, interview by Jeffrey P. Jones, February 2, 2004.

76. Shuger, "Comic Relief, 56–62."

77. Andrew Ferguson, "Politically Incompetent," *The Weekly Standard*, 27 October 1997, 20.

78. Again, see chapter 8 for the notion of "celebrity" as representative figure for audiences.

79. Cynics, of course, will say it is because these people are celebrities who crave the spotlight.

80. Networks have proven that they have no problem offering sexually or violently aggressive programming, but political controversy is something they have always been quick to avoid. CBS's repression of the special *The Reagans* in November 2003 is only the latest example.

81. Bill Maher, interview by Jeffrey P. Jones, 2 February 2004.

CHAPTER 5

1. The question actually makes specific reference to Leno and Letterman when referring to late-night talk shows. A different categorical response was available for *Po-*

litically Incorrect as a "comedy show," in league with *Saturday Night Live.* Which of these two response categories that programs like *The Daily Show* or *Dennis Miller Live* belong to in the respondent's mind is anybody's guess. See www.people-press.org/reports/display.php3?.ReportID=46.

2. As the Pew Center continued asking this question in the 2004 presidential election season, a reporter for *Newsday* showed yet again how this statistic could be mangled: "A recent study from the Pew Research Center for People and the Press . . . found that 8 percent of respondents *learned most everything they knew about a candidate* from shows like 'The Daily Show' and 'Saturday Night Live'" (emphasis added). Verne Gay, "Not Necessarily the News," *Newsday* (New York), 19 January 2004, B06.

3. Two examples that also involve young people include: the horror comics controversy of the 1950s, a moral panic resulting in congressional hearings that attempted to link juvenile delinquency to comic book readership, all fueled by flawed social scientific "data" produced by Dr. Frederic Wertham; and the social scientific study on children and Internet pornography by graduate student Marty Rimm, which was later publicized through a *Time* magazine cover story. See John Springhall, *Youth, Popular Culture and Moral Panics* (New York: St. Martin's Press, 1998), 21–146; and Tim Jordan, *Cyberpower: The Culture and Politics of Cyberspace and the Internet* (London: Routledge, 1999), 93–96.

4. This is related to the phenomenon of declining news readership among young people. See David Buckingham, "News Media, Political Socialization and Popular Citizenship: Towards a New Agenda," *Critical Studies in Mass Communication* 14 (December 1997): 344–66; Kevin G. Barnhurst and Ellen Wartella, "Young Citizens, American TV Newscasts and the Collective Memory," *Critical Studies in Mass Communication* 15 (September 1998): 279–305; David Buckingham, *The Making of Citizens: Young People, News and Politics* (London: Routledge, 2000).

5. The survey was conducted between 12–16 January 2000. Therefore, all the statistic really tells us is what advertisers are generally counting on—that young people watch late night television and are paying attention to some of the content found there (nothing too earth-shattering there).

6. Dana Milbank, "Tracking Laughs Is No Joke in an Election Year," *Washington Post,* 19 October 2000, C01; Michael Heaton, "Why Is Letterman Our Cronkite? Apparently Because That's The Way It Is On Tuesday, Election Day, 2000," *Plain Dealer* (Cleveland), 3 November 2000, 2; Margaret Talbot, "Mascaragate 2000," *New York Times Magazine,* 10 December 2000, 47–48.

7. Marshall Sella, "The Stiff Guy vs. the Dumb Guy," *New York Times Magazine,* 24 September, 2000, 72–80, 102.

8. Charles Schutz, *Political Humor: From Aristophanes to Sam Ervin* (New York: Fairleigh Dickenson University Press, 1977); Gerald Gardner, *All the President's Wits: The Power of Presidential Humor* (New York: Morrow, 1986); Gerald Gardner, *The Mocking of the President: A History of Campaign Humor from Ike to Ronnie* (Detroit: Wayne State University Press, 1988); Bill Hogan and Mike Hill, eds., *Will the Gentleman Yield? The Congressional Record Humor Book* (Berkeley, Calif.: Ten Speed Press, 1987).

9. John Street, *Politics & Popular Culture* (Philadelphia: Temple University Press, 1997), 60.

10. Walter Kaiser, "Wisdom of the Fool," in *Dictionary of the History of Ideas: Studies in Selected Pivotal Ideas,* ed. Philip P. Wiener (New York: Charles Scribner's Sons, 1973–74), available at http://etext.lib.Virginia.edu/cgi-local/DHI/dhi.cgi?id=dv4-70.

11. *P.I.* won several Cable Ace Awards; *Dennis Miller Live* won five Emmys for comedy writing; and *The Daily Show* won both an Emmy for best variety show and a Peabody Award for overall excellence.

12. Newspapers such as the *Los Angeles Times,* the *Boston Globe,* and the *Houston Chronicle* have run versions of Maher's "New Rules" commentaries that appear on his new show, *Real Time with Bill Maher,* as op-ed pieces. See, for instance, Bill Maher, "We Don't Need Laws about Love," *Boston Globe,* 14 February 2004, A15.

13. Caryn James, "They're Celebrities, and You're Not," *New York Times,* 8 February 2004, 2:28.

14. On CNN's *Wolf Blitzer Reports* (13 March 2003), Bill Maher and actor Ron Silver (*The West Wing*) were called on to debate the U.S. decision to eschew further diplomacy and move ahead with the invasion of Iraq.

15. Michael Mulkay, *On Humor: Its Nature and Its Place in Modern Society* (New York: Basil Blackwell, 1988), 26.

16. Mulkay, *On Humor,* 213–15.

17. When I asked Maher if he had "changed" since *P.I.* first went on the air, he noted, "I hope. I mean, if you're anyone over a ten-year period and you haven't changed, how awful." But he also went on to note that he is *allowed* to change in the public's eyes: "You can change your mind. That's one of the great things about being an entertainer as opposed to a politician. Because as a politician, of course, you can never change your mind because then you're 'waffling.'" Bill Maher, interview by Jeffrey P. Jones, 2 February 2004.

18. James, "They're Celebrities," 2:28. See also Alessandra Stanley, "Dennis Miller: Pranksters, Pundits, Political Animals All," *New York Times,* 30 January 2004, E1, and Rebecca Winters, "10 Questions for Dennis Miller," *Time,* 22 December 2003, 8, where Miller explains how 9/11 changed him and led to his ideologically rightward turn.

19. Dennis Miller, *I Rant, Therefore I Am* (New York: Broadway Books, 2000), 154.

20. Dennis Miller, *The Rants* (New York: Doubleday, 1996), 87.

21. Robert P. Laurence, "Room for Rant," *San Diego Union-Tribune,* 12 August 2001, F1.

22. Laurence, "Room for Rant," F1.

23. Schutz, *Political Humor,* 223.

24. Laurence, "Room for Rant," F1. Again, this has changed after 9/11, as he now clearly identifies himself with the Republican Party. California Republicans have even courted Miller to run for U.S. senator. Miller has also been flattered by attending luncheons with President George W. Bush (who called Miller his "friend"). See Tony Hicks, "Miller Talks Politics, But No Chance He'll Run," *Contra Costa* (Calif.) *Times,* 17 November 2003.

25. Miller, *The Rants,* 14.

26. Phil Rosenthal, "Worker Bee Dennis Miller Has Jokes, Not Answers," *Tampa Tribune,* 12 May 1996, Florida Television, 7.

27. Alex Witchel, "An Exceedingly Light Lunch with Dennis Miller," *New York Times,* 28 August 1996, C3.

28. Schutz, *Political Humor,* 228.

29. Dennis Miller, *The Rant Zone* (New York: Perennial, 2001), 123.

30. Miller, *I Rant,* 56.

31. Schutz, *Political Humor*, 230.

32. Miller, *I Rant*, 156.

33. Miller, *The Rants*, xi.

34. Roderick P. Hart, *Seducing America: How Television Charms the Modern Voter* (New York: Oxford University Press, 1994), 80–86; William Chaloupka, *Everybody Knows: Cynicism in America* (Minneapolis: University of Minnesota Press, 1999), 101–14.

35. Miller, *The Rants*, 4–5.

36. Miller, *The Rants*, 10.

37. Schutz, *Political Humor*, 78.

38. Schutz, *Political Humor*, 14.

39. Alan Wolfe, in a book review in the early 1990s, argued: "Americans are increasingly oblivious to politics, but they are exceptionally sensitive to culture. . . . Politics in the classic sense of who gets what, when and how is carried out by a tiny elite watched over by a somewhat larger, but still infinitesimally small, audience of news followers. The attitude of the great majority of Americans to such traditional political subjects is an unstable combination of boredom, resentment, and sporadic attention. . . . Culture, on the other hand, grabs everyone's attention all the time. . . . Because they practice politics in cultural terms, Americans cannot be understood with the tool kits developed by political scientists." Quoted in Jeffrey P. Jones, "Forums for Citizenship in Popular Culture," in *Politics, Discourse, and American Society: New Agendas*, ed. Roderick P. Hart and Bartholomew H. Sparrow (Lanham, Md.: Rowman & Littlefield, 2001), 194.

40. Lawrence Grossberg, *It's a Sin: Essays on Postmodernism, Politics & Culture* (Sydney: Power Publications, 1988), 40.

41. David Sheff, "Playboy Interview," *Playboy* 44, August 1997, 51ff.

42. Ana Marie Cox, "Lite Night with Bill Maher," *Mother Jones* 23 (January–February 1998): 67–68.

43. Renee Graham, "'Incorrect' Maher Must Be Doing Something Right," *Boston Globe*, 9 October 1996, F1.

44. Bill Maher, "Babes and the Beltway," *Playboy* 46, January 1999, 161.

45. Sheff, "Playboy Interview," 51ff.

46. Sheff, "Playboy Interview," 51ff.

47. David Rensin, "Bill Maher," *Playboy* 42, October 1995, 138.

48. David Wild, "Checking in with Bill Maher," *Rolling Stone*, 25 April 1999, 57.

49. Maher retains this populist impulse when discussing the major broadcast networks. When asked if there is any way for the networks to be as influential as they once were, Maher argues, "I think they could, if they would change their ways—if they'd get hip. They're sort of a mirror image of Washington, another example of so-called leaders being out of touch with the people they're leading." Quoted in Wild, "Checking In," 57.

50. Sheff, "Playboy Interview," 51ff.

51. Andrew Ferguson, "Politically Incompetent," *The Weekly Standard* 27, October 1997, 20.

52. Patrick Butters, "Maher, Comedically Correct," *Washington Times*, 4 November 1997, C10.

53. "'P.I.'s' Maher Hits the Road Recruiting 'Citizen Guests,'" *Pittsburgh Post-Gazette*, 15 February 1999, D7.

54. See Eric Alterman for an excellent review of the disconnect between pundit and public opinion, including a thorough accounting of the opinion poll numbers that show that disconnection. *Sound and Fury: The Making of the Punditocracy* (Ithaca, N.Y.: Cornell University Press, 1999), 262–78.

55. Wild, "Checking In," 57.

56. Scott Carter, interview by Jeffrey P. Jones, 2 February 1999, and 29 March 1999.

57. This monologue continued with more comedic material and political commentary, and it will be quoted and examined in its entirety in the following chapter.

58. James Wolcott, "Maher's Attacks," *Vanity Fair,* September 1997, 149.

59. Gennifer Flowers, Clinton's lover prior to his election as president, has been a guest on several occasions.

60. Not that Clinton himself wasn't capable of letting us all see and "experience" his id writ large.

61. Kaiser, "Wisdom of the Fool," available at http://etext.lib.Virginia.edu/cgi-local/DHI/dhi.cgi?id=dv4-70.

62. Sheff, "Playboy Interview," 51ff.

63. Wild, "Checking In," 57.

64. They indeed did talk when President Clinton telephoned Maher after Maher experienced his own "scandal" with his supposedly unpatriotic words following 9/11.

65. Wild, "Checking In," 57.

66. Comedy Central learned in 1996 that it would lose Bill Maher and *Politically Incorrect* to ABC. *The Daily Show* was created at that time to be the network's new flagship show.

67. As the show's correspondent Stephen Colbert puts it, "I never enjoyed that aspect of the show" (that is, mocking ordinary Americans). "I have no desire to club the equivalent of baby seals." Bruce Fretts, "In Jon We Trust," *Entertainment Weekly,* 31 October 2003, 35.

68. Compared with 1992, when neither the political parties nor the networks were interested in CC's contributions. Of course, one could argue the cynical view that the political parties are so desperate that they will take any free media coverage they can get, even if that involves a program whose sole purpose is to ridicule them.

69. "Comedy Central Hires Reich for GOP Reports," *Buffalo News,* 14 July 2000, 4c.

70. Sella, "The Stiff Guy," 72–80, 102.

71. Theresa Bradley, "Solidly Stewart," *ABCNews.com,* 14 November 2002.

72. Phil Rosenthal, "A Comic Koppel," *Chicago Sun-Times,* 15 December 2000, Features, 65.

73. For a nice summary of how competition between the cable news networks affected political reporting and commentary over the Clinton-Lewinsky scandal, see Alterman, *Sound and Fury,* 262–78.

74. Bradley, "Solidly Stewart," *ABCNews.com.*

75. John Thornton Caldwell, *Televisuality: Style, Crisis, and Authority in American Television* (New Brunswick, N.J.: Rutgers University Press, 1995); Jean Baudrillard, "Simulacra and Simulations," in *Jean Baudrillard: Selected Writings,* ed. and trans. Mark Poster (Palo Alto: Stanford University Press, 1988), 166–84.

76. Susan Douglas, "Daily Show Does Bush," *The Nation,* 5 May 2003. During the 2000 presidential election, comments by Stewart confirm that this is the approach

their comedy takes: "What we go after are not actual policies but the façade behind them. We work in the area between the makeup they're wearing and the real face. And in that space, you can pretty much hammer away at anybody." Sella, "The Stiff Guy," 77.

77. Simon Houpt, "The World according to Stewart," *The Globe and Mail* (Canada), 3 October 2002.

78. Steve Hedgpeth, "'Daily Show's Satiric Eye," *Plain Dealer* (Cleveland), 30 July 2000, 6I.

79. Transcript by author. Video clip available at www.comedycentral.com /tv_shows/thedailyshowwithjonstewart/videos.jhtml.

80. Transcript by author. Video clip available at www.comedycentral.com/ tv_shows/thedailyshowwithjonstewart/videos.jhtml.

81. Frank Rich, "Jon Stewart's Perfect Pitch," *New York Times,* 20 April 2003, 2:1.

82. Daniel Boorstin, quoted in Alterman, *Sound and Fury,* 282.

83. Alterman, *Sound and Fury,* 281.

84. Bradley, "Solidly Stewart," *ABCNews.com.* Ironically, CNN has picked up *TDS* for inclusion on CNN International. See Brian Lambert, "News Channel CNN Nabs Faux News Show: Stewart's *Daily Show* Goes Global," *The Gazette* (Montreal, Quebec), 24 July 2002, B9.

85. Stephen Armstrong, "'I Can Scratch the Itch," *The Guardian* (London), 17 March 2003, 8.

86. Matthew Gilbert, "On Topic of War, Most Late-Night Hosts Tread Lightly," *Boston Globe,* 13 March 2003, D1.

87. Jane Ganahl, "Comic Release," *San Francisco Chronicle,* 23 April 2002, D1.

88. Todd Gitlin, *The Sixties: Years of Hope, Days of Rage* (New York: Bantam Books, 1987), 35–36.

89. Aaron Wherry, "News and Laughs at 11," *National Post* (Canada), 5 October 2002.

90. Armstrong, "'I Can Scratch the Itch," 8.

91. Tad Friend, "Is It Funny Yet?" *The New Yorker,* 11 February 2002, 28.

92. Rich, "Jon Stewart's Perfect Pitch," 2:1.

93. Stewart also finds political parties to be of meaningless value: "Party affiliation has no more substance than when you were in school and they said, 'O.K., you're on the red team, you're on the blue team and whoever wins gets pie.'" Sella, "The Stiff Guy," 77.

94. Friend, "Is It Funny Yet?" 28.

95. Rich, "Jon Stewart's Perfect Pitch," 2:1.

96. Rich, "Jon Stewart's Perfect Pitch," 2:1.

97. Martha T. Moore, "Dole Lands a Comedy Central Gig," *USA Today,* 19 January 2000, 8A; Terry Morrow, "Daily Show Mixes Election Returns, Humor," *Plain Dealer* (Cleveland), 4 November 2000, 9E.

98. Robert Kahn, "The Laugh Track: War, Politics Grist for 'Daily Show' Anchor," *Newsday* (New York), 12 May 2003, A 14.

99. Ganahl, "Comic Release," D1.

100. Bill Maher, interview by Tom Snyder, *The Late Late Show with Tom Snyder,* Columbia Broadcasting System, 11 May 1998.

101. See David Harvey, *The Condition of Postmodernity* (Cambridge, Mass.: Blackwell, 1990).

102. Jean Baudrillard, "The Masses," 218–19.

103. Grossberg, *It's a Sin,* 40.

104. Baudrillard, "The Masses," 215.

105. Steven Best and Douglas Kellner, *Postmodern Theory: Critical Interrogations* (New York: Guilford Press, 1991), 121.

106. As Grossberg notes, this generation finds it "increasingly impossible to represent their moods and emotional contradictions, their affective relationships to the world, in those terms and at the same time, to seriously invest themselves in such values." Grossberg, *It's a Sin,* 40.

107. Miller, *Ranting Again,* 129.

108. Baudrillard, "The Masses," 215.

109. Steve Vineberg, "Political Satire in the Age of 'Letterman,'" *Chronicle of Higher Education,* 10 July 1998; Hart, *Seducing America,* 80–86.

110. Grossberg, *It's a Sin,* 42.

111. Schutz, *Political Humor,* 313.

112. Grossberg, *It's a Sin,* 39–40.

113. Mulkay, *On Humor,* 222–23.

114. Schutz, *Political Humor,* 14. Jerome Bruner discusses the ways in which narratives also serve this function: "Human beings, in interacting with one another, form a sense of the canonical and ordinary as a background against which to interpret and give narrative meaning to breaches in and deviations from 'normal' states of the human condition. Such narrative explications have the effect of framing the idiosyncratic in a 'life-like' fashion that can promote negotiation and avoid confrontational disruption and strife." Jerome Bruner, *Acts of Meaning* (Cambridge, Mass.: Harvard University Press, 1990), 67.

115. Schutz, *Political Humor,* 328.

116. Gerard Mulligan, a comedy writer for *The Late Show with David Letterman,* agrees: "Historically, if you think about it, comedians' behavior has been conservative. They point out anything that isn't normal." Sella, "The Stiff Guy," 102.

117. Schutz, *Political Humor,* 322.

118. Schutz, *Political Humor,* 327–28.

119. Schutz, *Political Humor,* 228.

120. The populist battle cry that Arnold Schwarzenegger used most recently to win an actual political campaign.

121. Schutz, *Political Humor,* 228.

122. Schutz, *Political Humor,* 197.

123. David Marshall, *Celebrity and Power* (Minneapolis: University of Minnesota Press, 1997), 243–44.

124. Marshall, *Celebrity and Power,* 17.

125. Mulkay, *On Humor,* 219.

126. Leah R. Vande Berg, Lawrence A. Wenner, and Bruce E. Gronbeck, *Critical Approaches to Television,* 2d ed. (Boston: Houghton Mifflin, 2004), 200.

CHAPTER 6

1. Original emphasis; James S. Ettema and Theodore L. Glasser, *Custodians of Conscience: Investigative Journalism and Public Virtue* (New York: Columbia University Press, 1998), 87.

2. Ettema and Glasser, *Custodians*, 105.

3. Ettema and Glasser, *Custodians*, 106.

4. Ettema and Glasser, *Custodians*, 109.

5. Let's not forget that a flood of detailed information was made available to the public by the U.S. Congress, including the entire Starr Report on the Internet within days of its delivery to Congress. The videotape depositions of the president were also broadcast on several cable television channels, again within days of their receipt by Congress. That doesn't mean the public read the data or watched the testimony, but it does mean that they were provided with much of the same information that members of Congress were operating from.

6. The network, of course, censored these last words. Maher later revealed what he said in a magazine interview. See David Wild, "Checking in with Bill Maher," *Rolling Stone,* 25 April 1999, 7. Transcript taken from *P.I.*'s web pages at www.abc.com.

7. The imitational form is what brings me to theories of parody. Entering the debates over literary forms of comedic presentation seems unproductive here, as scholars have devoted entire tracts to these debates, often beginning and ending their search in frustration. For instance, George Test begins the preface to his book on satire with: "This book assumes that what is commonly referred to as satire is merely the aesthetic manifestation of a universal urge so varied as to elude definition," and begins his first chapter with, "More than a quarter of a century has passed since a leading scholar of satire came to the conclusion that attempts to define literary satire had come to an impasse." George A. Test, *Satire: Spirit and Art* (Tampa: University of South Florida Press, 1991). For discussions of parody—ancient, modern, and post-modern—see Margaret A. Rose, *Parody: Ancient, Modern, and Post-Modern* (Cambridge, U.K.: Cambridge University Press, 1993).

8. Gary Saul Morson, "Parody, History, and Metaparody," in *Rethinking Bakhtin: Extensions and Challenges*, ed. Gary Saul Morson and Caryl Emerson (Evanston, Ill.: Northwestern University Press, 1989), 65.

9. Morson, "Parody, History," 65.

10. Morson, "Parody, History," 66–67.

11. Morson, "Parody, History," 71. Morson summarizes the point best when he notes, "parody is the etiology of utterance," 72.

12. Morson, "Parody, History," 70.

13. Another political satire that utilizes these same conventions for comedic effect is Warren Beatty's 1998 film *Bulworth*. For a discussion of populist films that insert into the mouths of fictional politicians the "truthful" words that publics wish politicians would say, see Jeffrey P. Jones, "Political Mythology in Film: Recurrent Hopes and Fears of the Media Populist" (paper presented at the annual meeting of the Society for Cinema and Media Studies, Atlanta, Georgia, 6 March 2004).

14. Mary Douglas, "Jokes," in *Rethinking Popular Culture*, ed. Chandra Mukerji and Michael Schudson (Berkeley: University of California Press, 1991), 296.

15. Douglas, "Jokes," 297.

16. Douglas, "Jokes," 294. See also Sigmund Freud, *Jokes and Their Relation to the Unconscious* (New York: W. W. Norton and Company, 1960); Martin Grotjahn, *Beyond Laughter: Humor and the Subconscious* (New York: McGraw-Hill, 1957).

17. We should also note, however, that parody need not be inherently subversive. Linda Hutcheon points out, parody can be "normative and conservative, or it can be provocative and revolutionary. . . . In Bakhtin's terminology, parody can be

centripetal—that is, a homogenizing, hierarchizing influence. But it can also be a centrifugal, denormatizing one." Linda Hutcheon, "Modern Parody and Bakhtin," in *Rethinking Bakhtin,* ed. Morson and Emerson, 101–102.

18. Morson, "Parody, History," 73.

19. Henri Bergson argues that humor develops from human attempts at control: "Humour consists in perceiving something mechanical encrusted on something living" (quoted in Douglas, "Jokes," 294).

20. Douglas, "Jokes," 67.

21. Erika Milvy, "Can't Get Enough of the Clinton Scandal? The Internet Runneth Over," *Los Angeles Times,* 20 August 1998, F47; Frank Ahrens, "The Bawdy Politic: President as Punch Line," *Washington Post,* 30 January 1998, D1.

22. Clifford Geertz, "Common Sense as a Cultural System," *Antioch Review* 33 (Spring 1975): 8.

23. Geertz, "Common Sense," 17–18.

24. Geertz, "Common Sense," 25.

25. Geertz, "Common Sense."

26. Boaventura De Sousa Santos, *Toward a New Common Sense: Law, Science and Politics in the Paradigmatic Transition* (New York: Routledge, 1995).

27. Michael Holquist, *Dialogism: Bakhtin and His World* (London: Routledge, 1990), 61. Bakhtin called this the "extraverbal context" of the utterance that makes it a meaningful locution for the listener.

28. Holquist, *Dialogism,* 47–48.

29. Holquist, *Dialogism,* 61.

30. Or, as Geertz would have it, "the temper its observations convey, the turn of mind its conclusions reflect." Geertz, "Common Sense."

31. Quoted in Holquist, *Dialogism,* 59.

32. Holquist, *Dialogism,* 60.

33. All quotes from a transcript of *Nightline* broadcast on 17 August 1998.

34. Indeed, such formulations are the rhetorical common sense of the political class as they seek to convince both voters and each other of what makes sense.

35. From transcript of *Nightline* broadcast on 17 August 1998.

36. Douglas, "Jokes," 296.

37. Michael Billig, Susan Condor, Derek Edwards, Mike Gane, David Middleton, and Alan Radley, *Ideological Dilemmas: A Social Psychology of Everyday Thinking* (London: Sage, 1988), 27.

38. Douglas, "Jokes," 302.

39. Douglas, "Jokes," 297.

40. For example, recent presidents have addressed the nation with Christmas greetings, indirectly spoken to us through the heroes of civil "religious" ceremonies (the Super Bowl, the Olympics), comforted and reassured the nation with words of condolence and resolution over terrorist attacks, and offered patriotic mobilizations during American military aggression overseas.

41. Douglas, "Jokes," 301.

42. Humor, jokes, and ridicule have been effective techniques of many successful populists in history, including Father Charles Coughlin, Huey Long, George Wallace, and Rush Limbaugh.

43. Douglas, "Jokes," 303, 305.

44. We should remember Geertz's note that common sense is the "interpretation of the immediacies of experience . . . subjected to historically defined standards of judgment" (Geertz, "Common Sense," 8).

45. Douglas, "Jokes," 305. Douglas argues further that the joker's "jokes expose the inadequacy of realist structurings of experience and so release the pent-up power of the imagination" (306).

46. Chris Powell and George E. C. Paton, eds., *Humour in Society: Resistance and Control* (New York: St. Martin's Press, 1988), xxi.

CHAPTER 7

1. A version of this chapter originally appeared as Jeffrey P. Jones, "Forums for Citizenship in Popular Culture," in *Politics, Discourse, and Society: New Agendas,* ed. Roderick P. Hart and Bartholomew H. Sparrow (Lanham, Md.: Rowman & Littlefield Publishers, 2001), 193–210.

2. Roderick P. Hart, *Campaign Talk: Why Elections Are Good for Us* (Princeton, N.J.: Princeton University Press, 2000); David Thelen, *Becoming Citizens in the Age of Television* (Chicago: University of Chicago Press, 1996); E. J. Dionne Jr., *Why Americans Hate Politics* (New York: Simon and Schuster, 1991).

3. Actual broadcast dates are 25 January, 1 February, 16 August, and 23 August 1998. The analysis was conducted from transcripts of these broadcasts.

4. Will's usage of "this man" is similar to the president's usage of "that woman" referring to Monica Lewinsky in his denial of the affair. Both are semantic moves to distance themselves from the object of referral. In Will's case, he seeks to distance Clinton from any legitimate place in the political system.

5. 23 August 1998.

6. Antonio Gramsci, *An Antonio Gramsci Reader,* ed. David Forgacs (New York: Schocken Books), 360.

7. Of the pundits on *This Week,* for instance, both of Roberts' parents served in Congress. Kristol's father is the conservative intellectual Irving Kristol. Will's wife was a manager in Bob Dole's 1996 presidential campaign. George Stephanopoulos was a senior advisor to President Clinton, and Sam Donaldson has been a senior White House reporter for over two decades.

8. John Dewey and Arthur F. Bentley, *Knowing and the Known* (Boston: Beacon Press, 1949), 270.

9. Dewey and Bentley, *Knowing,* 282.

10. For a helpful summary of opinion polls that demonstrate this see Eric Alterman, *Sound and Fury: The Making of the Punditocracy* (Ithaca, N.Y.: Cornell University Press), 275–76.

11. Gramsci, *Gramsci Reader;* Clifford Geertz, "Common Sense as a Cultural System," *Antioch Review* 33 (Spring 1975): 5–26; Boaventura De Sousa Santos, *Toward a New Common Sense: Law, Science and Politics in the Paradigmatic Transition* (New York: Routledge, 1995).

12. Quoted in Roderick P. Hart, *Seducing America: How Television Charms the Modern Voter* (New York: Oxford University Press, 1994), 15.

13. Michael Billig, Susan Condor, Derek Edwards, Mike Gane, David Middleton, and Alan Radley, *Ideological Dilemmas: A Social Psychology of Everyday Thinking* (London: Sage, 1988), 27.

14. Geertz too notes how intellectual ideas exist in the public imagination as common sense by using the example of science: "The development of modern science has had a profound effect . . . upon Western commonsense views. . . . [The plain man] has surely been brought round, and quite recently, to a version of the germ theory of disease. The merest television commercial demonstrates that. But, as the merest television commercial also demonstrates, it is as a bit of common sense, not as an articulated scientific theory, that he believes it" (Geertz, "Common Sense," 19–20).

15. P. David Marshall, *Celebrity and Power: Fame in Contemporary Culture* (Minneapolis: University of Minnesota Press, 1997), 72–73.

16. Marshall, *Celebrity and Power*, 247.

17. Joshua Gamson, *Claims to Fame: Celebrity in Contemporary America* (Berkeley: University of California Press, 1994), 195.

18. When alternative means of making sense were employed, such means were quickly pushed aside. For instance, in a highly unusual moment on the August 16 program, Sam Donaldson offered his reflections on the scandal in what sounded like commentary directly drawn from *Politically Incorrect*. "I'm not as mean a guy as I look, I think," he suggested. "I don't think my heart is as hard as some people think because all of us need some compassion at times. . . . I think the question now is not whether Bill Clinton deserves compassion as a human being, understanding we're all fallen angels. But is he qualified to be, and should he continue to be the leader, the man to whom we look up to in this country, if in fact, he's done these things? I say if he's done these things, he is not qualified to be a leader. Brother I will help you up, I'll give you a dollar if you need it but you cannot be the President of the United States." The next statement by George Stephanopoulos, however, not only brought this form of analysis and sense making to a close, but reestablished the proper direction and focus of how the scandal should be discussed. "There is a difference between a civil suit that's been dismissed and a grand jury," he quickly intoned. The discussion then careened through issues such as obstruction of justice, subornation of perjury, resolution of inquiry, impeachment, and indictments. This is a vivid, if limited, example of how certain ways of making sense are privileged over others—a privileging that similarly occurs on *Politically Incorrect*, but is based there on common sense.

19. Geertz, "Common Sense," 26.

CHAPTER 8

1. Interview at the studios of *Politically Incorrect*, CBS Television City, Los Angeles, California, 21 March 2000.

2. As one writer argued, "This is yet another letter pleading for the citizen panelist spot on your show. You'll note that your current method isn't exactly giving citizens the good name they deserve. It's too bloody democratic, you'll never get good people that way."

3. Again notice the way in which a viewer has inserted himself into the programming, taking Maher's critique of a certain guest author and his readers very personally, and in some sense feeling represented by this guest.

4. Maher interview in *The Onion*, www.avclub.theonion.com/avclub3209/av bonuesfeature3209.html.

5. One of the fascinating aspects of my interviews with viewers attending the citizen panelist auditions was how quickly the conversations could turn to discussions of political issues—from the Middle East crisis and abortion to Clarence Thomas and local politics.

6. Which is exactly the reason, as noted by Associate Producer Sheila Griffiths, that many politicians were reticent to appear on the show—it was spontaneous and unpredictable, and therefore too dangerous for them to participate. Sheila Griffiths, interview by Jeffrey P. Jones, 8 January 2004.

7. P. David Marshall, *Celebrity and Power* (Minneapolis: University of Minnesota Press, 1997), 243–44.

8. Marshall, *Celebrity*, 241.

9. Marshall, *Celebrity*, 240.

10. When I asked one male college student if *P.I.* was good for American democracy, he said, "No. It's television. It's just a TV show." When I asked another the same question, he replied, "I wouldn't go that far."

11. They felt fully informed about politics, but the others to whom they referred in their remarks obviously were not as engaged or knowledgeable.

12. Marshall, *Celebrity*, 246–47.

13. For instance, during the initial phases of the Clinton-Lewinsky scandal, guests on *P.I.* would regularly intone that Clinton was a "regular guy" (and therefore just like the citizens who supported him) because he liked to "smoke weed and chase women." Indeed, some said he was the kind of guy you would "want to hang out with."

14. For background information on Usenet, see M. Tepper, "Usenet Communities and the Cultural Politics of Information," in *Internet Culture*, ed. D. Porter (New York: Routledge, 1997), 39–54; Nancy K. Baym, "From Practice to Culture on Usenet," in *The Cultures of Computing*, ed. S. L. Star (Oxford, U.K.: Basil Blackwell, 1995), 29–52.

15. Usenet discussion sites are not created by corporations, but by individuals. Although CNN, NBC, and other media networks have created discussion forums on their websites, none originate from "fan" activity. Alt.fan.jon-stewart was created in January 1996, and has approximately 1,400 postings to date; alt.fan.dennis-miller was created in February 1995 and has approximately 7,000 postings to date. We should also note that the site dedicated to talk radio host Rush Limbaugh (alt.fan.rush-limbaugh) has been one of the most heavily used discussion forums for politics that is directly related to a media program in general. For an analysis of Limbaugh's site, see Jeffrey P. Jones, "The Aetherial Rush: Limbaugh's 'Textual' Movement on the Internet" (paper presented at the 82nd Annual Meeting of the Speech Communication Association, San Diego, California, 22–26 November 1996).

16. ABC began running a discussion forum on its website dedicated to *P.I.* in 2000, as did Bill Maher on his personal website, billmaher.com. ABC's site was terminated with the end of the program, but Maher continues to run his discussion forum. For statistics on Maher's discussion boards, see the appendix.

17 See Oldenburg's argument for how certain "third places" (as opposed to work and home) are central to community life, social conversation, and grassroots democracy. Ray Oldenburg, *The Great Good Place: Cafes, Coffeeshops, Community Centers, Beauty Parlors, General Stores, Bars, Hangouts, and How They Get You through the Day* (New York: Paragon House, 1989).

18. Nancy K. Baym, "Talking about Soaps: Communicative Practices in a Computer-Mediated Fan Culture," in *Theorizing Fandom: Fans, Subculture and Identity*, ed. Cheryl Harris and Alison Alexander (Cresskill, N.J.: Hampton Press, 1998).

19. That may simply be the product of this forum's participants portraying themselves as hip and slightly cynical toward popular culture. Comments of praise, though they do appear, are less often made public.

20. Michael X. Delli Carpini and Bruce A. Williams, "Constructing Public Opinion: The Uses of Fictional and Nonfictional Television in Conversations about the Environment," in *The Psychology of Political Communication*, ed. Ann N. Crigler (Ann Arbor: University of Michigan Press, 1996), 160.

21. John Thornton Caldwell, *Televisuality: Style, Crisis, and Authority in American Television* (New Brunswick, N.J.: Rutgers University Press, 1995).

22. Of course, for the Limbaugh forum, consider the source for where those discussions began. Jones, "The Aetherial Rush."

23. Caldwell, *Televisuality*.

CHAPTER 9

1. Samantha M. Shapiro, "The Dean Connection," *New York Times Magazine,* 7 December 2003, 56–61.

2. Laura Kurtzman, "Dean Turns Web into Gold," *San Jose Mercury News,* 21 July 2003.

3. Cartoonist Gary Trudeau, whose first statements on the national stage were inspired products of 1960s social and political activism, smirkingly ridiculed these twenty-somethings' newfound activist spirit in a series of cartoons on the young Dean campaign workers.

4. Peter Dahlgren, "Media, Citizenship and Civic Culture," in *Mass Media and Society*, ed. James Curran and Michael Gurevitch (London: Arnold, 2000), 310–28; Peter Dahlgren, "Reconfiguring Civic Culture in the New Media Milieu," in *Media and the Restyling of Politics*, ed. John Corner and Dick Pels (London: Sage, 2003), 151–70.

5. Dahlgren, "Reconfiguring Civic Culture," 152.

6. Dahlgren, "Reconfiguring Civic Culture," 155.

7. The etymology of *civic* obviously has connections here to civil society and its role as an important mediator between state and market.

8. Dahlgren, "Media, Citizenship," 322.

9. Dahlgren, "Reconfiguring Civic Culture," 158.

10. Michael Billig, Susan Condor, Derek Edwards, Mike Gane, David Middleton, and Alan Radley, *Ideological Dilemmas: A Social Psychology of Everyday Thinking* (London: Sage, 1988), 16.

11. Sonia Livingstone and Peter Lunt, *Talk on Television: Audience Participation and Public Debate* (London: Routledge, 1994), 29; Paolo Carpignano, Robin Ander-

son, Stanley Aronowitz, and William DiFazio, "Chatter in the Age of Electronic Reproduction: Talk Television and the 'Public Mind,'" in *The Phantom Public Sphere*, ed. Bruce Robbins (Minneapolis: University of Minnesota Press, 1993).

12. Doris A. Graber, *Processing Politics: Learning from Television in the Internet Age* (Chicago: University of Chicago Press, 2001); Lawrence Grossberg, *It's a Sin: Essays on Postmodernism, Politics & Culture* (Sydney: Power Publications, 1988).

13. Charles Schutz, *Political Humor: From Aristophanes to Sam Ervin* (New York: Fairleigh Dickenson University Press, 1977), 327–28.

14. Murray Edelman, *Constructing the Political Spectacle* (Chicago: University of Chicago Press, 1988), 66–68.

15. David Thelen, *Becoming Citizens in the Age of Television* (Chicago: University of Chicago Press, 1996), 77.

Index

Note: Page numbers appearing in italics refer to photographs.